CASTLES FROM THE AIR

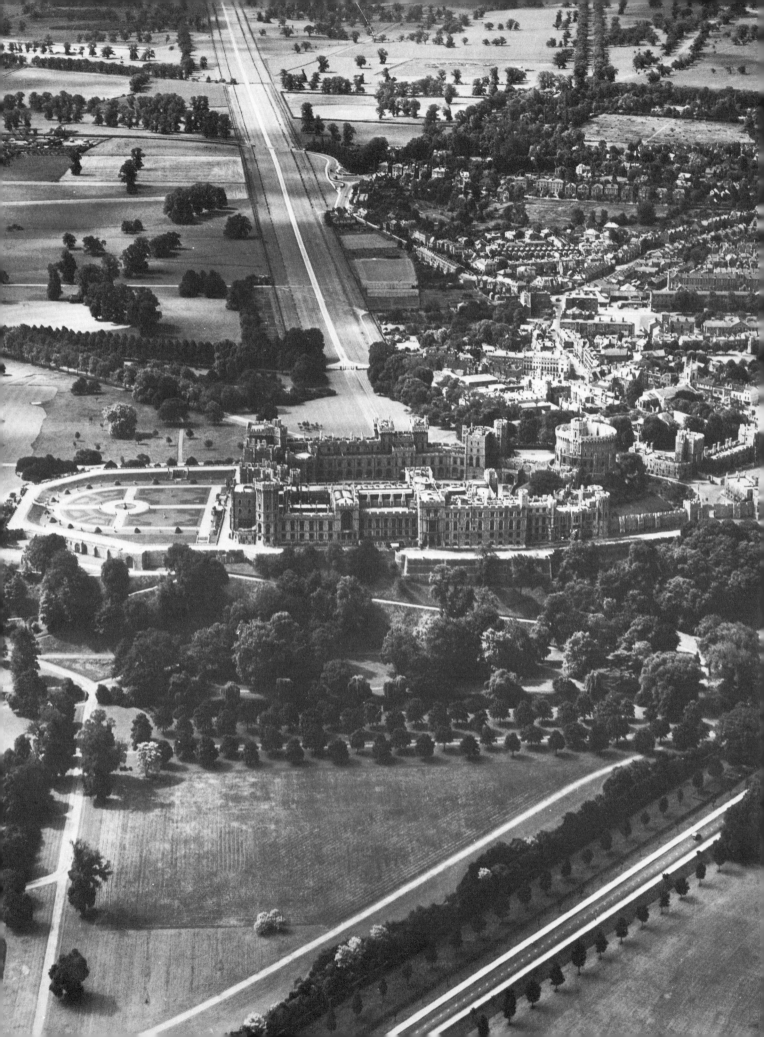

R. ALLEN BROWN

Castles
from the air

WITH PHOTOGRAPHS FROM THE
UNIVERSITY OF CAMBRIDGE COLLECTION

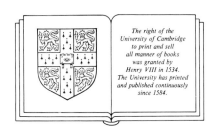

*The right of the
University of Cambridge
to print and sell
all manner of books
was granted by
Henry VIII in 1534.
The University has printed
and published continuously
since 1584.*

CAMBRIDGE UNIVERSITY PRESS

CAMBRIDGE

NEW YORK   PORT CHESTER

MELBOURNE   SYDNEY

Published by the Press Syndicate of the University of Cambridge
The Pitt Building, Trumpington Street, Cambridge CB2 1RP
40 West 20th Street, New York, NY 10011, USA
10 Stamford Road, Oakleigh, Melbourne 3166, Australia

© Cambridge University Press 1989

First published 1989

Printed in Great Britain at the University Press, Cambridge

British Library cataloguing in publication data

Brown, R. Allen (Reginald Allen), 1924–89
Castles from the air – (Cambridge air surveys)
1. Great Britain. Castles. Sources of evidence.
Aerial photographs.
I. Title
941

Library of Congress cataloguing in publication data

Brown, R. Allen (Reginald Allen), 1924–89
Castles from the air / R. Allen Brown.
          p.   cm. – (Cambridge air surveys)
ISBN 0 521 32932 9
1. Castles – Great Britain. 2. Great Britain – Aerial photographs.
3. Aerial photography in archaeology – Great Britain.
I. Title.   II. Series.
DA660.B843 1989
779′.9914100222 – dc 19   88–18934   CIP

ISBN 0 521 32932 9

To my friend and mentor

ARNOLD TAYLOR
maître de castellologie

Contents

Each photograph carries a north point (▲) for orientation. For dates of photography, see page 242.

Preface

The purpose and plan of this book having been discussed in the Introduction, nothing of consequence remains to be said here save to express my thanks to those who have brought it about. These include the Syndics of Cambridge University Press, whose invitation I could not resist although I had not intended to write another book on castles; the Curator, David Wilson, and his ever kind and hospitable staff at the Cambridge Committee for Aerial Photography, where I hugely enjoyed my many visits; and, not least, the staff of the Cambridge University Press, whose perceptive expertise in the unusually complex process of putting the book into print is most gratefully acknowledged. I am also glad to express my gratitude to my family, especially my wife who undertook the labour of typing and many editorial chores in what turned out to be difficult times; and to my ever knowledgeable friends, in England and in France, especially Mr Peter Curnow, sometime H.M. Principal Inspector of Ancient Monuments, whose particular knowledge is only exceeded by his generosity with it.

R. Allen Brown
Thelnetham, Suffolk

Introduction

The plates making up this book have been chosen almost exclusively from the collection of aerial photographs assembled and held by the Cambridge Committee for Aerial Photography, which has been systematically surveying the British Isles from the air since the last war. Relatively little new photography was possible, but by now the collection, although not devoted exclusively to archaeology or architecture, is close to comprehensive. Within its generous limits I have tried not only to illustrate the most famous and 'important' castles – Windsor or Arundel, Warwick or the Tower of London, or the great castles of Edward I in North Wales – but also to provide examples of all aspects of the siting, type, design and development of castles in England and Wales during the period of their ascendancy and viability, which here extends from c. 1066 to the sixteenth or seventeenth century. There is, however, much more to castles than topographical siting and physical appearance. Like all architecture they are a manifestation of the society which produced them. They stand above all for lordship. This consideration, too, has been a factor in selection, and is discussed no less than architecture and archaeology in the commentary which accompanies each plate.

An alphabetical arrangement of plates and castles has been chosen for simplicity and ease of reference. A topographical arrangement, county by county, would be inappropriate when the book is not intended as a gazetteer, and would have influenced the selection for no good reason. A chronological arrangement, which was at first envisaged, leads to difficulty. The typical architectural history of the typical castle in England and Wales is of an early foundation followed by development on the same site, often over a long period. Thus a Windsor or a Warwick could as well be listed among early motte-and-bailey castles as among 'later' castles of the fourteenth century, or indeed some other date. Further, though there may be trends and fashions, castles have no one central line of development, and they certainly refuse the standard labels affixed to medieval architecture by architectural historians – Romanesque, Early English, Gothic, Perpendicular and the rest – which, it may be noted, have been invented entirely for ecclesiastical buildings, of which the subject of medieval architectural history pretends exclusively and unreasonably to consist. Castles, one may suggest, are too important to be left to architectural historians who have largely neglected them.

Indeed, it can be suggested that castles are at once the best known and least understood of medieval buildings. Such houses of the period as survive require comparatively little interpretation, and most people still have some notion of the purpose and function of a church. With castles it is otherwise, and if they are viewed sensibly at all (there is no place in this book for prisoners languishing in dismal dungeons, maidens letting down their hair from towers, or robber-barons defending themselves with boiling oil) they are seen almost exclusively as fortresses, as grim as possible. In reality, it was the unique feature of the castle to combine the functions of both residence and fortress, and both were lordly. It is the combination of these otherwise disparate functions that makes a castle, and the residential role is every bit as fundamental as the military – more so perhaps, for the castle is the fortified residence of a lord (by no means necessarily the king or prince), and the first condition of the siting of any given castle is that the lord in question for some reason wished to have a residence and a presence in that place. That reason will seldom if ever be exclusively military, for in a world ruled by kings who were warrior princes aided by a warrior aristocracy there was no clear division between the civil and the military function. King John, we are told, planted Odiham castle where it is in Hampshire because of the hunting, and both Pickering and the Peak owed something of their popularity with their lords to their situation in the forest. The presence of the castle's lord will only be occasional, though on some scale, because any lord of substance will have duties at court and on campaigns, and will have also more than one residence, whether castle or unfortified house. Hence those great households moving through the countryside from castle to castle and manor to manor. And hence the lavish domestic accommodation in the castle, as lavish in any period as resources will permit – hall, chambers, chapels, kitchens and other domestic offices, for the several households of the lord and his guests. Hence also those ancillary amenities, gardens and vineyards, dovecotes and fishponds, warrens and chaces, forests and parks, with which the greater castles were surrounded. Castles were the stately homes of the medieval, more accurately the feudal, age, and those castles soaring romantically in the background of the illuminations in the *Très Riches Heures du Duc de Berry* were real. When in the sixteenth and seventeenth centuries the military importance of the castle falls away, we are left only with the basic residential role. Some castles thus still survive as the noblest of noble houses, not only royal Windsor but also ducal Arundel, and it is deeply significant that in France, where castles began, the word *château* is now applied to the larger country house.

Follow this train of thought and the military role of the castle appears almost secondary, which is perhaps unfair, for it is the degree of fortification which makes a castle, which distinguishes it, in the eyes of contemporaries and ourselves, from the unfortified or lightly fortified house. What fuse the two elements of residence and fortress are the functions and attitudes, and in due course traditions, of a warrior aristocracy in a society which saw itself divided into three, those who pray, those who fight, and those who labour. The second estate, the aristocratic warriors, whose proper habitat became the castle, had great powers of delegated authority, including military. Upon them rested not simply the defence but the control of the realm – and control is the operative word. The castle controlled the surrounding countryside, and did so by means of the heavily armed and mounted men within it. Its range was the range of the horse – about ten miles if one wished to return to base the same day. That base, of course, must be as impregnable as nature, art and science can effect, for it will inevitably be attacked in war. For warfare is about the control of land, and he who would control the land must first control, or take, the castles. In this way therefore it is certainly defence which

principally determines the castle's architectural form (though there will be sally ports and posterns – e.g. at Dover – because the best type of defence can be attack). However, it is a great mistake to think on that account that the military function of the castle was exclusively, or even primarily, defensive. It was not: the primary military purpose of the castle was active and offensive. There is, after all, nothing negative, passive or defensive in the ethos of chivalry, and castles are not thick on the ground in the Marches of Wales because the Normans were afraid of the Welsh, but because they were bases to hold down the land and assist further penetration and expansion. The point can never be better made, nor on so large a scale, than in England in and after 1066, when the raising of castles by the hundred was the very means whereby the land was taken over and the lordship of the alien few, a new ruling class from Normandy and France, imposed upon it.

For centuries, therefore, castles dominated contemporary warfare because they dominated the land, and their military value is enhanced when it is realized that they did so with a remarkable economy of manpower. Castle garrisons, when we can get at the figures through surviving accounts of the payment of wages or feudal surveys of knight-service owed in castleguard, are surprisingly small, and were generally not maintained at all in time of peace. They consist also predominantly of mounted men, knights for the most part, eked out later by horsed sergeants and men-at-arms. This small force could and did at will control the surrounding countryside, as we have seen, and it could be dislodged only by a serious and prolonged investment, a close siege involving much larger numbers, tedious and difficult to mount and to maintain. Yet, often enough, wars had to be

A vivid depiction of an assault on a castle in the Maciejowski Bible (Pierpont Morgan Library, New York, MS 638)

An imaginary siege in the early fourteenth-century *Roman du Saint Graal*: Mordred besieging the Tower of London (British Library, MS Add. 10294)

Seal of John de Warenne, Earl of Surrey, 1231–1304 (Public Record Office, Barons Letter)

won by these means. King Stephen, therefore, in his long struggle for the throne of England with his rival the Empress Mathilda, was not necessarily conducting a bad war because he spent so large a part of it moving from one siege to another (e.g. Corfe; Wallingford). The taking of Rochester after two months by John in 1215 was a climacteric in the civil war that followed Magna Carta and ended his reign: the king thereupon embarked on lightning campaigns taking one castle after another, for after Rochester, the Barnwell annalist stated, 'few cared to put their trust in castles'. Perhaps the ultimate demonstration in English medieval history of the superiority of defence over attack is the siege of Kenilworth in 1226, when that castle, doubtless aided by its broad water defences, held out for six months against all the force which the king and his government could bring against it.

Because castles dominated war they also dominated politics, the two not being sharply distinct in an age when political opposition could as a last resort appeal to arms, as a vassal might legitimately rebel in default of justice. For castles were the seats of lords and the centres of lordships, the recognized heads and *capita* of honours, and as such also had to be possessed or repossessed. Like the fief, but even more tightly circumscribed, the castle was held of a superior lord (usually but not always of the king: for mesne castles see e.g. Middleham, Prudhoe, Yelden), and if the feudal bond of fealty was broken then the castle must be taken back into the lord's hand. Hence confiscation and even, as the ultimate punishment and degradation of the contumacious vassal, demolition (see e.g. Bungay, Framlingham). Meanwhile, let us focus on the fact that castles as the fortified residences of lords in a world of lordship were the centres of local, and sometimes national, government and administration – royal castles in an age of personal and itinerant monarchy the scene of great councils and national events (Thomas Becket facing the king at Northampton in 1164; Mary Tudor marrying Philip of Spain at Winchester in 1554), or the headquarters and offices of the king's officials, sheriffs and others; the castles of other great lords than the king (the feudal suzerain, the lord of lords) the headquarters of their lordships and their honours. To the castle thus went vassals to give counsel to their lord and conduct the business of the community of his honour, knights to do their castleguard, and lesser men to plead their causes and to pay their rents. William of Newburgh, writing in the late twelfth century, said of royal castles that they were the bones of the kingdom, and so in effect were the others. A glimpse of the organization of this network in one respect is given by the *Anglo-Saxon Chronicle* for 1074, only a few years after the Norman Conquest brought castles into England. The English Edgar Aethling ('prince') was journeying with his household from his exile in Scotland to the new Norman king in Normandy – 'And the sheriff at York came to meet them at Durham and went all the way with them and had them provided with food and fodder at every castle they came to, until they got overseas to the king.'

The intangible but potent elements of status and prestige must also be included in the motivation of castle-builders and therefore in the purpose and function of the castle. As the fortified residence of a lord and the recognized centre of lordship the castle was a coveted status symbol. It became the symbol as well as much of the substance of authority and visually dominated the landscape as well as potentially dominating the land. And the fortification of the castle – walls and towers, battlements, gatehouse, donjon – is particularly important in this respect, for the ethos of the medieval and feudal aristocracy was military. A career at arms was the only honourable secular career, and the only career for nobles and gentry apart from the Church. So secular lords of whatever degree depicted themselves on their seals armed and mounted as knights, and on their tombs armed *cap à pie*. So in thirteenth-century England the bureaucrats of medieval government decided that crenellation was the demarkation between a fortified and an unfortified house, and those on their way up sought licences to crenellate their houses as a sure sign of mounting social eminence. Further, most if not all castles had one deliberately dominant feature, in French architectural terminology the *pièce maîtresse*, which was at one and the same time the ultimate military strongpoint, to be held if the rest of the castle fell (e.g. the siege of Rochester in 1215), and the inner and privy residence of the castle's lord. In many early castles this was the motte and its superstructure, in many others the great tower, in others an architecturally emphasized inner bailey. The contemporary word for it was *donjon*, derived from the Latin *dominium* meaning lordship, of which it was the supreme expression. Without doubt these considerations of pride and display were as important in the

The castle of Saumur, in a scene from the early fifteenth-century *Très Riches Heures du Duc de Berry*, depicting the month of September (Musée Condé, Chantilly/Giraudon)

The tomb of John de la Pole (d. 1491) and his wife, St Andrew's Wingfield, Suffolk (F. H. Crossley)

The tomb of Sir Thomas Arderne (d. 1391) and his wife, St Peter's, Elford, Staffordshire (Anthony Kersting)

earlier period of the castle's history as in the later, and it is erroneous to suppose that kings and barons, lords and knights in the eleventh and twelfth centuries were somehow more primitive in this, or any other, respect than their successors. Lordship was authenticated by legitimate display and building was a principal medium. And we may see these concepts and practices, of course, as much operative in the subsequent development of castles as in their initial raising, as when after 1138, and his marriage to Alice the queen (young widow of Henry I) and his creation as earl of Sussex, William of Albini II expressed his soaring social eminence not only in the building of two new castles, at New Buckenham and Castle Rising, but also in the grandiloquent development of Arundel, which he had acquired in right of his wife.

Finally, though one should perhaps put it first, the castle is essentially feudal, and the more one thinks about it the more feudal it becomes – the fortified residence of a lord in a society dominated by the lordship of a military aristocracy; if not royal (and the majority were not) then held of the king or superior lord, like the fief but more straitly, in return for loyalty and military service. The castle is also essentially feudal in that it went with, worked in conjunction with, knights who were its *force de frappe*, and were also, as professional and above all mounted warriors, both the military and the social élite of feudal society. One may say that in the beginning what we call feudalism was all about the provision of a specialist heavy cavalry of knights, and castles were another characteristic manifestation of feudal society. And of course if not all knights were great lords, all great lords who held castles were knights themselves, with retinues of knights in their households or at their call. The feudality of the castle, moreover, is not mere theory but fact. While there is obviously no divine rule which prohibits the fortified residence of a lord in any other type of society than that which for other reasons we call feudal, the fact remains that in the West and Latin Christendom (to which it is unique) the castle exactly coincides with the feudal period. The earliest known castle sites, at Doué-la-Fontaine and Langeais, both date from the second half of the tenth century in northern France, which is when and where one would be wise to place the first establishment of a feudal society. The end of feudalism may be more difficult to date than the beginning, but most would agree with its waning in the sixteenth and seventeenth centuries, which witness also in most western countries the final decline of the castle. In England the coastal forts of the Tudors, Camber, Deal and the rest, are not castles, because they have no residential function save as public barracks, and they are all royal or, as we may say, national defences. What is happening is that military power and capacity, once delegated to the king's vassals and their vassals, are being gathered together again as the monopoly of the sovereign state.

In England (and subsequently Wales and southern Scotland and, in the twelfth century, Ireland) castles were a Norman innovation, and the only castles known here before 1066 are those very few – Richard's Castle, Ewyas Harold, Hereford, and at least one other, all in Herefordshire, and Clavering in Essex – which were raised by Norman and French lords already here, the friends of Edward the Confessor and the harbingers of the Conquest. The first acts of the Norman invasion force in the autumn of 1066 included the raising of a castle at Pevensey, where they landed, and another at Hastings, to which they moved. Immediately after the victory at Hastings the crucial burgh of Dover was occupied and a castle placed within it. Castles, no doubt including the future Tower, were placed in London, before the Conqueror entered the city for his coronation on Christmas Day. From then on the pattern of Norman penetration and settlement is marked by the castles which were raised; Norwich, for example, in East Anglia in 1067, Exeter in the far west in 1068, Cambridge and Huntingdon, Warwick and Nottingham, Lincoln and York itself in the course of the new king's expedition to the north in the same year. If these, and others, were the king's castles, others

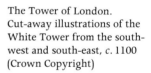

The Tower of London. Cut-away illustrations of the White Tower from the south-west and south-east, c. 1100 (Crown Copyright)

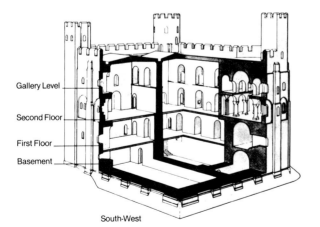

Gallery Level

Second Floor

First Floor

Basement

South-West

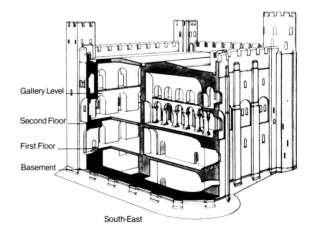

Gallery Level

Second Floor

First Floor

Basement

South-East

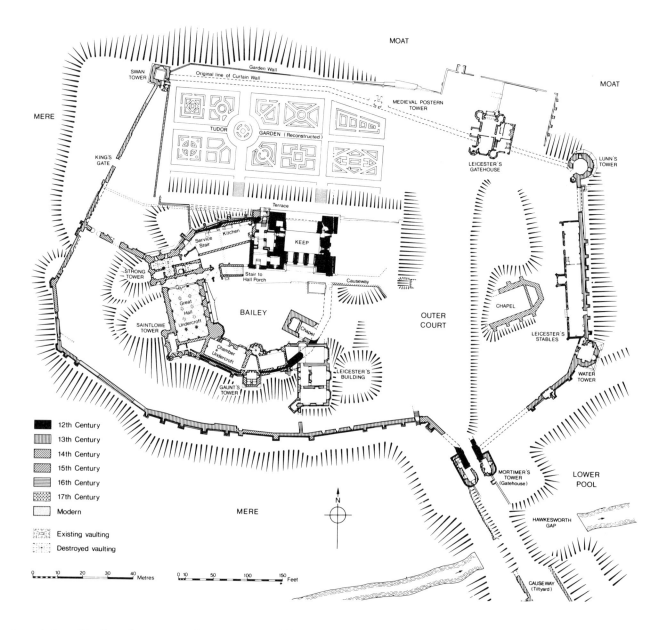

Ground plan of Kenilworth
Castle, Warwickshire (Crown
Copyright)

again were raised by his vassals, and their vassals, all over England as the
headquarters of the lands they now acquired. Castles no less than knights
rendered the Norman settlement permanent. Over and over again in the examples
illustrated in this book the pattern of a castle's history is revealed as one of early
foundation soon after 1066 and thereafter continuing development. Domesday
Book (1086), which does not systematically record castles, nevertheless makes
casual reference to some fifty by the end of the Conqueror's reign, and no less
casually surviving written references of all kinds record some eighty-four by the
end of the eleventh century, both totals being certainly only a fraction of the
contemporary reality. There can have been nothing like the scale and concentration of Norman castle-building in England and Wales (e.g. Chepstow, from the
beginning) in the first generation of the Conquest anywhere else in Latin
Christendom, for not even the Norman conquest of southern Italy or the arrival of

the crusading Franks in Outremer will quite compare. In England and Wales the process of the foundation of new castles will continue, by ongoing expansion of the latter, or by the establishment of new lordships in the former (e.g. Albini at Old Buckenham in the reign of Rufus, or Clinton at Kenilworth by Henry I) until the maximum number of many hundreds of castles (perhaps even a four-figure total) was reached in the first half of the twelfth century. Thereafter, while the overall number declines for economic and political reasons – the cost of building and even maintenance soared, and the contemporary historian Robert of Torigny gave the curiously precise yet unbelievable number of 1,115 castles demolished as unlicensed at the end of Stephen's reign – the addition of a new castle on a new site is comparatively rare.

Orderic Vitalis, writing in the earlier twelfth century, gave their lack of castles as one reason for the English defeat in 1066 and after. The remedying of that situation by the Normans on such a massive scale is dramatic and concrete evidence not just of a change in military organization and tactics but of a social revolution also, the former following from the latter. No castles and no cavalry in pre-Conquest England, where an ancient, Germanic society survived, presided over by a Carolingian-type monarchy. Anglo-Saxon fortifications were communal and national: *i.e.* the burghs of Alfred and his successors were or became fortified towns and cities and all of them were royal, clean different from the residential fortresses of individual lords, the king included. Sociologically the Norman Conquest was the imposition not just of a new ruling dynasty but of a new ruling class, as the Anglo-Saxon or Anglo-Scandinavian aristocracy vanished almost overnight, slain, exiled or suppressed. The new men from northern France with their knights and castles, fiefs and honours, homage and vassalage, brought new attitudes and customs, laws and institutions, and a new military system, and imposed and integrated them on and with the old. Castles and the sites of castles survive in their hundreds all over England and Wales (and southern Scotland and Ireland) as visual evidence of the new order, as they also show the change when we can see them inserted in innumerable instances into pre-existing burghs or walled towns and cities.

Far and away the commonest type of early castle, at least in England and Wales, is the so-called 'motte-and-bailey'. (The descriptive phrase is modern though both words are contemporary. From the Latin *mota* we derive the English 'moat' as a kind of back-formation for the ditch about it.) In the classic motte-and-bailey castle the larger area of the bailey is enclosed by ditch and bank with a timber palisade crowning the latter, and contains all those buildings, assumed to be at first of timber, which a great feudal household required – hall, chambers and chapel, stables and kitchens and other domestic offices. The motte is smaller in area than the bailey but rises above it, is usually placed to one side and has its own ditch about it. Connected to the bailey by a timber bridge, it is often an artificial mound of earth but may be natural in whole or part. It, too, has a timber palisade about the summit and within this a timber tower (p. 10, Plate). But in thus describing the classic motte and bailey it should be emphasized how much we generalize from the particular. Sites abound in every quarter of the kingdom, but very few have been systematically excavated using modern methods (Hen Domen is an exception) and very many sooner or later were rebuilt in stone, their earthworks often to become the mere foundations of towering later structures like Windsor or Arundel, Warwick or Alnwick – or Sandal, though there the masonry has gone again. Apart from archaeology we have only occasional stray literary or documentary references, or the rare description of a particular castle, or the rarer illustration, such as the stylized representations of mottes and their superstructures upon the Bayeux Tapestry. There is inevitably a paucity of detailed evidence to enable us to get back to the eleventh century or the early twelfth.

The timber tower upon the motte might be elaborate, and often if not always contained the apartments of the castle's lord. At South Mimms in Hertfordshire an elaborate tower was taken down to natural ground level within the motte, and the motte, which must have been added to the tower and not vice versa, was itself revetted in timber – arrangements which were reproduced in stone at Farnham. At Abinger in Surrey the timber tower rose from four stout posts, presumably so that the defenders could move freely beneath it on the confined platform of the motte top, after the manner of the tower shown at Dinan on the Bayeux Tapestry, or the tower described by prior Lawrence at Durham in the mid-twelfth century. One method of stabilizing an artificial motte, apart from revetment, was to construct it in a series of rammed-down layers, as shown on the Bayeux tapestry at Hastings, and as is known to have been done at Pleshey and the Old Baile at York. Two or more baileys are common, as at Cainhoe, Clare, Kilpeck and Yelden, though two baileys in line with the motte between them, after the manner of Windsor, Arundel, Rockingham, and perhaps Okehampton, are comparatively rare. More than one motte is very rare indeed, known only at Lewes and Lincoln, and must betoken not a doubling-up of military strength but dual lordship – like the uncommon *donjons jumeaux* in France (e.g. Niort). For the motte with its superstructure, the two integrated in a way we find difficult now to envisage, will be the donjon of the castle which possesses it, i.e. the ultimate expression of lordship, and is sometimes explicitly referred to as such.

The castle of Dinan, from the Bayeux Tapestry. A timber tower and palisade are shown on top of the motte, a ribbed bridge being provided for access. (Ville de Bayeux)

Hastings, from the Bayeux Tapestry. The layered construction of the motte, and the fortification crowning it, are clearly depicted. (Ville de Bayeux)

There is no doubt therefore of the importance of the motte both practically, as the ultimate refuge, and symbolically (on the Bayeux Tapestry most castles are represented simply by their mottes). Nor is there any doubt of the existence of the motte-and-bailey type of castle in northern France before 1066 and its introduction into this country by the Normans; but perhaps its particular predominance here may be due to the unique demands of the Norman Conquest and the ability of this type of castle to meet them. Very large numbers of castles were needed quickly to render the new Norman settlement permanent, while it seemed only a little less important to assert and proclaim the legitimacy of this new lordship. Nevertheless, not all early castles had a motte, nor did they in Normandy (e.g. Le Plessis-Grimoult). Many were simply enclosures of ditch, bank and presumed palisade about the necessary residential buildings – in a word, they were simply baileys. No motte is known, for example, at Pevensey, Dover or the Tower of London, nor at Old Sarum or Rochester, Richmond or Ludlow. Yet so potent was the concept of the donjon that it may seem difficult to conceive at least an early castle of any lord of substance without some ultimate strong-point and inner sanctum, architecturally emphasized as *pièce maîtresse*, though some later castles appear to have nothing of the kind – Harlech or Beaumaris, for example, or quadrangular castles like Bodiam or Bolton. Certainly early castles without mottes appear often to have had an alternative form of donjon, not least the great tower of stone (below), which may be added later, or an inner bailey as at Restormel, Barnard Castle, or the first phase of Castle Acre. And a donjon, once established, of whatever form, seems always to have been kept up as a point of particular pride.

Not all early castles, thus, even in England and Wales, were motte-and-bailey castles, nor, it should be emphasized, were all early castles constructed of

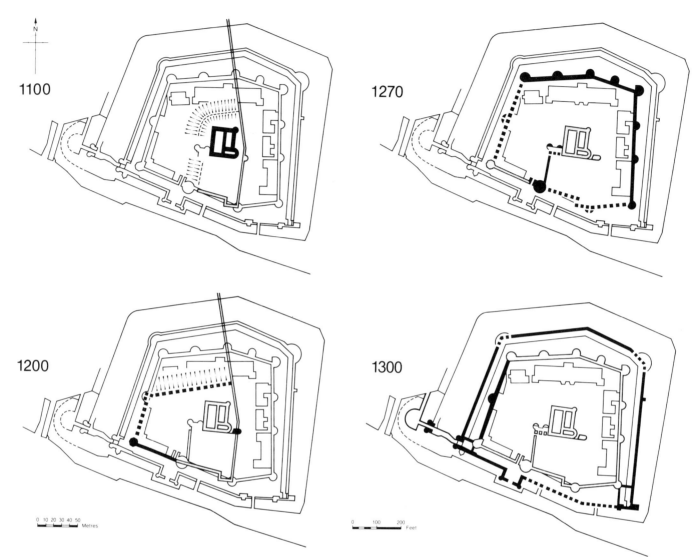

1100

1200

1270

1300

0 10 20 30 40 50 Metres

0 100 200 Feet

```
═══  Building existing before
     this period
███  New building in this
     period
■■■■ Conjectural new building
     in this period
───  Outline of present Tower
     buildings
```

Plans showing the development of the Tower of London in 1100, 1200, 1270 and 1300 (Crown Copyright)

earthwork and timber only, though that is often stated or implied. Masonry was there from the beginning, at Doué-la-Fontaine and Langeais, the earliest surviving castles known, each with a great tower of stone from the late tenth century, or in Normandy in the great tower of the ducal castle at Rouen, dating from the second half of the same century. In England and Wales masonry, i.e. building and fortification in stone, was in some known cases present from the beginning also, or as immediately thereafter as was practically possible – at Richmond, the Peak, and Bramber, for example, and at Ludlow and Chepstow. On the other hand, timber construction, which we tend to associate with the early period, can survive very late: the timber tower upon the motte at royal York evidently stood until 1228, when it was blown down by the wind and had to be replaced by the present Clifford's Tower, while as late as 1302 Edward I built his pele at Linlithgow in timber (albeit as an economy measure). Nor can there easily be a castle, built however late, which does not make use of earthworks at least for its ditches. In short, there is no neat progression from earthwork and timber to masonry as one theme of the castle's development. Instead there will be overlap and piecemeal applications of building techniques and materials (and brick must be added to timber and stone from the thirteenth century). Since in fact the principles of medieval fortification remain much the same throughout, we certainly should not speak of 'the castle of earthwork and timber' or 'the timber castle' as though it were entirely different from something else called 'the stone castle'.

Nevertheless we have good reason to suppose that the great majority of the castles of the first generation of the Norman Conquest in England and Wales were of earthwork and timber, and many, if not all, were raised on the motte-and-bailey plan. Some, we have seen, had stone fortification and/or buildings from the start, and most of the rest were converted earlier rather than later, the process being generally thought to have been especially concentrated during the twelfth century. Conversion, rather than rebuilding, would seem to be the word, for what is involved is often simply the replacement of the palisades about the bailey(s) and the summit of the motte with stone walls, and the rebuilding in stone of any timber gatehouse and such buildings as stood within the bailey(s). The fortification in

Ground plan of Dover Castle, Kent. Though a fortification already existed here in 1066, work on the stone-built castle began only in 1168, during the reign of Henry II. By 1180 a massive £7,000 had already been spent. (Crown Copyright)

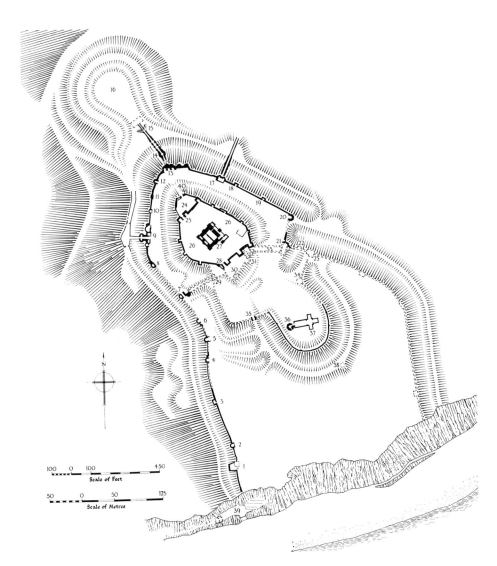

Key

1 Tudor Bulwark
2 Rokesley Tower
3 Fulbert of Dover's Tower
4 Hurst's Tower
5 Say's Tower
6 Gatton Tower
7 Peverell's Tower and Gate
8 Queen Mary's Tower
9 Constable's Tower and Gate
10 Treasurer's Tower
11 Godsfoe Tower
12 Crevecoeur Tower
13 Norfolk Towers
14 St John's Tower
15 Underground passages
16 Outwork
17 Fitzwilliam Gate
18 and 19   Mural towers
20 Avranches Tower
21 Penchester Tower
22 Godwin Tower
23 Ashford Tower
24 North Barbican
25 King's Gate
26 Inner Bailey
27 Keep
28 Palace Gate
29 Harcourt Tower
30 Well Tower
31 Armourer's Tower
32 Arthur's Gate
33 Walled passage between Penchester's and Arthur's Gate
34 Clinton's Tower
35 Colton's Gate
36 *Pharos*
37 Church of St Mary-in-Castro
38 Stone tower-mill
39 Moat's Bulwark
40 Medieval causeway

stone of the motte where one exists generally takes the form of the so-called shell keep (the phrase is modern, not contemporary, and the English word 'keep' for the French 'donjon' dates only from the sixteenth century), i.e. a ring wall about the summit in place of the timber palisade. As a variation, the ringwall revets the motte at Berkeley and at Farnham instead of encircling the summit, and at Tamworth and elsewhere is polygonal, not circular. In what is regarded as the classic shell keep the stone-built residential buildings of the inner sanctum of lordship are disposed about the inner circumference of the wall and thus about a central courtyard, as at Restormel, which in its final form is thirteenth century. At Windsor, where everything survives intact, though the shell-wall was unfortunately heightened in the early nineteenth century, the residential accommodation is timber-framed and fourteenth-century (Edward III). If this analysis is correct, the problem is that the classic shell keep lacks the lofty timber tower which was evidently such a feature of an early motte with timber superstructure. The answer would seem to be twofold: first, the difficulty and structural danger of placing a masonry tower upon an artificial mound of earth, and, second, that nevertheless this was done more frequently than is always realized. Both shell keep and tower keep, the latter within the former, exist or existed, for example, at Clun, Farnham, Guildford, Launceston and Tretower. Further, the shell keep may have an entrance tower (Arundel) and/or other mural towers or turrets (Berkeley, Lewes, Tamworth), and be built up into something much more impressive than a mere crenellated wall crowning a motte, as with the 'Seven Towers of the Percies' at Alnwick, or the great complex formerly standing at Sandal. Such a donjon could

Successive levels of residential accommodation in William de Corbeil's keep at Rochester, Kent, begun 1127 (Crown Copyright)

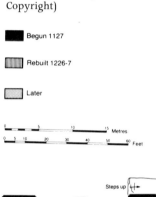

■ Begun 1127

▨ Rebuilt 1226-7

▤ Later

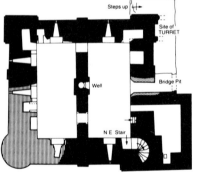

GROUND FLOOR (BASEMENT)

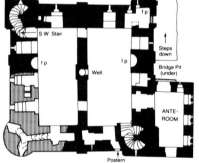

FIRST FLOOR

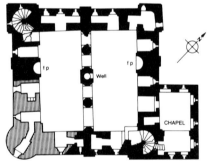

SECOND (PRINCIPAL) FLOOR

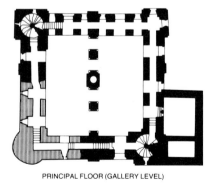

PRINCIPAL FLOOR (GALLERY LEVEL)

THIRD (TOP) FLOOR

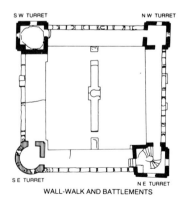

WALL-WALK AND BATTLEMENTS

14

be at least as impressive as a tower keep and it is significant that at Builth, at Rockingham and at Windsor the shell keep is referred to as the 'great tower'. It is also significant for the lasting viability of the type that Edward I, a prince not given to built-in obsolescence, raised a shell keep on the ancient motte when he rebuilt his castle of Builth in and after 1277.

Nevertheless that alternative form of donjon which in contemporary parlance is *magna turris*, the great tower, and in modern archaeological usage the tower keep, was a much favoured feature of the early stone castle, not least in the twelfth century, when many were built and added to existing castles. They straddle that century from Corfe, let us say, via Rochester and Castle Hedingham to Dover, the last by Henry II who was a notable builder of them (cf. Peak, Richmond, Scarborough). But the stone-built great tower goes back to the beginning, in England and Wales to the Conqueror's day at London, Colchester and Chepstow, and in France and Normandy to the tenth century at Doué-la-Fontaine, Langeais and Rouen. Nor is it either obsolete or obsolescent by *c.* 1200, as is often said, but on both sides of the Channel triumphantly goes on to the end as architecturally perhaps the ultimate expression of lordship – in England, for example, at Tattershall or at Warkworth, both of the fifteenth century. Nor should this be surprising, for if one wants an impressive strong house, which is what a castle is and what a keep is, then to draw all the units of halls, chambers and chapel (two chapels at Dover and at Rochester: plus kitchen at Norwich and Castle Rising; garderobes everywhere) into one defensible tower block is one obvious and effective solution. This is especially obvious with that type of keep, evidently beginning at Langeais and found here at Chepstow in the eleventh century and Norwich and Castle Rising in the twelfth, which is oblong rather than vertical, more a very strong hall and chamber block, of two storeys only, than a high tower. Shape varies also. All the earliest known, and almost all the early, tower keeps are rectangular: without doubt the cylindrical tower keep becomes fashionable in the thirteenth century and as from *c.* 1200. Especially is this so in France but in England and Wales we have, for example, Pembroke, Tretower and Launceston amongst others; we may add in practice Henry III's Wakefield Tower at the Tower of London (p. 16); and we may certainly add Conisborough in spite of its buttresses. But the earliest known (though not well-known enough) cylindrical tower keep in England at New Buckenham dates from *c.* 1140, i.e. in the middle of the rectangular period, and the French, at least, date Fréteval to 1040, while in the later medieval period the rectangular great tower comes back again, e.g. at Tattershall, and, of course, had never vanished. Clearly there is fashion here as

Floor plans of William II of Albini's keep at Castle Rising, Norfolk, begun 1138. The prominence accorded the hall is in stark contrast with Rochester. (Crown Copyright)

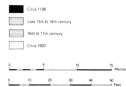

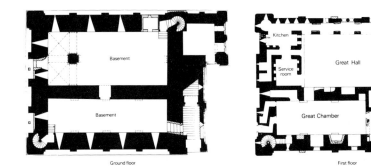

Ground floor   First floor

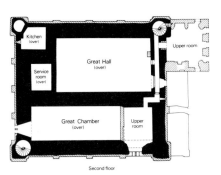

Second floor

The Wakefield Tower at the Tower of London, built in two phases between c. 1220 and c. 1240. The vaulted first-floor hall served as the king's inner or privy chamber. (Crown Copyright)

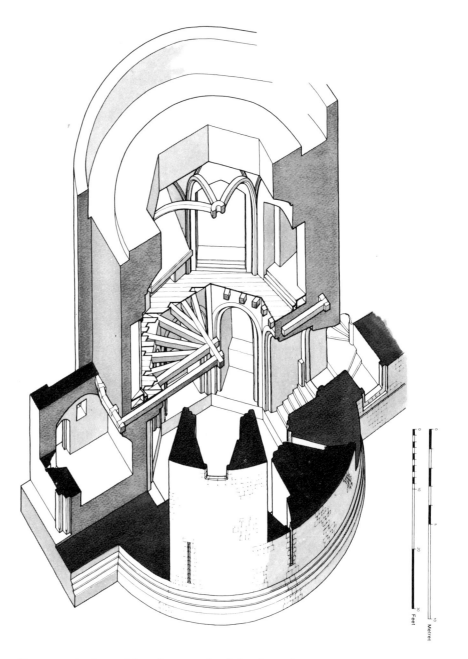

well as practical considerations; and while the cylindrical tower does not offer sharp or blind angles to pick and bore and mine, nor flat surfaces vulnerable to the pounding of artillery, it is much less convenient for the planning of residential accommodation within. And clearly with so sweeping an overlap of date between rectangular and round, we should not label as 'transitional' those great towers which are neither, but polygonal, like Chilham and Orford, Richard's Castle, Tickhill and Odiham. All these, as it happens, are late twelfth or early thirteenth-century, and are perhaps best thought of as experimental, though that category, if it is one, is not confined to that period, as witness the unique keep at Warkworth dating from the fifteenth century, which also produced the polygonal keep at Raglan. Orford was certainly the work of Henry II (as Chilham may have been) and

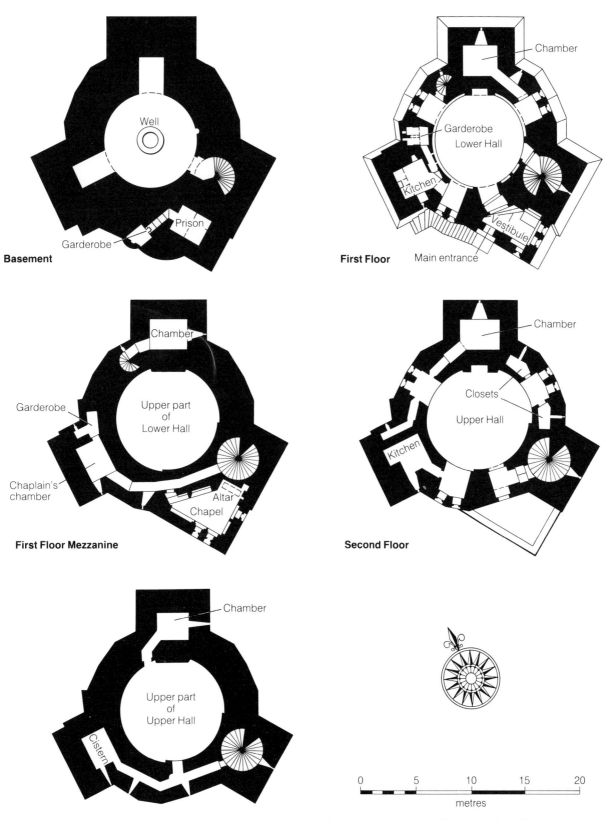

Basement

First Floor

Well

Garderobe
Prison

Chamber

Garderobe
Lower Hall

Kitchen

Vestibule

Main entrance

First Floor Mezzanine

Second Floor

Chamber

Garderobe

Upper part
of
Lower Hall

Chaplain's
chamber

Altar
Chapel

Chamber

Closets

Upper Hall

Kitchen

Second Floor Mezzanine

Chamber

Upper part
of
Upper Hall

Cistern

0   5   10   15   20

metres

The keep at Orford, Suffolk. The residential accommodation lay
on the first and, somewhat grander, second floors.

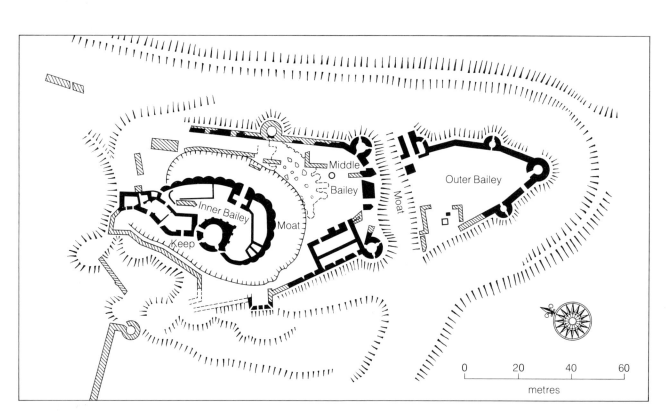

Ground plan of Château-Gaillard, Normandy. One of the finest castles in the west, Château-Gaillard cost Richard I some £7,000–£8,000 between 1196 and 1198. (after Malençon)

just antedates his Dover, the finest of the rectangular keeps: to deduce on that account that Dover keep was obsolete when built is surely absurd. Of the more fanciful shapes than the polygonal, some instances of which are on either side of 1200 but others not, there appears to be no analogy with the quadrilobe French Etampes (*c.* 1140?) in this country until Henry III's Clifford's Tower at York in the later thirteenth century, and no example of the French *en bec* design applied to keeps (e.g. La Tour Blanche at Issoudun, *c.* 1202), though Richard I chose that plan, with embellishments, for his remarkable donjon at Château-Gaillard.

One might say that the two basic principles of medieval fortification were the enclosure and the tower. The first, whether by palisade or wall, is obvious. The second a little less so: we have already seen its ultimate form as the great tower, *magna turris*, but have yet to see it applied to the defence of the enclosure and its entrance. It would be tempting to state that the architectural development of castles lies in the increasingly sophisticated application of those principles were it not for the awkward fact that we are dealing all the time with individual buildings (and usually with the piecemeal development over centuries of those buildings) and in each case so much depends upon particular circumstances, topographical, political and other, and upon the particular intentions, resources and capacity of the lord or patron, and, of course, the capacity of the master mason. It may be true that to look at Conway and Caernarvon, Harlech or Beaumaris, is to know that they were built at the turn of the thirteenth and fourteenth centuries, yet more than technique and design determine their appearance, while Richard I's Château-Gaillard is at least as sophisticated as they are although built a century earlier.

The use of towers to strengthen the enclosure, whether of castle or of walled town, is crucial to medieval fortification. Mural or flanking towers projecting from

18

the exposed outer face of the curtain wall – or palisade – enabled the defenders to cover it without exposing themselves. The summit of the tower was also a fighting platform rising above and thus commanding the summit of the curtain wall or palisade should that be gained by escalade. A series of towers on the circuit of the enclosure also acted as a series of strongpoints to divide it up into commanded sections to contain any breach that might be made. Mural towers in castles also contained useful and prestigious accommodation – never a tower without its chambers at the Tower of London, or anywhere else – for the castle was a residence in terms of its constituent parts as well as of the whole. The technique of the flanking tower was inherited, of course, from the classical past (e.g. Portchester) and was never lost. Recent excavations have shown the use of timber flanking towers in the palisade of Hen Domen and mural towers are there from the beginning also in the eleventh-century curtain at Ludlow and Richmond. An early example of their systematic use and scientific disposition survives at Henry II's Dover (the inner bailey especially) and another very similar at earl Roger Bigod's Framlingham of c. 1190, where the fixed lines of shooting ('fire' and 'firing' are inappropriate words before the use of gunpowder for propulsion) from the arrow slits at various levels have been worked out to cover the whole perimeter to devastating effect. The twelfth-century towers at Framlingham and Dover are open-backed, though doubtless closed originally by timber-framing (cf. the Byward Tower or gate with this arrangement surviving at the Tower of London). They are also rectangular, as are those at Richmond and Ludlow. Shape, however, varies, and the variations coincide with those of the great towers or tower keeps already discussed. That is to say that while the rectangular plan predominates in the eleventh and twelfth centuries, cylindrical is very fashionable from the thirteenth century, though the rectangular may recur later (e.g. Pickering). The rare tower *en bec* occurs at Dover (the Norfolk Towers), and polygonal towers

Ground plan of Edward I's castle at Conway, north Wales, 1283–7 (Crown Copyright)

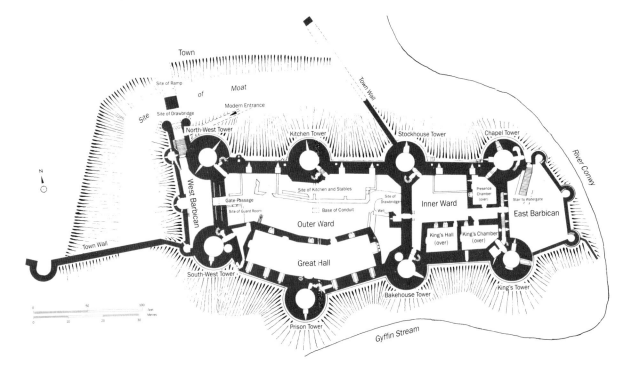

Charles, duke of Orleans, imprisoned in the White Tower of the Tower of London after his capture at Agincourt. This miniature, of. *c.* 1500, shows St Thomas's Tower in the foreground and the public buildings, including the hall, behind and to the right. (British Library, MS Royal 16.F.II)

occur less rarely from the late twelfth century, but without much other regard to date. Two classic single instances are the Avranches Tower at Dover and the Bell Tower at the Tower of London, both of the late twelfth century, but those at Raglan are fifteenth-century. The polygonal towers of Caernarvon, unique in Edward I's castles in North Wales and deliberately evoking the Theodosian Wall at Constantinople, show that in the plan and design of towers there may be other considerations than those of military science and ballistics or even fashion. Of course it is broadly true that mural towers become bigger, better and more sophisticated as time passes, until a kind of apogee is reached, in this as in so many ways, in the late thirteenth century, at e.g. Caerphilly, or at Conway and Caernarvon, Harlech and Beaumaris – or that mural tower to end all medieval mural towers which is Marten's Tower at Chepstow – though it must be remembered that Edward I's castles in North Wales (and Caerphilly scarcely less) are the unique products of unique circumstances, great castles built new from the foundations to hold down new territory acquired from the Welsh, with little

The earl of Salisbury arriving at Conway castle, as depicted in an early fifteenth-century miniature (British Library, MS Harley 1319)

regard to expense, by a rich and powerful prince (or by the greatest magnate in the realm, the Clare lord of Glamorgan, earl of Gloucester, earl of Hertford, lord of Tonbridge and lord of Clare). It is further to be remembered that Edward I's castles in North Wales were built mostly under the direction of a man of genius, Master James of St George, from Savoy, 'master of the king's works in Wales', master mason and therefore their architect.

The principle of the tower was also applied throughout the castle's history to the defence of the gate. The entrance to the castle was a potential weak point and must therefore be made as strong as possible. The earliest form of gate-tower (*sic*) was evidently just that – a single tower pierced by the entrance passage, and thus a strongpoint in the perimeter like any other tower. The gateway at Exeter, which may well be as early as *c*. 1068, is of this type, and so was that at Ludlow in the eleventh century, before its conversion into a tower-keep in the twelfth. The similar gate-tower at Framlingham is as late as *c*. 1190, but by then we can see what now at least appear to be the precursors of the more formidable twin-towered gatehouses in the two gates of Henry II's inner bailey at Dover (King's Gate and Palace Gate). Here a pair of mural towers are brought together on either side of the entrance more strongly to defend it. Make those towers more boldly projecting half-cylinders (as is usually the case – octagonal e.g. at Raglan), join them together to the rear in a block containing the gate-passage, with its defences and porters' lodges at ground level and chambers above, and one has the great gatehouse of the later Middle Ages. Thus, for example, at Caerphilly or Harlech or Beaumaris, where that which was once a weak point is so strong as to contain some of the best residential accommodation in the castle. There is also a third type of gateway found in all periods (and from which the twin-towered type is likely to be derived), in which the gate itself is simply set in the curtain wall but with one or more mural towers nearby to cover it. This, though simple, is by no means a primitive arrangement but is found in some of the finest and most sophisticated castles, including Conway of the late thirteenth century and Bolton of the late fourteenth. It even occurs at Coucy-le-Château (Aisne), of all places, and at the Tower of London, where the first phase of what is now the Bloody Tower was once a water-gate of this type guarded by the majestic Wakefield Tower.

Aerial photography is obviously not the medium to illustrate the details of medieval military architecture and fortification which must therefore only briefly be dealt with here. Curtain walls, mural towers and the great tower itself needed a wall-head consisting of at least a wall-walk and crenellated parapet in order to be effectively manned, and the same is true of the generally earlier and always vanished palisades. The sophistication of stone machicolation, which is a corbelled-out gallery about the summit to defend the base of walls and towers and gateways, is a development of the later Middle Ages and evidently, to judge by surviving remains, commoner in France than in this country; even so it is found on the late twelfth-century keeps of Château-Gaillard and Niort (the latter, Henry II) and is itself only a masonry form of the timber hoarding found from the earliest periods on both sides of the Channel (Rochester keep is one of many places where the beam holes for a timber hoarding can still be seen). While mural towers will have loops for shooting at more than one level other than the summit, walls also in some cases are pierced by shooting galleries, as at the Tower of London (west inner curtain and the so-called Main Guard, both towards the city) and the south front of Caernarvon. Gunports for defence by guns appear in walls and towers from the fourteenth century onwards. The defences of the vulnerable gate can scarcely be better summarized than by listing those provided or intended in the King's Gate at Caernarvon – two drawbridges, one each end, five great doors, six portcullises, loops at various levels, nine *meurtrières* or murder-holes above, and a right-angled bend (for the rare bent entrance in this country, see Denbigh and the inner gate at Pembroke). The barbican or outwork which keeps an enemy at his distance from the gate, or pins him down at his approach, occurs from an early date (e.g. Castle Rising, *c.* 1140) and may be seen at various stages of development at Arundel, Goodrich, Portchester, Prudhoe and Warwick.

If aerial photography is less good for architectural detail, it excels in showing not only the whole building – and sometimes what has gone as well as what remains – but also the relationship of the building to the countryside. Really dramatic mountainous sites, castles perched like eagles' nests on crags, are rare in England, and even in Wales, though the castle of the Peak is one such and a certain drama attaches to those castles situated, sometimes with their attendant towns, on isolated hills or prominent spurs, like Cause or Corfe or Dover, Harlech or Montgomery, or Durham on its river-girt rock. Indeed, although, granted the purpose of castles and the short range of contemporary artillery, we may often find castles seemingly commanded by high ground, the siting of early castles at least on promontories and spurs was very common. By cutting off the area of the castle by a ditch or ditches, and placing the motte, if any, on the end or highest point, a strong and isolated position was at once obtained. Windsor is a famous instance, Okehampton a particularly dramatic one, but there are many others. Similar advantage of natural features is taken by those fewer castles, again sometimes with their attendant towns, which occupy a loop in a river or an isthmus between two waterways, as is the case at Bungay or at Warkworth or Christchurch, while Durham and Pembroke have the best of both these worlds by occupying rocky promontories themselves surrounded by water on three sides. It may well be that some castles are larger than one would expect them to be, as fortified residences rather than fortified towns, because, having been sited on a natural feature which is a natural fortress, they have been compelled by military logic sooner or later to take over the whole position. This is surely the case at Scarborough, for example, while in similar fashion Dover, Old Sarum and perhaps Bamburgh were eventually obliged to occupy all the Anglo-Saxon burgh or city in which they had been founded.

Nevertheless many castles were necessarily founded on relatively flat terrain and without the advantage of any natural defensive features. Their strength then depended wholly upon their construction, and additional defensive elements might be added. One of these was water. Water was always used where possible to fill the ditches, neighbouring streams or rivers being dammed, tapped or even diverted, but sometimes its defensive capacity to keep an enemy at his distance was more extensively exploited. The most devastating instrument of siege warfare against the stone-built castle was the mine: the most effective resistance was to build your castle on the living rock (e.g. Caernarvon, Conway, Goodrich, Harlech), or to provide extensive water defences. The classic examples of the latter in England and Wales are Kenilworth, Leeds and Caerphilly, with Bodiam on a smaller scale, and all are late (Kenilworth in its final phase of development). However, water defences more elaborate than moats are known from earlier periods and, indeed, from the beginning as at York (Clifford's Tower, very extensive but now vanished), while other early examples include Bungay, Clavering, Framlingham and evidently Yelden. The doubling-up of lines of defence to gain added strength, which finds its ultimate expression in the scientifically planned concentric castles of the late thirteenth century – Beaumaris, Caerphilly (concentric fortification combined with wide water defences) and the Tower of London as Edward I developed it – where the outer *enceinte* is low enough to be commanded by the inner, is basically an ancient and obvious device. It is applied on a large scale in the late twelfth century at Richard I's Château-Gaillard and Henry II's Dover, and is surely manifest in those few early 'motte-and-bailey' castles which have double ditches. These – Berkhamsted and Helmsley, Hen Domen and Cause – are rare, and it is probably worth remarking that they were founded in the lordship of the highest in the land and the closest to the new Norman king, namely by Robert, count of Mortain, and Roger of Montgomery; for they may be examples of the *castellum trium scannorum* (two ditches produce three banks) listed in the early twelfth-century law-book, the *Leges Henrici Primi*, as a closely guarded royal right.

Though it may, of course, add to their strength, the planting of castles by rivers, of which there are innumerable examples (Chepstow, London, Ludlow, Rochester, Wark, York), is chiefly to be seen in the context of the control of communications, as castles may be similarly placed by roads, or combine both functions by commanding river crossings (e.g. notably Rochester among those cited above, or Norham or Barnard castle, or Hen Domen for the vital Ford of Montgomery). There are castles also, of course, guarding ports and in communion

with the sea. Matthew Paris called Dover 'the key of England' in the thirteenth
century, Pembroke commanded the passage to Ireland, and Henry II built his new
castle of Orford on the Suffolk coast where the Dunwich river then had its outlet.
Edward I's great castles in north Wales, Conway and Caernarvon, Harlech and
Beaumaris and Flint, were all built upon tidal waters which added to their
impregnability as they could be relieved by sea, while at Rhuddlan the river
Clwyd was diverted through a new cut between two and three miles long so that
sea-going vessels could reach the new castle.

The close association of castles and towns is made more striking by aerial
photography. Usually at once in and after 1066 castles were placed in important
cities – thus London and York, Winchester and Norwich, Lincoln and Rochester –
as they were also placed in Anglo-Saxon burghs and towns of consequence,
amongst others Bamburgh, Dover and Durham, Exeter, Hastings and Pevensey,
Portchester and Old Sarum, Totnes and Wallingford. Often but not always the
castle was placed in one corner of any pre-existing fortifications. But the Norman
Conquest was also the occasion of the foundation of new towns in England and
Wales on some scale, and just as Edward I planted towns and castles together as the
means of the conquest of north Wales, so the Norman *conquistadores* and their
successors planted new towns, often fortified, to go with their new castles to
establish their lordship in and over the kingdom – at Barnard Castle and Castle
Acre, for example, or at Cause and Kidwelly, Launceston and Ludlow and Pleshey.
Castles in any case attracted settlement in offering security and thereby
prosperity, and lords sought settlement not only for prestige but also for the
profits of rents, tolls and services. In this way towns developed at the foot of
castles in the mutual benefit of a true community, though sometimes the old pre-
Conquest world might suffer from the new régime, as when Domesday records that
Robert Malet's new market at Eye has taken trade from the bishop's market at
nearby Hoxne. Still today the market town of Eye is bigger and more important
than neighbouring Hoxne village; but in other cases by now the attendant 'vill' or
township has vanished more completely than the castle, so that aerial photography may reveal the association of known castle sites with 'deserted villages',
as at Anstey, Kilpeck and Pulverbatch, Richard's Castle and Yelden. Indeed
although not all castles were associated with what we would call towns, and there
were towns of consequence like Dunwich or Ipswich without castles, there can have
been few if any castles devoid of closely adjacent settlement after the manner of
eighteenth- and nineteenth-century stately homes which pushed the plebs away.

The castle was also closely associated with the Church. By this is meant more
than the invariable presence of at least one chapel within as a necessary part of the
castle's residential accommodation; or the usual close proximity of the parish
church, often enough supplied by the lord, who was in any case its patron, as part
of his lordship; or even the comparatively rare but by no means unknown
episcopal castle (e.g. Durham, Farnham, Norham), as bishops had temporal
authority thrust upon them. Nor should the association of castles and organized
religion occasion surprise upon reflection, for this was an integrated society in
which the upper echelons of the Church, and the monasteries, were manned by the
same aristocratic families (with daughters in the nunneries) who held the castles,
and it is unwise in any case to underestimate the piety of individual lords. Orderic

Vitalis, commenting on the extraordinary number of new religious foundations in Normandy in the Conqueror's day, and upon that generation of Norman magnates who in making them followed the duke's lead (St Stephen's and Holy Trinity at Caen), wrote that 'the most powerful nobles held themselves cheap if they had not on their domains some establishment of monks or clerks provided by them with whatever was necessary for the service of God'. In that monastic age those same nobles setting up their new lordships in England not only made rich benefactions to the monastery of their patrimony at home, but sometimes, if they did not take on the patronage of an existing religious house, founded a new one on their new demesne, often but not always as a dependency of the Norman convent, as William and Robert Malet founded the Benedictine priory of Eye as a cell to Bernay, or Judhael of Totnes (a Breton) founded his priory, also Benedictine, as a cell to St Serge at Angers. The best known of these new foundations is that of St Pancras at Lewes by the first Warenne lord and Gundreda his wife, who also founded another Cluniac priory at Castle Acre, the *caput* of their East Anglian honour. As further examples, Roger de Busli founded Blyth (Benedictine) in *c.* 1088 as well as his castle of Tickhill, and a little later (for Norman England, like Rome, was not built in a day) the great Roger Bigod in 1103–4 founded his Cluniac priory at Thetford near to his castle there. Monastic houses and great churches were not much less a sign of lordship than castles themselves, and the patronage of monks and clerks was very much an element in contemporary notions of *noblesse oblige*. The nexus of lordship is emphasized the more when it is found that some of these early post-Conquest religious foundations were initially made within the castle itself, only later moving out to a more ample site nearby, as was the case at Castle Acre and at Clare, i.e. the later Stoke-by-Clare. One may sometimes feel that the ideal *caput* of a great honour in the eleventh and twelfth centuries would have been (in the best regalian tradition, like so much else) a fair castle with a fortified town and a great church, preferably monastic. Even in that early period, however, the seigneurial foundation might be merely collegiate, as Robert d'Oilly founded the collegiate church of St George within Oxford castle in 1074. In the later Middle Ages this type of foundation, more domestic and more easily contained within the castle, seems to have become more fashionable, and while St George's Chapel at Windsor now stands alone and supreme, others once existed or were intended to exist, e.g. at Barnard Castle, Warkworth and Tattershall (just outside the castle).

Any survey of castles in England and Wales (or anywhere else) must find room for what English-speaking historians call the fortified manor or, better, the fortified manor-house, and the French the *maison forte*. The castle-proper, in French *le château-fort*, is to be defined as the seriously or heavily fortified residence of a lord, but there were of course no set standards of maximum or minimum strength, and the degree of fortification varied according to individual circumstances and resources. Not everyone required, or could aspire to, a castle strong enough to withstand the assault of armies, nor would it have been appropriate for lesser men to do so. At the lower end of the scale, therefore, we find houses with some pretensions to nobility, which was a nobility of the sword, but without sufficient fortification really to rate as castles and in need of some other term, like fortified manor-house or *maison forte*. Though status was undoubtedly an issue, pro-.

claimed by battlements and towers, the practical motivation was chiefly mere domestic security, and the spirit behind the *maison forte* was that articulated by Patrick Forbes at Corse Castle in Aberdeenshire in *c.* 1500 – 'Please God, I will build me such a house as thieves will need to knock at ere they enter.' This, then, is the context of Stokesay in Shropshire, built by Laurence of Ludlow, a wool-merchant and financier moving into the ranks of the country gentry, Acton Burnell in the same county, built by a bishop, Robert Burnell of Bath and Wells, also Chancellor and friend to Edward I, or Little Wenham in Suffolk, built by John de Vaux, a man of considerable substance yet of the second rank. All these three examples date from the later thirteenth century, but it is important to stress that the *maison forte* can be found in the English kingdom at any period between *c.* 1066 and *c.* 1600. In this country there has been a conventional view that the 'fortified manor' belongs only to the later Middle Ages, the fifteenth century especially (e.g. Oxburgh Hall), and is itself symptomatic of the decline of the castle at that time; while in France a new and improbable-sounding thesis is currently being hammered out, that the *maison forte* is a phenomenon of the mid-thirteenth century, and represents a movement by mere knights to usurp something of the authority and privilege of their social superiors. We should therefore add to the English examples of 'strong houses' from the thirteenth and the fifteenth centuries, already given, the explicit references to *domus defensabiles* in Domesday Book (1086, Herefordshire ff. 184d, 187a), the first phase of Castle Acre, also from the late eleventh century, or Henry of Blois' episcopal palace of Wolvesey from the twelfth, and place all these and others in what is obviously a continuum of comparative strength running according to particular circumstance, and without significance of date, from, let us say, the totally unfortified Wingfield in Derbyshire to Caernarvon or Caerphilly. We must also surely add to the unavoidably ill-defined category of *maisons fortes* the so-called pele towers of the north, dating from the fourteenth century and later, like Belsay, Edlingham, or Sizergh. One may quarrel with the term 'pele' in any case, in that its root meaning is enclosure, not the tower which stood within it, but it is more misleading still if it obscures the fact that these northern peles are strong houses, built by lesser men than great lords in their castles, in self-defence against the raids and burnings of the Scottish border in the later Middle Ages. But finally it is an over-simplification to suppose that the fortified manor as opposed to the castle invariably denotes the lesser man. Ralph, lord Cromwell, in the fifteenth century, amongst other works, built both the fortified Tattershall castle and the unfortified Wingfield manor, and there is nothing at all of the second-rank about William of Warenne, later earl of Surrey, who in the Conqueror's time built both the *maison forte* of Castle Acre and the strong castle of Lewes with its two mottes.

EPILOGUE

The decline of the castle in England and Wales was a slow and piecemeal process ultimately caused by a change in the whole nature of society, namely the decline of feudalism. Certainly it was not due to the introduction of gunpowder in *c.* 1300: the use of heavy guns in warfare had little effect upon military architecture in this country (beyond the insertion of gunports for the castle's own defence) for some two centuries, until the appearance of Tudor coastal forts in the sixteenth century, and the improvisation of earthwork defences to receive the shot about more ancient fabrics in the seventeenth. Indeed, we may take the seventeenth-century Civil War as our epilogue, for, while a good number of castles still survive as stately homes, it is difficult to think in terms of lingering feudalism after 1660. The Civil War, following Tudor neglect, brought about the end of so many castles that it is hard to decide whether to rejoice or deplore that they had that Indian Summer. Nobles who were still vassals in theory and sentiment defending their castles for the king (which is the usual pattern) may seem a fitting end to the history of English feudalism, but the price paid was appalling. Vicious Parliamentary slighting after the war (e.g. Corfe, Montgomery), much of which in any case must seem to us unnecessary, did more brutal damage than the sieges and assaults themselves, which were often amateur by the standards of contemporary Continental warfare, and abandonment and stone-robbing thereafter did the rest. In extreme cases like Basing (no longer strictly a castle by the 1640s) or Sandal almost nothing remained standing save bare earthworks, and even they were not always spared, for the motte at Rockingham was cut down. At Colchester attempted demolition of the great keep in 1683 decapitated what is arguably the most important secular Romanesque monument in the kingdom. To list these sad destructions would be dispiriting, but aerial photography is good on dilapidations (as it is also for modern encroachments on sites) so that Civil War participation and slighting is noted in the commentaries on the individual castles which follow. Meanwhile a better and more buoyant end is made by citing two apposite lines from Browning –

> Boot, saddle, to horse and away!
> Rescue my castle before the hot day.

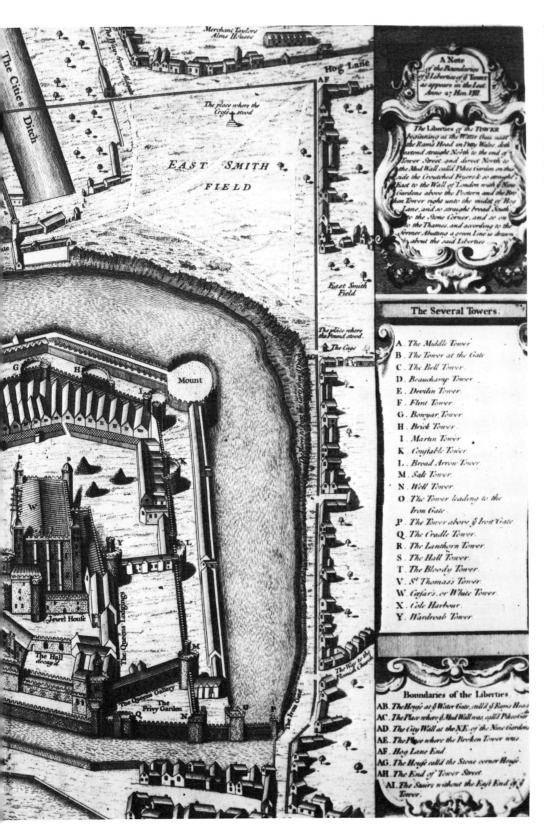

The bird's-eye survey of the Tower of London made in 1597 by Haiward and Gascoigne shows the castle as it was finally developed in the later Middle Ages, but with decay already apparent. Edward I's landward entrance remains, but Ordnance Office stores and workshops disfigure the outer ward to the north, and the palace buildings south of the White Tower are decayed.(Society of Antiquaries)

Château-Gaillard, *Normandy*

Richard I's Château-Gaillard at Les Andelys in Normandy needs no excuse to be included in a book of 'English' castles, for it was built by a king of England who was also the Norman duke (duke also of Aquitaine and count of Anjou). In any case castles in England came from France and more particularly Normandy, so that Château-Gaillard is no more foreign than, say, Henry II's Dover or the Conqueror's Tower of London. Further, it is a masterpiece showing how far the art and science of fortification had progressed by the end of the twelfth century, to create one of the very finest castles, not just in the Anglo-Norman world but also in all Europe, yet this a whole century before such comparable masterpieces as Conway and Caernarvon, Harlech and Beaumaris. The occasion and the context of the great new castle were the wars between Richard Coeur de Lion and the French king Philip II Augustus for the Angevin lordships in France, the protection of Normandy, and more particularly the control of the disputed territory of the Vexin. Richard himself, the foremost soldier of the age, chose the site (belonging to the archbishop of Rouen) and was often present to urge on the work which to a degree he directed.

Château-Gaillard from the north-west, the inner bailey with its great cylindrical keep nearest the camera. Compare the plan on page 18.

The accounts survive and appear to show that the building was achieved in the two years 1194–6, which is almost unbelievable, still more so when it is realized that the castle was only the crown of a whole new complex fortification comprising also the fortification of, and building of a royal residence upon, the Isle of Andeli (left on the photograph), and a new and fortified town (now Le Petit Andeli) opposite the island on the right bank of the Seine and at the foot of the rock on which the castle stands. The defences of the new town included the flooding of the cultivated land to form a lake between it and the old town (now Le Grand Andeli) one mile inland, crossed by a causeway which still bears the modern road (clearly shown on the larger photograph); and the Seine was crossed and barred by a stockade and bridges from the left bank (off the photograph) to the new town via the two islands of Gardon (extreme left) and Andeli. The castle itself, 'the Saucy Castle' and 'the Fair Castle of the Rock', beggars all description in the sophistication of its design and execution. Outer bailey, middle bailey and inner bailey, each separated by a rock-cut ditch, are lined up on a ridge one behind the other in the only direction from which attack can come. The inner bailey stands within the middle bailey, and the keep within the former, applying thus the principle of concentric fortification. Boldly projecting drum towers adequately cover the outer curtain, 'Butavant' thrust forward at the prow on the forward edge of the rock (nearest the camera); but the extraordinary eliptical construction of the inner curtain of the inner ward obviates the need for flanking towers which are, so to speak, incorporated within it. Lastly the keep or donjon, as close as one can get to the dangerous word 'unique' in architectural history, cylindrical but *en bec*, its solid beak pointing towards an enemy, wedge-shaped corbels rising from the circumference to carry the arcades of a now vanished war-head. (A slightly earlier primitive version of this design without corbels or arcades survives at the French castle of La Roche Guyon a few miles further south up-river). 'Behold, how fair is this year-old daughter of mine!' Richard is said to have exclaimed as the castle approached completion, at astonishing speed and prodigious cost, and he is said also to have been so pleased with it as to boast that he could hold it even if its walls were made of butter. In the event, his successor, John, could not; yet when Château-Gaillard eventually surrendered on 6 March 1204, it was only after a siege and complete investment of three months duration, with the exhaustion both of supplies and hopes of relief; and when it fell to Philip Augustus the duchy of Normandy fell with it.

Doué-la-Fontaine, *Maine-et-Loire*

Here, in the Loire valley, what is now the earliest known and visible castle site in France and Europe enables us almost to see the origin both of the castle itself, and of the rectangular, stone 'great tower' or tower keep which is the best known type of castle donjon. Saved in the nick of time from the bulldozers sent to raze it in 1966, the motte was excavated between 1967 and 1970 by Professor Michel de Boüard of the University of Caen (Centre de Recherches Archéologiques Médiévales), with spectacular results. Beneath and within the motte there was discovered, first, a rectangular stone building measuring some 23 m by 16 m, its walls still standing to a height of 5 or 6 m on a roughly north–south axis. The principal doorway was to the west with another south, and there had been a window in each of the south and north walls. An east–west cross-wall had been inserted at a slightly later date dividing the interior into two very unequal parts, the larger to the north. This building, which itself stood upon the site of a vanished Carolingian royal palace (*palatium*), was identified as the hall of an early princely residence, built about the year 900, and probably pertaining to Robert I, who became king of the West Franks in 922. The discovery thus of a late Carolingian, stone-built, ground-floor hall was exciting enough, but even more exciting were

The Carolingian hall at Doué-la-Fontaine, precursor of the rectangular tower keep of the full medieval period

the revealed facts that, having been burnt out towards the middle of the tenth century (930 × 940?), this unfortified lordly residence was soon afterwards restored and fortified, *i.e.* transformed into a castle. Further, the fortification comprised the blocking of the original groundfloor doorways and windows and building up the former hall into a strong tower of one or probably more storeys above what became the ground floor basement, entrance being henceforth provided at first-floor level, covered by a timber forebuilding. In other words, Doué-la-Fontaine becomes not only the earliest castle but also the earliest tower keep, 'great tower' or donjon. The context of the firing of the unfortified hall-type dwelling is thought to have been the wars between the early counts of Blois and Anjou, and the fortification and construction of the great tower to have been by the former against the latter. In short, in so far as Doué-la-Fontaine represents the origin of the castle in Europe, its advent both in place and time is almost exactly where we should expect to find it, namely in northern France in the mid-tenth century, with the origins of feudal society and the break-up of the Carolingian kingdom.

From our point of view the remaining history of this site at la Chapelle is inevitably an anti-climax. Early in the eleventh century a motte was added about the base of the hitherto free-standing great tower by the count of Blois, but soon afterwards, the town having fallen to the rival count of Anjou along with Saumur in 1025, the tower was demolished to the level of the motte and a new castle founded on a new site, i.e. the present one, about a kilometre away.

FURTHER READING

Michel de Boüard, 'De l'aula au donjon: les fouilles de la motte de la Chapelle à Doué-la-Fontaine (x^e – xie siècle)', *Archéologie Médiévale*, III – IV.

Langeais, *Indre-et-Loire*

Until the discovery of Doué-la-Fontaine in the late 1960s, Langeais was the oldest known surviving castle site in Europe – again in northern France and the Loire valley. It is attributed to Fulk Nerra, count of Anjou, in c. 994, and again the context is the rivalry in the formation of their feudal principalities between the counts of Anjou and Blois. Again what survives (generally but not universally taken to be part of the original castle) is a stone building, in fact the donjon of Fulk's castle. But if Langeais, like Doué-la-Fontaine, is to be considered a prototype of the rectangular tower keep, it is of that type which is more oblong than vertical, more a strong first-floor hall than a tower proper, such as is described by William of Poitiers at Brionne in the mid-eleventh century – 'a stone hall serving as a keep (*arx*)' – or such as survives from the late eleventh century at Chepstow and from the twelfth century at e.g. Castle Rising, Norwich and Falaise. Such a design further emphasizes the residential function of donjon and castle alike, whatever their military strength. What remain now are the east wall (the

33

The donjon at Langeais, thought to have been erected *c.* 994 by Fulk Nerra, count of Anjou

longer) and the north wall of a rectangular building whose interior measurements are 16 × 7 m. The walls now stand 12 m high and there were two principal storeys, a blind basement and a well-lit *étage-noble* or residential floor above. Altered in other respects also later, the buttresses of the east wall are thought to be an addition of the earlier twelfth century and a now vanished forebuilding was added to the south end of this east wall in c. 1100. The entrance was at first-floor level. The building stands upon a natural rise, not a motte, adjacent to the better-known *château* of 1465. The rest of the ancient castle was destroyed in 1427 and the donjon itself was partly demolished in 1841. It is not, unfortunately, open to the public but belongs to the Institut de France.

Acton Burnell, *Shropshire*

Acton Burnell, a few miles south-east of Shrewsbury, is at the low end of the scale of the fortified residences of lords, scarcely a castle at all but, as befits a bishop, an elegant example of what we call the fortified manor and the French (more accurately) the *maison forte*. It was built in the late thirteenth century, beginning in 1284, by Robert Burnell (d. 1292), bishop of Bath and Wells from 1275, Chancellor from 1274, friend and counsellor of Edward I both before and after that king's accession in 1272. Though more or less self-contained (there are no kitchens nor obvious service rooms and in the latest and best analysis of the building no chapel is identified), the present house cannot have stood alone, but is best envisaged as the principal lodging for the bishop within an enclosed manorial complex. Indeed, to this day the gable ends of a great aisled barn of similar date stand 100 yards to the east. The parish church, stylistically a few years earlier than the house and immediately to the west of it, was presumably outside this enclosure though built or rebuilt by Robert Burnell in what had been his family manor.

The strong house as we have it (cf. Little Wenham and Stokesay) is finely built of red sandstone, rectangular in plan with square angle turrets and a similarly projecting gardrobe block in the centre of the west front. It has been little altered though it was damaged in the eighteenth century when it was used both to contain and screen farm buildings (and the attractive but entirely incorrect roofs of the gardrobe block and south-west turret put on). It measures 23 m on the east – west axis and 17 m north to south, its lateral bays marked by bold buttresses and its four turrets and western gardrobe block rising above the general level. Its strength

was minimal, denied by its windows and largely confined to the crenellated parapets of its wall walks and turrets. Nevertheless that crenellation marks the lordly status of the building and its owner. Inside, the principal apartment was the great hall at first-floor level, where it occupied three-quarters of the space available, was open to the roof, and was reached from the main entrance in the north-east turret. (The entrance lobby within the turret at this level has formerly been identified as the chapel.) West of the hall were the bishop's chambers on two levels. On the ground floor, beneath the bishop's suite, was a lower hall with chambers to the west, perhaps forming the suite of the steward of the manor and estates. Thought to have been quite early abandoned as a residence after Robert Burnell's time, the building was taken into guardianship by the then Office of Works in 1930.

Alnwick, *Northumberland*

In many ways to see Alnwick is to think of Arundel, and vice versa. Both are now grand, ducal castles, the stateliest of stately homes, standing above all for a splendid continuity of occupation. Yet both (like Windsor) have paid heavily for their continuance, outright rebuilding in the nineteenth century eventually following the inappropriate alterations of preceding generations. In the case of Alnwick, whatever was done (and it was much) by the first duke of Northumberland when the castle's fortunes revived in the later eighteenth century was undone a century later by Anthony Salvin for the fourth duke. The result, however, bears much more than a passing resemblance to the great medieval border castle as it had been developed principally in the twelfth and fourteenth centuries. The original lay-out of motte and two baileys is still there. The motte is still crowned with the great donjon, however much rebuilt, taking the form of an inner enclosure, crammed with state apartments and heavily defended, after the manner of Norham or Barnard Castle. It probably began as a shell keep of mid-twelfth-century date and was developed with the seven towers of the Percies – very much still there and emphasized by Salvin – in the fourteenth century, when the gateway took on its present form from the 'Norman' original. The towers and curtains of the two baileys, east and west, retain vestiges of twelfth-century work and much of the fourteenth – notably the main outer gate to the town (west) with its long, elaborate barbican (cf. Warwick), the integrated whole dating probably from the later fourteenth century, and perhaps from 1377 when the then Percy lord of Alnwick was created earl of Northumberland.

The first reference to the castle, as 'very strong indeed', occurs in 1138, but its foundation is earlier, usually attributed to Ivo de Vesci in *c.* 1100, and probably going back to his father-in-law, William Tyson, the first post-Conquest lord of Alnwick. Ivo was succeeded by Eustace fitz John who had married his daughter and heiress Beatrice, their son William adopting the name of Vesci from his mother. Thenceforward the house of Vesci were the lords of Alnwick until 1297. Eustace fitz John (d. 1157) is thought to have built and fortified the castle in stone, and the most famous incident in its history occurred in the time of his son, William I de Vesci (d. 1183), when William the Lion, king of Scots, besieging the castle in

1174, was surprised and captured by a relieving force under Ranulf de Glanville. In 1309 Alnwick passed to the Percies, a house in the ascendant, in whose hands, with deviations and diversions, it has ever since remained. They were responsible for much work here, though Warkworth rather than Alnwick became their principal seat and the headquarters of their government of the March after their acquisition of it in 1332. By the mid-sixteenth century the castle was in decay, and the first Percy line ended in effect in 1670, both to await their renaissance in the mid-eighteenth century.

Anstey, *Hertfordshire*

Anstey, now in the grounds of Anstey Hall which it dwarfs, is a fine example of a so-called 'motte-and-bailey' castle, not least when seen in an aerial photograph. That is to say, that although the castle in its heyday did not look like this, and comprised much more than the naked earthworks now alone surviving, those fundamental earthworks do survive very impressively – the ditched and banked enclosure of the divided bailey north-east and south-east of the motte, and the great motte itself, once the donjon, its ditch still water-filled, rising some 10 m from the base, flat-topped, the area of its summit some quarter of an acre. At Anstey there is also a small, subsidiary mound south-east of the motte by its junction with the bailey, called the Barbican Mount and possibly indicating the position of the entrance. There are also distinct traces of a bank striking off west of the motte which may be the remains of the enclosure of a thus fortified vill or township (cf. Pleshey). There is no visible masonry and the site has never been scientifically excavated.

The castle has little known history. It is traditionally ascribed to Eustace, count of Boulogne, who held the manor in demesne in Domesday – though it may be worth noting that the present church is dated only from the later twelfth century on architectural grounds. The manor remained a member of the honour of Boulogne thereafter, and as such was held by king Stephen as count of Boulogne, who granted it to Geoffrey de Mandeville in 1141. By the later twelfth century, at least, the castle was in existence, held, as tenants of the lord of the honour, by the family of Anstey–Hubert, who died in 1210, and Nicholas, who may have died in 1225. While tenurial references (e.g. land held of the castle etc.) continue into the later Middle Ages, the only known direct references to the castle as a going concern occur in the thirteenth century, and the first is of considerable interest in showing that it was of military and political significance in the reign of John. Nicholas of Anstey joined the opposition to the king, and in consequence his lands were confiscated in 1215. After the civil war they were restored, but a writ of November 1218 orders that the fortifications of his castle of Anstey are to be reduced to the *status quo ante bellum*. Nicholas may do this himself, and have respite until Easter for doing it, but anything erected after the outbreak of war is to be demolished by view of the sheriff, and nothing is to remain which was not there of old.

Arundel, *Sussex*

Arundel castle, at the end of a high ridge above the river Arun (and then with access to the sea), was raised here by Roger II of Montgomery soon after December 1067. Second only to William fitz Osbern in the Conqueror's friendship and favour, he had been left behind in the autumn of 1066 to help the duke's wife and son in the government of the duchy in his absence, but now came to England in the triumphant king-duke's train, ripe for rich reward. He received what was henceforward the rape of Arundel (which then included Chichester, where he planted another castle) and, in addition, in 1071, the county of Shrewsbury – where he has left the name of his Norman patrimony in the town and castle of Montgomery. Earl Roger (d. 1094) is responsible for Arundel's foundation and plan of two baileys, one on either side of the motte, after the manner of Windsor, and he and/or his son earl Robert (of Bellême) for its first stone fortification and masonry buildings, the core of the present gatehouse (less its barbican) being attributed to the eleventh century together with traces of presumed residential buildings at the south end of the towering modern block in the lower (eastern) ward.

The castle was besieged, taken and confiscated from the house of Montgomery-Bellême by Henry I in 1102, because earl Robert supported the king's rival, Robert Curthose, duke of Normandy, the Conqueror's eldest son and expected successor, and remained in royal hands until 1138 when it passed to the young William of Albini (Aubigny) II as the dower of the queen, Alice of Louvain, second wife and widow of Henry I, whom he married in 1138. He was created earl of Sussex (or

Arundel) by the new king, Stephen, and celebrated his brilliant marriage and social elevation with an architectural display which included two new castles, New Buckenham and Castle Rising, in Norfolk, and what was evidently the second major phase in the development of Arundel. To him, soon after 1138, the fine shell keep upon the motte, with its richly ornamented doorway, is now attributed, and he was evidently responsible for, amongst other things, a new or extended residential range, still traceable beneath the modern one at the south-east end of the castle, and for some or all of the walling-in at least of the upper ward with towered and buttressed curtain.

On William of Albini's death in 1176 Arundel was retained from his heir by Henry II who is known to have carried out some works here and may be responsible for the two-light windows which can still be seen in the outer face of the south-east front and presumably mark Albini's hall. But in spite of this, and similar difficulties in regaining the castle and lordship from Richard I, the Albini earls of Sussex remained at Arundel until 1243 when the last of them, earl Hugh, died without male heirs and the inheritance was divided among sisters and co-heiresses. Isabel then brought Arundel to the house of fitz Alan, but it was not until 1289 that the new lord, Richard fitz Alan, was created earl of Sussex by Edward I. And it was evidently this social elevation in turn which marks the third known and major phase of the castle's medieval development, thus demonstrating

40

again how personal a matter building is, of castles no less than other and unfortified houses. Of what remains of the medieval fabric of Arundel, as yet insufficiently studied, the great barbican of the gatehouse, and the latter's alteration and heightening to accommodate it, is attributed to earl Richard fitz Alan, and so is the alteration of the keep upon the motte by the closing of the Albini entrance and the addition of the present stairway, entrance vestibule and adjacent Well Tower. We may be sure of much more but know little about it.

It is often said of Arundel, as it has been said of Windsor, that what we see is a nineteenth-century castle. Again the observation is unjust, though certainly general views and distant vistas largely display a deliberate modern creation and certainly Arundel has suffered both negatively and positively in the modern period. Much damage was done by slighting following the Civil War siege of December 1643 to January 1644, and thereafter a long period of neglect was followed by the extensive works of the eleventh duke, between c. 1790 and c. 1810, and the overwhelming works of the fifteenth duke, in the 1890s, which combined almost to obliterate the medieval residential ranges in the lower ward and heavily to restore much else. Nevertheless within Arundel there is still a fine medieval castle waiting to get out, though there has never yet been a St John Hope to help it. Meanwhile Arundel, again like Windsor but also like Alnwick, stands for the continuity of the lordly residential role of castles, and is still satisfyingly occupied, as it has been since the sixteenth century, by the Howard dukes of Norfolk, indirect descendants of fitz Alan and Albini if not of Montgomery-Bellême.

Bamburgh, *Northumberland*

Worse things than neglect, decay and ruination can happen to medieval buildings, as Bamburgh amply demonstrates. The rock site by the sea could not be more dramatic, nor its history more romantic, yet little that is original or authentic is now to be seen upon it. The place has been called 'the birth-place of England' (i.e. derived from Angles rather than Saxons) and the long summit of the basalt rock was once occupied by the royal city of the kings of Bernicia and ancient Northumbria. On the highest point of the rock (north-east), where the castle chapel came to stand, was the church of St Peter, whose most precious relic was the right arm of St Oswald. After Athelstan's conquest in 926, Bamburgh became the headquarters of the earls rather than the kings of Northumbria, and so remained until late in the eleventh century. Within it the Normans placed their castle, on the analogy of Dover or more nearly Durham, its foundation perhaps being by the Conqueror himself. At least the earlier architectural history of the castle is in fact obscure because of the frequent failure of historians (and, less culpably, their sources) to distinguish between the castle and the ancient burgh in which it stood. Clearly the castle was what came to be the inner ward to the east with the keep on its west or city side, and may not have taken in the whole position until the thirteenth century (cf. Dover) if, indeed, it ever did. The rectangular tower keep is

(or was) twelfth-century and may have been raised by the Scottish Henry earl of Northumberland (son of David I, king of Scots) who held Bamburgh in Stephen's reign. From 1157, when Henry II resumed it, until 1610, when James I alienated it to one Claudius Foster, it was a royal castle. The most dramatic events in the active history of the castle are the siege of 1095, when William Rufus took it from Robert de Mowbray, the last Norman earl of Northumbria, and 1464, when the earl of Warwick took it for the Yorkists, his great guns 'Newcastle' and 'London' doing great damage. That damage was never wholly to be made good, and throughout the sixteenth and seventeenth centuries the castle was allowed steadily but honourably to decay. In 1704 it was bought by Lord Crewe, bishop of Durham, the trustees of whose estate thereafter did terrible things in the name of charity (cf. Framlingham). A century later Fate struck again with Lord Armstrong's 'restoration' of 1894–1905, of which it has been said that it combined 'the acme of expenditure with the nadir of intelligent achievement'.

Barnard Castle, *County Durham*

Barnard Castle in Teesdale, both castle and attendant town, are the product of the Norman settlement of the north, founded on a 'green field' site as the *caput* of a lordship conferred upon Guy de Balliol (Bailleul-en-Vimau, dep. Somme, arr. Abbeville) in *c.* 1095 by William Rufus, who also granted him the future barony of Bywell. These lands and their lordship had previously been centred upon Gainford, and had probably pertained to the Old English earldom of Northumberland (of which the Norman Robert de Mowbray was deprived in that year) while certainly before that they had belonged to the churh of St Cuthbert. Hence the repeated but unsuccessful claims of the bishops of Durham to overlordship in the following centuries, and hence the fact that in Guy de Balliol's time the new church of St Mary in his new town was a mere chapelry of the parish church at Gainford. That Guy de Balliol founded both castle and town seems clear, though both take their name from his nephew and successor Bernard, who is known to have succeeded by 1130 but on charter evidence cannot have done so before 1112. This Bernard I de Balliol (d.*c.* 1150) granted the first borough charter to the town (its liberties modelled on those of Richmond), and no doubt carried out substantial works at the castle as well. The house of Balliol was established at Barnard Castle for almost exactly two centuries, in 1233 making a great leap forward socially when John I de Balliol married Devorguilla, co-heiress of the lord of Galloway (they jointly founded Balliol College, Oxford). As the result of that marriage his successor, John II, became king of Scotland in 1292. The result of that in turn was his forfeiture at the hands of Edward I, whereafter castle, town and lordship were granted to the Beauchamp earls of Warwick who in the fifteenth century were succeeded by the Nevilles. After the death of Warwick the King-Maker in 1471 Barnard Castle reverted to the Crown, and so remained until one Sir Henry Vane bought it and in 1630 dismantled it for the materials which he used in the reconstruction of his castle at Raby.

The castle, which in Leland's words 'stondith stately apon Tese', was planted on a high cliff sheer above the river, by an ancient ford a little to the north of the later bridge, and the town laid out to the east of it. In spite of extensive excavations in the last decade there is almost no firm date in its subsequent development. Eventually, at least, it covered a very large area, now encroached upon, with four wards, *viz.* the Inner Ward with the Town Ward to the east of it, the Outer Ward to the south, and the small Middle Ward between the Outer and the Inner. From start to finish the Inner Ward was the core of the castle, a veritable donjon (cf. Alnwick) combining its principal strength and its principal accommodation, the great rock-hewn ditch about it a (twelfth-century) enlargement of the first moat. Here stood the hall (several times rebuilt) and chamber block (twelfth-century, but its oriel windows attributed to Richard III – cf. Middleham) and here the great Round Tower was added, which still dominates the castle and is thought to mark the elevated marriage of 1233. In spite of current archaeological theories, it still seems reasonable to suppose that at least the present Town Ward went with this inner enclosure from the beginning as its necessary outer bailey. Its stone curtain is dated to the twelfth century and it contained a principal gateway to the castle (north), and another (lesser and twelfth-century) hall. The Middle Ward was a kind of barbican to the entrance to the Inner, and the evidently thinly defended Outer Ward (not archaeologically investigated) one might not take seriously had not Leland noted a 'fair chapelle' in it. Leland also noted two chantries in it, and one may perhaps wonder if this vanished edifice, most inconveniently distant from the state apartments, was not the remnant of the collegiate church founded in his castle by Richard, duke of Gloucester, the future Richard III.

FURTHER READING

David Austin, 'Barnard Castle, co. Durham', *Château-Gaillard*, x.

Old Basing, *Hampshire*

The end of what by then was Basing House, stormed, sacked and burnt by Cromwell himself on 14 October 1645, is better known than the beginning, though the total destruction of the great house so long and gallantly defended has laid bare the earthworks of the former castle whose site it occupied. This was the castle of Hugh de Port (Port-en-Bessin, Calvados), the Domesday lord of Basing and much else, who died a monk at Winchester in 1096. It was the *caput* of the honour held by him and his descendants who, in the thirteenth century, adopted the name of St John (St-Jean-le-Thomas, Manche) through marriage. It took the form of a formidable inner enclosure, as opposed to a motte (cf. Castle Acre), and two baileys still tolerably preserved in spite of sixteenth-century terracing and building, and seventeenth-century outworks dating from the Civil War. In spite of extensive modern excavation almost nothing is known of the medieval buildings. The castle and lands passed to the family of Paulet in 1428, created earls and then marquesses of Winchester in the 1550s, and John Paulet and his family were the heroes of the siege. 'Basing stands for loyalty' declared the marquis, and that was its undoing when the times were out of joint.

Beaumaris, *Anglesey*

Amongst Edward I's castles in Wales Beaumaris lacks the dramatic profile of Harlech, or Caernarvon or Conway, because it lies in flat, marshy ground, and because even less than Caernarvon was it ever finished, not one of the great towers of the inner *enceinte* rising to its full height nor surmounted by its turret. Yet the concept and plan were as impressively formidable as anything produced by the warrior king and his master mason, Master James of St George, and the circumstances of the inception of this, the last of their Welsh castles, were dramatic enough. In September 1294 the Welsh broke into revolt against the new English rule, and amongst other outrages overran Anglesey and hanged the royal sheriff, who was also the king's friend, Roger de Pulesdon. Retaliation was swift in the devasting winter campaign of 1294–5, and by the spring the island was re-occupied and preparations put in hand for the raising of the new castle and borough which had doubtless been envisaged in 1283 but never undertaken. Edward himself was there from *c.* 10 April to 6 May, staying at the ancient Welsh township of Llanfaes nearby, now to be razed to the ground and its inhabitants moved lock, stock and barrel to a new settlement twelve miles away at Newborough. Throughout the summer, men, money and materials were poured into Beaumaris. 'Never before . . . had so much treasure been applied so swiftly to one single operation' (A. J. Taylor). By the autumn over £6,000 had been received and spent, almost every (silver) penny upon the castle, for the new town also founded was not to receive its walls for another century. A letter of Master James of St George and his clerk of works, Walter of Winchester, to the Treasurer, dated at Conway on 27 February 1296, reports that the castle was already defensible as the king had required, with the curtains of the main inner enclosure and the flanking towers of its two gates standing from 6 m to 8.5 m in height. Already, however, more money was urgently required, and to maintain the progress which the king desired they estimated a need for at least £250 a week in the coming season. This pace, however, proved impossible to sustain, as the king's energies and resources were diverted more and more into his Scottish wars. In the season of 1296 only £742 were received though £2,323 were spent. In the years immediately following both receipts and works declined even more sharply and virtually ceased after 1298. In 1306, however, they were resumed and continued at a reduced rate until 1330, by which time a total of some £14,400 had been spent on the still unfinished castle, and its planners, Edward I (1307) and Master James of St George (1309), were both long dead.

One should not, however, think only negatively, in terms of incompletion, about this magnificent building so nearly achieved. Beaumaris is, above all, in conception and almost in execution the perfect concentric castle (cf. Caerphilly – and the Tower of London), the chosen site with no natural advantages save the sea requiring a doubling or, rather, trebling of defences – outer moat (filled with controlled tidal waters), outer curtain (formidably equipped with turrets and loops and complete save for the North Gate) and the massively fortified Inner Ward, the ultimate strength of the castle. The Inner Ward had four cylindrical towers, one at each angle, and two D-shaped towers, one in the centre of each of the two sides without gatehouses. They were intended to be three storeys high, a

basement and two residential floors, though all lack their top storeys and turrets. At Beaumaris there were two massive gatehouses, north and south, each on a very similar plan to the great gatehouse at Harlech but even bigger. Neither was completed: the Northern Gatehouse stands almost to its full height to the field but lacks the top hamper of its rearward section; the Southern Gatehouse rises no higher than the curtain walls at the front and now at least has little more than its foundations at the rear. The Southern Gatehouse had in front of it a barbican as well as the outer gate in the outer curtain (the Gate next the Sea) and by the latter a defended dock so that sea-going ships could unload straight up to the castle. Finally, Beaumaris was planned to contain even more lavish accommodation than usual, with no less than five suites of hall and chambers for those of high degree, two in each gatehouse at first- and second-floor levels and a fifth in the north-east section of the Inner Ward, served directly by the chapel (still in the Chapel Tower at first-floor level) and thus presumably intended for the lord of the castle, *i.e.* the king or Prince of Wales.

A more or less adequate maintenance in the fourteenth and fifteenth centuries followed by outright neglect in the sixteenth was to be the pattern of the future. In 1534 there was said to be 'scarcely a single chamber . . . where a man could lie dry', and by 1609 Beaumaris, like Conway, was reported to be 'utterlie decayed'. Nevertheless, it was put into a state of defence in the Civil War and held for the king until its surrender on 14 June 1646. Some dismantling followed, not under the Republican régime but at the Restoration, and the rest is silence until the relatively enlightened conservation of our own day.

FURTHER READING

A. J. Taylor, *Beaumaris Castle*, Cadw Official Handbook, Cardiff.

Belsay, *Northumberland*

The principal interest at Belsay is the tower (top left), usually listed as one of the
'pele towers' of the North, though the term is a misleading misnomer which should
not be used as a term of art (p. 26 above). It may be dated on architectural grounds
to the late fourteenth century and may well have been added as a stronghold to an
existing unfortified hall-house after the manner of Edlingham in a period when
warfare and forays between the English and the Scots imposed security and
defence upon landlords and all who could afford it in the Marches. Certainly it
would not have stood alone but within an enclosure, called for no good reason in
the case of pele towers a 'barmkin'. In the Middle Ages also there was a vill or
settlement adjacent, which was finally moved outside what had become the park
in the 1830s and '40s. The present house adjoining the tower on the west is dated

49

1614, though refurbished in 1862, and once had a large projecting wing, west again, of similar or early eighteenth-century date, whose walls now are mere stubs. Finally the present Belsay Hall was built at a distance on a new site (right centre) east of the castle by the then owner between 1807 and 1815, in a heavy Neo-Classical style entirely inappropriate to the history, landscape and climate of the country.

The tower is one of the finest of its kind, of sophisticated masonry with machicolated parapets and with a corbelled-out and machicolated turret at each angle, that at the south-west angle being larger and higher than the others to contain the vice which connects all floors. It was entered at ground-floor level on the west, i.e. house, side, and had three storeys, each consisting of one large, main apartment with ancillary chambers to the west. It is well equipped with fireplaces and garderobes and, though very strong and eminently defensible, its residential function is further emphasized by wall-paintings (of early fifteenth-century date?) at the principal, i.e. first-floor level. From start to finish the place, including the present Hall, has belonged to the Middleton family, save for a political break between 1318 and 1371.

FURTHER READING

S. Johnson, *Belsay*, English Heritage Handbook, London.

Berkeley, *Gloucestershire*

The first reference to this famous castle, the notorious scene of Edward II's murder in 1327, occurs in Domesday Book (1086) where under Berkeley, then royal demesne, we read that earl William fitz Osbern had put out or taken out (*misit extra*) five hides in Sharpness to make a small castle (*ad faciendum unum castellulum*). This castle, which is still small – some half an acre – in terms of the overall area of its motte (now encased in the keep) and (inner) bailey, was subsequently held of the king by Roger de Berkeley and his successors until the mid-twelfth century, when Henry of Anjou, shortly before his accession as Henry II in 1154, was able to take it from Roger III de Berkeley, a supporter of king Stephen, and grant it, together with a substantial part of the former's lands, to a supporter of his own, Robert fitz Harding. In the first of three charters relating to this affair, Henry also engaged himself to fortify the castle at Berkeley according to Robert's will (*firmare ibi castellum secundum voluntatem ipsius Roberti*). Henceforth the first and reduced family of Berkeley made their centre and *caput* at the castle of Dursley, Gloucestershire, and the family of fitz Harding, though they evidently had some difficulty in retaining their lordship and tenure in the Angevin period, have remained at Berkeley until the present day. What one sees now is principally of the fourteenth century, when the castle was again largely rebuilt, but enough traces of twelfth-century work remain to show that in c. 1154 the original motte-and-bailey of the Conquest period was refortified and rebuilt in

stone and the remarkable keep (north towards the church) first constructed. This may be described as a shell keep, with the difference that the perimeter wall is built, not on the crest of the motte, but up from ground level about it (cf. Farnham), thus encasing and revetting the motte which was also lowered to accommodate the new structure. The whole was strengthened by four semi-circular turrets, one (east) housing the apse of the chapel within and another (north) now replaced by the fourteenth-century Thorpe Tower, and entrance was by an external stairway on the east side, now encased in the fourteenth-century forebuilding. There is, however, the enigmatic feature of a line of stone columns, revealed by excavation in the 1920s and bisecting the keep internally, suggesting the intention of a proper great tower like Clifford's Tower at York as opposed to a hollow shell, though in fact the arcade is too far from the outer walls for the span of floors and roof.

The keep was severely damaged in and after the Civil War siege of 1645 and the outer bailey now shows nothing upstanding save the outer gatehouse towards the town.

FURTHER READING

P. A. Faulkner, *Archaeological Journal*, CXXII, 197–200.

Berkhamsted, *Hertfordshire*

Though the railway (which affords a splendid view) came close to mutilating it, Berkhamsted remains one of the best examples in England of a motte-and-bailey castle, albeit with a difference. That difference is its double banks and double ditches (cf. Helmsley), which form of defence is thought to be an especially royal prerogative and here may surely be attributed to Robert count of Mortain, the Conqueror's half-brother, who held the manor and the town in 1086 and was evidently the founder of the castle. Since count Robert's time Berkhamsted has been held by the earl or duke of Cornwall when there was one, and in 1337 was attached to the duchy of Cornwall then established as the inalienable appanage of the king's eldest son. In the absence of such an heir, castle and honour were held by the king himself, or, not infrequently, by the queen in dower. So much said, there is little to add. The earthworks are the splendour of Berkhamsted, the poor remains of masonry being attributed to the twelfth and thirteenth centuries. The shell keep upon the motte was almost certainly in position by the middle of the former, together with the curtain wall of the bailey. The bailey was formerly divided into two by a cross-wall to make the much smaller northern section a kind of forecourt to the donjon (cf. Farnham). It has been not too fancifully suggested that the series of eight earthern platforms on a third and outermost bank about the motte and north-east quarter of the castle were for siege-engines in the siege of 1216, when prince Louis of France, leader of the opposition to king John, took the castle in two weeks.

It is thought that Berkhamsted has not been occupied since the end of the fifteenth century: when in 1580 Elizabeth I leased the estate to Sir Edward Carey

he in fact built a new residence nearby, now part of Berkhamsted Place. The castle still pertains to the duchy of Cornwall but has been in the guardianship of the Office of Works and its successors since 1930.

Bodiam, *Sussex*

At Bodiam one thinks of Bolton, and vice versa, for both are perfect specimens of the neat and tidy, late fourteenth-century, quadrangular castle, strong towers at the four corners with lesser towers central on the longer sides, all requirements, both of defence and sumptuous residence for large numbers, the latter especially, brought together into one integrated whole about a central and rectangular courtyard. There are, of course, differences. Bodiam's angle towers are cylindrical, it has, so to speak, a proper gate-tower (north centre: there is also a lesser postern tower south centre), and generally the building is less high than Bolton so that there is more light and air in its courtyard. It lacks, indeed, something of the external bleak austerity of the northern Bolton, though what chiefly gives it an almost paradoxical beauty are the wide water defences in which it stands – the best answer to undermining short of placing one's castle upon the living rock. (Periodically the water-lilies are cleared away as giving too much of the wrong

impression.) The main approach was suitably elaborate, by bridge from the north-west across the lake to the small, artificial, polygonal island shown at the foot of the photograph, and so through a right-angled turn straight to the gate-tower via a barbican tower and drawbridges. Both the main gate and the postern are boldy machicolated, and the former is very strong indeed, with gun-ports, three gates, three portcullises, and *meurtrières*. Within, as Patrick Faulkner (who has also analysed the accommodation here) said of Bolton, it contained 'every luxury known to the time' – and almost all of it for men of high degree.

The castle was built towards the end of the fourteenth century, in the reign of Richard II, the licence to crenellate, in favour of Sir Edward Dalyngrigge (Dalling Ridge near East Grinstead), being dated 1385. Sir Edward, who had done well in the wars in France, serving under Sir Robert Knollys, had acquired the manor of Bodiam through marriage a few years previously, and now came home seeking to express his risen estate in a manner acceptable to the military aristocracy of the age. In doing so he also fulfilled a public duty, for his licence specifically refers to the defence of the countryside against the king's enemies, i.e. the French. French coastal raids were a new feature of the times. The river Rother was then navigable up to the bridge at Bodiam, which was regarded as part of Winchelsea, itself sacked and burnt in 1380.

This, then, is the context of Bodiam, purpose-built on a new site, the old manor house, it is thought, being marked by the 'homestead moat' a little way off near the church. It was bought and saved from further dilapidation by Lord Curzon (cf. Tattershall) who gave it to the nation on his death in 1926.

Bolton-in-Wensleydale, *Yorkshire,*

Bolton-in-Wensleydale, we know, was a new castle on a new site, built in the last quarter of the fourteenth century by Sir Richard Scrope, later lord Scrope, Steward of the Household and thereafter Chancellor to Richard II. The licence to crenellate survives, dated 1379, and so does the contract with the master mason John Lewin, to build a part of it, dated 1378. According to Leland, who saw it still in its glory in the early Tudor period, it took eighteen years to build, was finished in 1399 and cost £12,000 ('the expencis of every yere came to 1000 marks'). He made a good shot at describing it also, with the comment that 'all the substance of the lodgyns [in] it be includyd in 4 principall towres'. For this, in spite of mid-seventeenth-century Parliamentary slighting, and subsequent ruination including the collapse of the north-east or Kitchen Tower in 1761, is a very fine specimen, sufficently complete for analysis, of a late medieval quandrangular castle (cf. Bodiam), with a tower at each angle and a lesser turret in the centre of the two longer sides (north and south) and all its accommodation and domestic offices symmetrically integrated about a central courtyard. The gatehouse was a noble and defended passageway, facing east, due north of the south-east tower. The brilliant architectural analysis by Patrick Faulkner in 1963 showed how a medieval Stately Home of this type worked, and thus the manner of life of the

Beautiful People within it – Great Hall with kitchens (north) and chapel (south), and suite after suite (four very grand indeed) for the lord and his principal guests and the lord's high steward, a separate complex (south-east) for the permanent staff with their own hall (the origin of the servants' hall?), and at least twelve lesser lodgings for lesser men, though none lower than esquires and the chantry priests of the chapel (two to a chamber). There is no provision here for any garrison in the modern sense, for this was a military society in which gentlemen bore arms and knew how to defend themselves, their ladies and their houses. Nor is there any separate provision for mere servitors, who presumbly slept where they could in the domestic offices and service rooms, which were almost entirely confined to the ground floor, with the residential suites, chambers and public apartments at first-floor level and above. As Patrick Faulkner observed: 'Stark and uncompromising in exterior appearance, the castle contains within every luxury known to the time.' And that luxury, which the informed architectural eye can see in halls and chambers, fireplaces and garderobes (some of the latter warmed by some of the former), is confirmed by the will of Richard lord Scrope, who died in 1403 aged seventy-six, with its lists of rich stuffs and furnishings and tapestries, chalices and vestments in the chapel, gold and silver plate for dining in the hall, fine sheets and heraldic hangings on the beds.

Such luxury and conspicuous expenditure was not, of course, confined to Bolton, though Bolton affords us a glimpse of it, for this was good lordship everywhere. Nor was it confined to this period, nor to castles of this type, more fortified manor than fortress. And if Bolton can be regarded as a great *maison forte* rather than a castle proper, its end was nonetheless military and honourable. Held for the king by the young John Scrope, son of the eleventh baron, after the defeat of Marston Moor in 1644, it was besieged for over a year before surrendering on 5 November 1645, in the process severely damaged, and after that 'rendered untenable'. But still, more or less as Leland saw it, 'the castell standithe on a roke syde', a splendid monument to late medieval northern lordship, its attendant village trailing to the east like the train of some robe of state.

Bramber, *Sussex*

Bramber was one of the Sussex rapes – from west to east, Arundel, Bramber, Lewes, Pevensey and Hastings – unusually compact lordships or castellanies, each based upon a principal castle from which it took its name, set up from as early as

the winter of 1067–8 to guard the south-east invasion coast and the ports and passages to Normandy. It is possible that Bramber was formed slightly later than the others, though before 1073, from parts of Arundel and Lewes, rather as the lordship of Battle Abbey was also inserted into this strategic organisation some time after 1070 (Chichester was split off from Arundel only in the thirteenth century). In any case the lordship of Bramber was conferred upon the Norman William de Braose (Briouze, Orne) of whom almost nothing previously is known, though his neighbours in Sussex were already great magnates in Normandy, close friends and relations of the duke. He died between 1093 and 1096, but his family and descendants were lords of Bramber until 1326, when division of the honour between two daughters and co-heiresses may perhaps have led to a decline of the castle. It passed to the Mowbrays and so to the Howards but was stated by Camden to be a total ruin in 1586. Local tradition rather than evidence has it held for the king in the seventeenth-century civil war and slighted afterwards.

The castle stands upon a natural hill as a deeply ditched enclosure of about three acres, with a small earthwork annexe to the south-east enclosing the eleventh-century Norman church of St Nicholas contemporary with it (obscured by trees on the photograph). It has several claims to distinction and all of them are early. The motte, its ditch now almost vanished, stands centrally within the bailey instead of to one side – though this is partly a modern optical illusion since in the beginning the motte and its ditch effectively divided the castle site into two baileys, north and south. The castle had an early stone gatehouse and presumably an early stone curtain though the latter was much rebuilt. The shattered remains of a tall rectangular tower (11 o'clock on the photograph), of inward projection, by the present entrance and near the church, is thought to have been first an eleventh-century gatehouse comparable to Lewes, later (but not much later) heightened and converted into a tower proper or keep after the manner of Ludlow.

FURTHER READING

K. J. Barton, E. W. Holden, 'Excavations at Bramber Castle, Sussex, 1966–7', *Archaeological Journal*, CXXXIV.

New Buckenham, *Norfolk*

William II of Albini raised this castle, at the other end of his park some $1\frac{1}{2}$ miles south of his castle at what then became 'Old' Buckenham, to mark his marriage to Alice the queen in 1138 and his elevation to an earldom (first Lincoln, then Sussex) in *c.* 1139. It might seem reasonable to assume that the work was done or well advanced before the demolition of the old castle in *c.* 1146, but the fact that he acquired Arundel and was building Castle Rising at the same time complicates the issue. Things were done on the grand scale and, as at Rising, a new town laid out to go with the castle, here to the east, symmetrical and rectangular, its common land still beyond it, the symmetry bent only by the church of St Martin to the north,

added by a later lord in the mid-thirteenth century. Before that, it seems, the townspeople used the chapel, taken in by the thirteenth-century expansion of the castle, and in modern times degraded to a barn, the remains of which can be seen on the bend of the road among the farm buildings by the castle ditch.

The new Albini castle comprised a large and circular inner enclosure of ditch (still water-filled) and most impressive banks which, however (as at Rising) are thought to have been later heightened. To the east, towards the new town, there was an outer bailey, its ditch joining the town ditch, containing the entrance to the castle and the entrance to the inner bailey. Another outer bailey to the south (where it extended to the modern road) and west, taking in the chapel mentioned above, is thought to have been added in the thirteenth century when the present entrance to the inner enclosure on the west was also made. Within the formidable earthworks of that inner enclosure, again as at Rising, stood the great tower of William II of Albini, the ultimate symbol of his lordship. But here it was cylindrical, and is thus the earliest known cylindrical tower keep in England. Nothing but a truncated stump remains, left featureless save for a cross-wall so unusual in towers of this kind as itself to be a mark of early date.

When the last Albini earl of Sussex, Hugh, died 'in the flower of his youth' in 1243 his great possessions were divided among his four sisters and co-heiresses, Buckenham passing to Robert de Tatteshall as the husband of Mathilda, the eldest of them. After other changes of lordship it came in the fifteenth century to the Knyvet family, one of whom, Sir Philip Knyvet, demolished it in 1649.

Old Buckenham, *Norfolk*

The castle site at Old Buckenham represents the second generation of Norman settlement in the person of William (I) of Albini (St-Martin d'Aubigny, Manche), its founder and first lord. Though two of his uncles, Nigel of Albini of Cainhoe in Bedfordshire and Richard, abbot of St Albans, were of the first generation of Norman settlers, William's father, Roger of Albini, doubtless the eldest brother and head of his house, had stayed on the Norman patrimony in and after 1066. William arrived in the time of Rufus who established him in East Anglia, and his younger brother, Nigel, soon followed him. Both were the founders of great families here, Nigel being the ancestor of the house of Mowbray. Both gained enormously from the patronage of Henry I, and William, made the king's butler (hence William of Albini *pincerna* in charters and genealogies), marked his arrival among the new lords of the land by founding, in true Norman fashion, both a castle and a religious house. The former was at Old Buckenham, thus the *caput* of his honour, and the latter at Wymondham some six miles to the north, established as a priory and cell to St Albans, where his uncle was abbot, in 1107. William I of Albini died in 1139, but meanwhile his son and heir, William II, was rising to far greater heights. In 1138 he married 'Alice the queen', as contemporary Albini charters proudly call her, i.e. Alice ('la Belle'?) of Louvain, the young queen, second wife and widow of Henry I, receiving also in her right the castle and rape of

Arundel and becoming earl of Sussex. To mark his meteoric social ascent the first Albini earl carried out prestigious works at Arundel, built two new castles in Norfolk, and founded another religious house. The new castles were Castle Rising and New Buckenham, and the religious house the priory of Augustinian canons at what henceforward became 'Old' Buckenham. This was the end of the first Albini castle of Buckenham, for the foundation charter of the priory, dating from *c.* 1146, records the grant to the canons of, among other things, eighty acres within the park of Buckenham and the site of the castle which was to be demolished (*castellum diruendum*). That this was done admits of no doubt, and all that remains of the castle now, adjacent to the remains of the priory, is a double rectangular enclosure of water-filled ditch and bank, still impressive in its size. Investigation might be especially rewarding, for it is in a sense a sealed site, with a firm *terminus ad quem* of *c.* 1146 and a life-span of less than fifty years.

Builth · *Breconshire*

Builth must be regarded as one of Edward I's new royal castles in Wales, of which it was the first and is the smallest. In the south, on the bank of the Upper Wye, like Aberystwyth it lay outside the chain of great castles about Gwynedd on which the king's main effort and expenditure was to be concentrated. Now a total ruin without one stone upon another, only an aerial photograph, short of excavation, can do it justice.

A product of the First Welsh War, it was begun at once in early May 1277, before the main army under the king in the north had assembled to move forward

from Chester to Flint. It took the form of a complete refortification and rebuilding of an early Norman motte-and-bailey castle (cf. Cambridge) raised by Philip de Braose (son and successor of William de Braose of Bramber) when he seized the cantref of Buellt from the Welsh in the late eleventh century. That castle had had a stirring history and had several times been refortified or developed, but was finally taken and demolished to the foundations by Llywelyn in 1260 when in fact it was in the lordship of the lord Edward, i.e. the future Edward I, no less. Now it was to be rebuilt stronger than before, and no doubt even the formidable earthworks, upon a natural bluff, owe something to Edward, for diggers (evidently including women) under a master *fossator* were among those employed. The site is roughly circular, with the motte surrounded by its own deep ditch to the north and two platform baileys of unequal size, the larger south and east of the motte, the smaller to the west, separated from each other by a third and transverse ditch joining the inner motte-ditch to the outer. What Edward's masons, carpenters and others did we have little means of knowing, for the surviving accounts of the works which extended from May 1277 to the autumn of 1282 give little architectural detail. They began however with temporary timber-framed buildings of which a hall and chamber were raised upon the motte (*donio loco*) as a clear sign of reasserted lordship. Thereafter there are specific references especially to the raising of the 'great tower' of masonry, thought to have been what we call a shell keep upon the motte, and also to a stone wall with six mural towers surrounding the castle (i.e. an outer curtain?), a twin-towered gatehouse with turning bridge, a stone wall enclosing the inner bailey, and another to enclose the outer bailey. In August 1282 the works ceased for lack of funds (*pro defectu pecunie*), and that the defences were never entirely completed is proved by a reference in 1343 to the twin-towers of the gateway still unfinished.

No new borough was founded with Builth though the existing town was doubtless affected by the new work. In Leland's time the castle was still 'a fair castel of the Kinges' and the present ruination is thought to have been begun in Elizabeth I's time by robber gentry robbing stone for their new and fashionable mansions.

Bungay, *Suffolk*

Though they were all early castles, the early history (which in the cases of the last two is all there is) of Bungay, Framlingham, Thetford and the now-vanished Walton (under the sea near Felixstowe), is very ill served because of the surprising neglect by historians of the great family of Bigod, earls of Norfolk from 1141. There is no doubt that each was a Bigod castle (though the fact is not always recognized), and little doubt that all four were founded by Roger Bigod, the first of his line. Roger, who died in 1107, rose very fast in the East Anglia and England of the Conqueror, serving as sheriff and profiting from the fall both of Ralph de Gael (whom his son Hugh was to succeed as earl) and Odo of Bayeux. At Walton he is known to have given the church of St Felix to Rochester cathedral priory before his death, and at Thetford he founded the Cluniac priory in 1103. There appears to be no evidence to support the statement that Bungay was granted to him with Framlingham in c. 1101, yet there is no good reason to doubt the attribution of both the castle and fortified town of Bungay to him. The principal manor of Bungay (which was then neither a burgh nor a flourishing town though sometimes said to be both) had belonged to the deposed archbishop Stigand in 1066, and was thus in the king's hand in Domesday though held as *terra Regis* by Roger. The first known reference to the Bigod castle occurs only in 1140 when king Stephen attacked and took it from earl Hugh. Regained by the same earl Hugh it thereafter figures prominently and dramatically in the politics of the reign of Henry II, being confiscated with the earl's other castles in 1157, restored in 1165, but taken again and demolished in 1176 as punishment for his leading part in the rebellion of 1173–4. Subsequent refortification may have taken place after 1189 when Framlingham was certainly rebuilt by earl Roger Bigod following its restoration to him by Richard I, but the present shell keep and gate-towers about the demolished tower keep upon the mound are usually and reasonably associated with a licence to crenellate issued by Edward I to the last Bigod earl in 1294. After the latter's

death in 1306 the castle passed, via Thomas of Brotherton (fifth son of Edward I) and his daughter Margaret, to the Mowbrays and thence, in 1483, to the Howards.

Castle and town were sited in a naturally defensible position at the entrance to a narrow isthmus formed by a long loop in the River Waveney and thus had water and marsh on two sides to east and west. The castle, now partly built over and degraded, comprised a large motte or mound with a strongly entrenched inner bailey to the west reaching down to the marsh and river, and an outer bailey to the south which joined the town ditch at the present Castle Hills. Excavations in the 1930s dramatically revealed the lower courses of a large rectangular tower keep with forebuilding on the summit of the motte, thought to date from 1165 on analogy with the similar keep at Scarborough and to have been demolished in 1176 (the ineffective mine gallery under the south-west angle, however, is much more likely to be associated with the attempted demolition by a Mr Mickleborough in the eighteenth century than by Henry II in the twelfth).

In local legend the castle is forever associated with the great earl Hugh, and no account of it should end without at least a few lines from the traditional poem celebrating his exploits against the king of London –

> Were I in my castle of Bungay
> Upon the Waveney,
> I would ne care for the King of Cockney.

Caernarvon, *Caernarvonshire*

Of the four greatest new royal castles of Edward I in North Wales – Caernarvon and Conway, Harlech and Beaumaris – Caernarvon was meant to be and is the finest, and deliberately and significantly differs in appearance from the others. From the start it was intended as the centre of the new royal government imposed by the Statute of Rhuddlan in 1284, and was required therefore to be especially impressive as well as virtually impregnable, with ample and appropriate accommodation for the king and his queen, and his court and his household which

were in most respects the government of the realm. Further, Caernarvon was the ancient centre of the Welsh principality of Gwynedd, and its entry therefore by Edward's forces in the early summer of 1283 was the culminating act of the Second Welsh War (1282–3) which had become the outright conquest of Wales. Further yet, Welsh Caernarvon had been Roman Segontium, and was a place still steeped in imperial traditions at a time when imperial notions of ultimate sovereignty were paramount in royal circles. To a twelfth-century writer it was 'the old city of the Emperor Constantine, son of Constans the Great', while in the current Welsh legends written down in the *Mabinogion* it was the city of the dream of Maxen Wledig, i.e. the Emperor Magnus Maximus (whose body, it was believed, was found there in 1283 and reburied in the church at Edward's orders) – a great fortified city at the mouth of the river, and a great fort in the city, the fairest man ever saw, and great towers of many colours on the fort, and in its hall a chair of ivory, and the image of two eagles in gold thereon. It was this *imperium*, and thus the legitimacy of Edward's rule, that the architecture of Caernarvon especially expressed. The Eagle Tower at the west had three turrets each with a stone eagle thereon (now vanished), while the polygonal towers used throughout (as opposed to the cylindrical towers of Edward's other castles) and the banded masonry of the south front (intended on the north side also but not accomplished) were a deliberate evocation of the Theodosian Wall at Constantinople, Constantine's own city and the Second Rome. Thus Caernarvon was intended, as Arnold Taylor writes, 'to be both the fulfilment of the tradition and the interpretation of the dream'. Yet even this does not exhaust the propaganda element of the new castle, which at great inconvenience incorporated in its Inner Ward (its donjon and ultimate sanctum of regality) the motte of earl Hugh of Chester's castle, raised here in the eleventh century when the Normans first reached this place, to be driven out again in 1115. In this way too, therefore, the legitimacy of Edward's lordship was symbolically expressed. To emphasize its permanence, Eleanor, Edward's faithful queen, was brought here to bear their son on 25 April 1284, the future Edward of Caernarvon and first Prince of Wales of the modern succession.

There is something very impressive about all this concentration upon Caernarvon, not only of effort and money and resources, but also of history, tradition, legend and politics. The result was one of the most sophisticated exercises in medieval military architecture that can be found. The cost was almost prohibitive, some £27,000 (nearly double the second most costly of Edward's works at Beaumaris) spent over some fifty years and the castle still not finished. Like many of Edward's castles it was combined with a walled town or burgh, the two planned and raised together as one integrated whole. Like others it had direct access to tidal waters to add to its impregnability and the effectiveness of its command. Castle and town were on a peninsula almost surrounded by water, a fact which modern urban development has obscured. The castle itself, separated from the interior of the town by a great ditch much wider than now, rises tailor-made from the rock which is levelled and scarped to take it, and this accounts for its irregular shape and narrow waist which made division into two wards easy. The whole is bound together by the careful disposition of mural towers of varying sizes, the most impressive being the Eagle Tower at the west end and angle, which housed the accommodation for the Justiciar or regent of North Wales, at first

Edward's close friend Otto de Grandson. There were two gates, the Queen's Gate on the east leading direct into the royal or princely Inner Ward from the open country, and the King's Gate on the north meant to serve either ward from the town. Neither was ever finished within and nor were the ranges of lodgings in the Inner Bailey if indeed they were ever begun. The elevated entrance, reached by ramp and drawbridge, of the Queen's Gate was to accommodate the ancient motte which remained inside the Inner Bailey until the nineteenth century. The strength of the King's Gate was at least as formidable, intended to employ every known defensive device, all of them in multiples – two drawbridges, five doors, six portcullises, nine *meurtrières* and countless loops. But perhaps the most formidable single strength of Caernarvon is the concentration of medieval 'fire-power' along the south front where two shooting galleries, one above the other, pierce the walls in addition to the loops in the towers and the warhead of the whole curtain.

The architect, i.e. the principal master mason in charge of the work at least in its earlier and vital phases was, of course, Master James of St George (p. 21). The castle was evidently maintained in reasonable state until the seventeenth century when (mercifully abortive) orders were issued for its demolition together with the town walls. Neglect followed until the later nineteenth century, and it became an Ancient Monument in 1908.

FURTHER READING

A. J. Taylor, *Caernarvon Castle and Town Walls*, Cadw Official Handbook, London.

Caerphilly, *Glamorganshire*

Caerphilly in Glamorgan can be claimed to be the finest castle in the English realm, at least rivalling, perhaps excelling, the greatest of Edward I's castles in North Wales, which it also ante-dates. The fact therefore that this is not a royal but a 'baronial' castle should make one pause to think (not necessarily disapprovingly) of the nature of English society in the late thirteenth century and the role of castles in it. Caerphilly was built by the greatest baronial house of all, the Clare lords of Glamorgan, who were also earls of Gloucester and of Hertford and lords of Tonbridge in Kent and Clare in Suffolk, whence they took their name. It was begun, we know, on 1 June 1271 as a new centre of their lordship of Glamorgan, from which they had expelled the native Welsh prince, Gruffyd ap Rhys, in 1266, and in answer to the mounting threat of Llywelyn, prince of Wales. We also know this was the second attempt to raise a castle here, a first castle begun in 1268 on a site probably just north-west of the present one (remains of earthworks) having been destroyed by Llywelyn in 1270. After 1271, however, any detailed knowledge of Caerphilly and its building can be derived only from what we see, for no accounts survive to record the progress of the works, though we can be quite sure that such were kept. We do not even know when it was finished (as

Two views of Caerphilly showing it before and after the Marquis of Bute's restorations and the re-flooding of the water defences

finished it was, unlike Beaumaris or Caernarvon), though we may suppose this was substantially before 1283, by which time the conquest of Wales had altered the circumstances which brought it into being.

In substance the Clare castle of Caerphilly is a grand exercise in concentric fortification, after the manner of Beaumaris. It adds extensive water defences, standing completely within a huge lake, created by the great Barrage or screen of walls and sluices on the east, its unique feature, which dammed the waters of the streams, Nant y Aber and Nant y Gledyr, to make the lake and control its level, as well as barring the main approach to the castle from the east and the borough which was founded with it. There is also, to the west and still within the waters, a hornwork, to protect the western approach, fortified and connected by draw-bridges to the land, and to the main gate. The outer ward of the main castle, like that at Beaumaris, is little more than a narrow platform revetted by a low outer curtain, here crenellated but without towers save for those of the two outer gates, east and west, and a water-gate to the south (with perhaps originally another to the north). The main strength of the castle is, of course, the inner ward, an irregular rectangular enclosure bound together by four great drum towers at the angles (each designed as a separately defensible unit), the gigantic and much ruined Kitchen Tower to the south, and the twin-towers of the two great gatehouses, east and west, fully comparable to those at Beaumaris and Harlech and more particularly resembling the great Clare gatehouse at Tonbridge of comparable date. The principal residential accommodation, of great hall (now much restored) with subsidiary chambers and offices, was along the south inner curtain, with further residential suites and chambers provided in the drum towers and in the gatehouses (the east gatehouse housing, it is thought, the constable). Caerphilly has little or no dramatic military history (how could it have?). The fabric is thought to have been neglected from the fifteenth century, and certainly Leland found it an impressive ruin in *c.* 1536. It was probably slighted by Parliamentary decree in or after 1647 and thereafter left to decay until the restorations of the marquis of Bute in the earlier part of the present century.

FURTHER READING

William Rees, *Caerphilly Castle, a History and Description,* Cardiff.

Cainhoe, *Bedfordshire*

The castle of Cainhoe, in the parish of Clophill, consists of a motte and two (or three) baileys, classically sited on an isolated spur. The large enclosure to the south-west, whose vestigial bank and ditch show up on an aerial photograph, must be that of the former vill. Cainhoe is entered as a separate manor in Domesday, held, like the adjacent Clophill, by Nigel d'Albini or d'Aubigny (St Martin d'Aubigny, Manche, arr. Coutances), one of the first arrivals of a family which was to establish itself in great place in several branches in England after the Conquest. His brother, Richard, became abbot of St Albans, while, in the next generation, his nephew Nigel was to become the ancestor of the second house of Mowbray, and his nephew William the ancestor of the Albini earls of Sussex (for the castles of the latter see Arundel, Buckenham Old and New and Castle Rising). Only by comparison with their great fortune does his seem modest (thirty manors

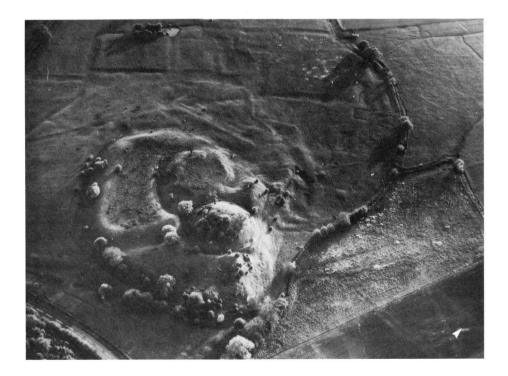

in Domesday Bedfordshire alone), and Cainhoe was the *caput* of his honour, which answered for twenty-five knights' fees in the early thirteenth century. Nigel's male descendants in the direct line were lords of the honour until 1233, when it was divided among co-heiresses, and the manor remained undivided in the female line of Albini of Cainhoe until 1272. The castle appears to have no other known history and never to have been archaeologically investigated, 'rescue' excavations arising from recent roadworks to the south being confined to a section of the outer enclosure. The township is thought to have become deserted after the Black Death (1349).

Camber, *Sussex*

Camber on the Sussex coast near Rye is not a castle (though mistakenly called such) and is included here to show the difference. It is purely and exclusively military, an artillery fort for guns, built also to resist the same, with no residential function save as a barracks for its garrison. This is no fortified lordly residence, no stately home, and the point is emphasized by its isolation, with no adjacent settlement or vill, no church, no park or chace. Also its military function is merely defensive, to defend and thus command what is in range of its guns, in this case what were the open waters of the Camber, against penetration by hostile ships, and it has no

offensive function of its own as the castle had. Finally it is royal. So, of course, were many castles; but many more were not, held of the king as part of their fiefs and honours by great lords with delegated authority, or even held of other great lords than the king. Camber, by contrast, is one of a great series of coastal forts and defences built by Henry VIII against the fear of invasion, notably in and after 1539, a national system of defence constructed by what is becoming a national monarchy.

Camber in fact is a complex building of three phases. A low, round artillery tower with many gun-ports was first built here between 1512 and 1514 at a cost of some £1,300. This, much modified, is now the lower part of the central tower of the elaborate fortress built in two phases, with further modification and change of plan, between 1539 and 1543 at a further cost of some £15,750. First (1539–40) an elaborate concentric structure was created about the modified central tower, with four equi-spaced bastions, backed by four horseshoe shaped towers and connected by an octagonal curtain, with a bastion-shaped gatehouse additionally to the north-west. Then (1542–3) all this was modified and altered at great expense, the present four immensely strong bastions built to replace the earlier ones, the curtain between them thickened and strengthened, and all the fortress heightened in the process.

The whole thing was, characteristically, a waste of money. The waters of the Camber silted up within a very few years, the garrison was disbanded and the guns removed in 1637, and in 1643, exactly a century after its completion, the lead was stripped from the roofs and the Henrician fortress abandoned to its long decay.

Cambridge

Almost nothing remains of Cambridge castle save the memory (e.g. Castle Street) and the motte (south of the Shire Hall – top centre – in what was the bailey) which, having borne the great tower built upon it by Edward I, is unlikely even to retain its original contours. William the Conqueror founded the castle at Cambridge with others on the return from his first northern campaign in 1068, and chose the high ground commanding the crossing of the Cam where the Romans had planted their town centuries before. Twenty-seven houses were demolished (*destructe*) to clear the site of the new castle which was presumably raised on the motte-and-bailey plan. Little more is heard of it until the Angevin period when a steady series of minor payments credited to the sheriff show the maintenance of the fabric but no major work, though some £200 was later credited to William earl of Salisbury for the work of the hall and chamber in the last years of John's reign when he held the castle for the king. During the long reign of Henry III the only recorded expenditure is upon the gaol, and it seems that the castle of 1068 was never developed and had little function beyond the sheriff's headquarters for local government. Then in the summer of 1284 Edward I embarked upon a total rebuilding evidently intended to make Cambridge castle one of the strongest in his kingdom, and which had cost a total of some £2,630 by 1298 when the works

ceased. The result was a major fortress in the latest fashion, a roughly quadrangular enclosure with a cylindrical tower at each angle, a gatehouse with bridge and barbican in the south-west curtain, and a cylindrical great tower or keep upon the ancient motte. Yet, once more, anticlimax seems to follow. Edward I's rebuilding was never entirely finished, in respect of the two angle towers on the west side, and the fourteenth-century evidence is of bare maintenance at best. In the fifteenth century the castle was in ruins, and in 1441 Henry VI allowed the roofless hall and chamber to be demolished and the stone used for the building of King's College. This was a precedent for the extraction of further materials for Emmanuel and Magdalene colleges in the sixteenth century, and by 1604 even the curtain walls were said to be 'rased and utterly ruinated'. Hasty refortification in 1643 took the form of earthworks and bastions, plus a brick barracks where the hall had stood, and led to a Parliamentary order for slighting in 1647. In the eighteenth century only the gatehouse stood, and that because it was used as a gaol until it too was demolished in 1842.

Castle Acre, *Norfolk*

Castle Acre is a monument to the Norman Conquest and the Norman settlement of Norfolk and East Anglia, more specifically to the great family of Warenne (Varenne, Seine-Inf.). William I de Warenne, companion of the Conqueror at Hastings, was rewarded with vast estates in England in some thirteen counties, and was created earl of Surrey by Rufus in 1088, just before his death the same year from wounds received at the siege of Pevensey in that king's service. His castles at Conisborough, Lewes and Reigate became the respective centres of his other great lordships, as here in Norfolk Acre was raised as the *caput* of his East Anglian honour. All the attributes of new Norman lordship on the grand scale are shown by an aerial photograph – the prodigious earthworks of the castle, the attendant town (centre) west of the castle, laid out on a grid plan with its own defences which survive in ditch and bank and the thirteenth-century north gate, now the Bailey Gate (the southern gateway was demolished in the nineteenth century), and a new religious house, Castle Acre Priory, on the other side of the town (now village) to the west again (bottom left). This was a house for Cluniac monks founded probably by William II de Warenne in 1089, colonized from his father's foundation at Lewes, and placed first in the castle but very soon moved to its present spacious and agreeable site. The road which runs through Castle Acre, roughly south-east/north-west, and crosses the River Nar (now a mere stream) at that point, is the ancient Roman road long since called the Peddars Way (peddars to Walsingham forked right just north of Acre).

William I de Warenne began all this and planted the castle by the river, then navigable up to Acre, soon after 1066. His wife Gundreda is known to have died in childbirth within it on 27 May 1085. Recent (1972–7) and meticulous excavations have shown, however, that the architectural history and development of the castle, if not entirely unusual did we but know it, are certainly the reverse of what

Vertical view of Castle Acre showing the castle earthworks in relation to the town and, top right, the priory

we might at first thought have expected. The great stone building or keep, uncovered and shown on the photograph within the circular perimeter of the Upper Ward, began in the eleventh century as a mere *maison forte*, a very grand 'strong-house', not in fact very strong, and standing within a bank and palisade of no great strength either, and with a timber gatehouse. Since French 'castello-logists' are currently proclaiming a new phenomenon of the *maison forte* raised by knights of moderate standing in the mid-thirteenth century, the fact that Castle Acre was raised in this form in the second half of the eleventh century by one of the greatest magnates in the land certainly requires emphasis. At Castle Acre serious fortification, at least of the Upper Ward where one would expect it most, came not in the beginning but later, and only in the twelfth century, probably in the 1130s and 1140s, was the house converted into a keep by doubling the thickness of its walls and raising it in height, while the perimeter bank was heightened also and a curtain wall built on top of it (the original timber gateway having been rebuilt in stone some time previously). In the event it appears that this intended great keep, which might have been almost on the scale of Rochester, was never completed (perhaps because of the death of the third earl William de

Warenne on the Second Crusade in 1148) but was reduced and cut back to its northern half beyond the cross-wall. At which point the bank of the Upper Ward was heightened again to north and west and the curtain wall heightened also.

Apart from these dramatic changes the overall plan of Castle Acre is of a comparatively small inner or upper bailey taking the place of a motte as the donjon, with a larger outer bailey connected by a bridge. In addition, there was and is an outwork or barbican to the north-east, presumably to defend the main entrance. Two other gateways have been revealed, an east gate and a west gate, leading into the outer bailey and placed where its ditches and banks meet those of the Upper Ward.

Though there are complications and qualifications, one may say that the Warenne earls of Surrey held the castle until 1347 when it passed to the Fitzalan earls of Sussex and lords of Arundel. They in turn held it until 1558 when they sold it to Sir Thomas Gresham. The last lords of Castle Acre were the Coke earls of Leicester, who held it until 1971. Meanwhile it is thought that the castle declined in importance, and thereafter structurally, as from the fourteenth century. The buildings visible beneath the grass of the Lower Ward await investigation.

FURTHER READING

J. G. Coad and A. D. F. Streeten, 'Excavations at Castle Acre Castle, Norfolk, 1972–7', *Archaeological Journal*, cxxxix.

Excavations in progress in 1976 on the Upper Ward and keep at Castle Acre

Castle Bytham, *Lincolnshire*

Only an aerial photograph can do justice to the formidable earthworks and buried ruins of Castle Bytham, classically situated on a hill above the village. Almost nothing is known of its architectural history, though an amateur survey and trial excavations in 1870 produced a plan and posited a 'keep', i.e. the roughly rectangular enclosure which dominates the site, with a great cylindrical tower 16.5 m in diameter immediately attached to the east (8 o'clock on the photograph), stone curtains and outer wards, and outworks including water defences drawn from the neighbouring beck and local springs. There appears also to be a town bank. This then is no mere motte-and-bailey, was certainly fortified in stone by the time of the siege of 1221 when miners as well as siege-engineers were brought against it, and was then said to have been demolished (*funditus eradicatum* in Walter of Coventry, ed. Stubbs, Rolls Series, ii, 249) though evidently thereafter rebuilt. A charter of 1226 refers to at least two chapels there, 'St Mary in the castle'

and 'St Thomas the Martyr in the barbican', together with 'St Mary Magdalene beneath the castle'. In Leland's time there yet remained 'great waulles of buildinge' (c. 1540).

The castle is first mentioned in 1141 but is thought to be of an early foundation, at the time of the Norman settlement and in Domesday's 'West' Bytham. The manor, with a pre-Conquest vill already established, had belonged to earl Morcar, after whose dispossession in 1071 it was granted to Drogo de la Beuvrière, the Domesday tenant, a Fleming and lord also of Holderness, to which honour it became attached. Drogo returned to Flanders just before the death of the Conqueror, who then granted Bytham and Holderness to the husband of his sister Adelaide, Odo count of Aumale and former count of Champagne. They were the founders of a line whose best known representative in England is William 'le Gros', count of Aumale, staunch supporter of king Stephen who made him earl of Yorkshire also. After his death in 1189 his daughter and heiress, Hawise, eventually brought his lands and lordships to William de Forz (de Fortibus; Fors, arr. Niort, Deux-Sèvres) and their descendants; but meanwhile the lady's first husband, William de Mandeville earl of Essex, had granted Bytham to his tenant, William de Coleville, to be held of the lords of Holderness for the service of $2\frac{1}{2}$ knights' fees. Thus Bytham became a mesne castle, which is important for the understanding of the siege of 1221.

In the political struggles which closed the reign of John and produced Magna Carta, William de Coleville joined the rebels while the new young count of Aumale, William II de Forz (succeeded 1214) remained loyal. John took the castle in 1216 and very properly placed it in the custody of count William, the direct lord. In 1217, William de Coleville having made his peace with the government of the boy king Henry III, the count was ordered to restore Castle Bytham to him but, not surprisingly, objected. Eventually he was foolish enough to rebel outright, and hence the siege of the castle, which was taken in a few days, restored to Coleville, and thenceforth held in chief. In 1369 the castle with the manor passed from the Colevilles to the Bassets, and in 1394 is said to have been occupied by Joan, countess of Hereford, with her grandchildren who were also the children of Henry Bolingbroke, the future Henry IV. Nothing else seems to be known of the castle, which Leland found a ruin.

FURTHER READING

Rev. John Wild, *History of Castle Bytham*, Stamford.

Castle Hedingham, *Essex*

Castle Hedingham has two particular claims to fame, that it has one of the finest twelfth-century rectangular tower keeps in the country, and that it was held continuously by the one great Norman family, of Vere (Ver, Manche, arr. Coutances), to survive right through the medieval into the so-called 'modern'

period. The twentieth and last Vere earl of Oxford died in 1703 without male heirs. The castle stands on a natural hill or spur rising to the west, and by its keep especially dominates in proper feudal fashion the township at its foot and the surrounding countryside. It consists of two baileys or courts of which the inner, containing the keep and the reportedly excavated remains of a great hall and chapel, occupies the highest ground and is cut off from the outer to the east by a ditch, now partly filled in and crossed by a brick bridge of early Tudor date. Both inner and outer baileys are or were surrounded each by its own bank and ditch, those of the outer bailey being damaged by the terracing of the Georgian house (1719?) which now stands within it. It is thus worth noting that the different terrain and the hill-top site produced a different type of castle at Hedingham from that of the other Vere strongpoint at Great Canfield where there is a, so to speak, standard motte-and-bailey site.

There is reason to suppose (though there is no direct proof) that the castle was founded by Aubrey I de Vere, the Domesday tenant-in-chief who kept Hedingham (and Canfield) in demesne, and, in default of documentary evidence, it is as certain as these things can be that his successor, Aubrey de Vere III, built the great tower keep to mark his elevation to an earldom (of Oxford) by the empress Maud in July 1141. His new social eminence was also marked by the foundation, with his wife Lucy (who became the first prioress), of Castle Hedingham Priory (St Mary, St James and Holy Cross) for Benedictine nuns, and by the building or rebuilding of the present splendid parish church (tower rebuilt 1616), seen on the photograph below the castle. The keep, dated to the 1140s, has close affinities with Rochester. Wanting two of its four angle turrets and most of its forebuilding on the west face (see photograph), and damaged by fire in the present century, it is otherwise complete, with floors and roof. There are three residential storeys above a basement, the second rising through two levels with a mural gallery as at Rochester. The first floor is the entrance floor (from the forebuilding) and both it and the floor above are distinguished by great arches thrown centrally across in place of the dividing cross-wall usual in such great towers.

Castle Rising, *Norfolk*

There is no doubt that the castle here was raised soon after 1138, in what had been a mere berewick or outlier of his manor of Snettisham, by William II of Albini to mark his marriage in that year to queen Alice and his elevation to an earldom in 1139. For the same reason and at approximately the same time he carried out important works at Arundel and raised another new castle at New Buckenham, granting the site of his former castle there to his new foundation of 'Old' Buckenham priory. There is no doubt either that all the impressive earthworks at Rising pertain to the castle, no part of them being of an earlier age, as used to be maintained. As part of the work on the chosen site, the existing settlement was moved, lock, stock and barrel, slightly north of the new castle to the present village, which is thus another Albini new town (cf. New Buckenham), dated by the splendid parish church (top right) also provided by the new earl. The former church of early eleventh-century date was taken into the castle where it long stood just inside the northern bank of the inner bailey (on the photograph partly obscured by the shadow of the keep) until finally engulfed by its erosion – to be discovered with great excitement in the nineteenth century.

The castle of Rising consists or consisted of three enclosures covering twelve acres in all, a large oval-shaped inner bailey with a lesser outer bailey respectively to east (right) and west. The prodigious scale of the earthworks of the inner bailey owes a good deal to their heightening in *c.* 1200, and though very impressive in their own right they must have detracted from the intended dominant majesty of the keep as they still do. At the same time the western outer bailey was levelled up to the kind of platform it now is by the dumping of the surplus spoil obtained from the deepening of the ditches about the inner enclosure. The eastern outer bailey remains as in effect a barbican or outwork covering the entrance to the main ward via a bridge and gatehouse contemporary with the keep.

The principal residential accommodation was always in the inner ward, comprising the keep and a complex of ancillary buildings – hall, chambers, chapel and kitchen – recently archaeologically investigated. The keep itself is splendid, though here in traditional rectangular shape as opposed to the cylindrical tower at New Buckenham. It is the oblong type of rectangular tower keep (cf. plans, p. 15), of two principal storeys only, a basement and a residential suite above, hall and great chamber on either side of the cross-wall, with chapel, kitchen (in the north-west angle), other ancillary rooms and an excellent arrangement of garderobes (on investigation the earliest distinction between Ladies and Gents known to the present writer). In plan and design it is very close indeed to Norwich, as both resemble Falaise, and it may not be too fanciful to suggest that the affinity is due to queen Alice, widow of Henry I, to whom Norwich and Falaise are attributed. The entrance was at first-floor level on the east side, covered by a forebuilding which is perhaps the finest surviving in England, and clearly shown on the photograph. This, too, was very similar to the former 'Bigod's Tower' at Norwich and contained at first-floor level, at the head of a great flight of defended stairs, an entrance vestibule above a basement probably always entered from outside. This entrance vestibule, like that at Norwich, was originally an open arcaded loggia, and still contains the splendid entrance to the keep proper with a richly decorated arch of three orders, now blocked by a Tudor fireplace (*sic*) and a display of glazed tiles put there in the nineteenth century. The open arcading of the vestibule is now converted into a series of glazed windows all save one with stone mullions and transoms of fifteenth- or sixteenth-century date. The vaulted ceiling was inserted probably in the early fourteenth century when the forebuilding was heightened by one storey and its present inappropriate roof. The external decoration of the forebuilding is to be noted as unusual and again reminiscent of Norwich.

Rising continued to have a very distinguished social history after the demise of the last Albini earl of Sussex in 1243. It passed first to the Montalt family through Cecily, youngest of the co-heiresses, but they sold the reversion of all their property to the Crown in 1327. The first royal occupant in consequence was queen Isabella, murderess and widow of Edward II, who spent much of her time here from 1331 to her death in 1358 (though in no wise a prisoner, in spite of local guide-books). Then Edward the Black Prince entered into possession, for to him Edward III had granted the reversion in 1337, tying castle and lordship explicitly

and inalienably to the duchy of Cornwall. There they should still be, but Henry VIII granted both to Thomas Howard, duke of Norfolk, in 1544, and the Howards continued to hold them (though in a cadet branch from 1693) until modern times. The castle finally passed into the custody of the State in 1958. Meanwhile ruin and decay had set upon it at least in the sixteenth century, when one suspects the estate was chiefly valued for the hunting. One may cherish a last glimpse of Rising as the scene of gracious living afforded by a surviving letter of 1538, by the duke of Norfolk to the duke of Suffolk, 'written upon a molehill in Rysyng Chase, 8 August, 11 o'clock'.

FURTHER READING

R. Allen Brown, *Castle Rising*, English Heritage Handbook, London.

Cause, *Shropshire*

The dramatic site of Cause is more reminiscent of the Normans in southern Italy than in England or even Wales. Here on a detached ridge or hill rising some 213 m a castle and fortified vill were placed as a new centre of lordship in the former royal manor of Alretone. The foundation is attributed to Roger fitz Corbet, Domesday tenant of Alretone under Roger of Montgomery, earl of Shrewsbury – though it may equally have been Corbet the father. 'The earl himself holds Alretone', says the Survey, 'and Roger holds of him. King Edward held it . . . In this manor five of Roger's knights have $6\frac{1}{2}$ ploughs in demesne . . .'. The Corbets were important vassals of the great Montgomery fee of which they held some thirty-eight manors, and they named their stronghold 'de Caux/Cause' from that district of Normandy whence they came. Their lordship was held in chief after the fall of Robert of Bellême in 1102, and they continued to hold it until 1347 when it passed to the barons Stafford for lack of male heirs. One of the last of that family (though his son, Henry, afterwards resided much at the castle in reduced circumstances) was the unfortunate Edward duke of Buckingham whom Henry VIII executed for no good reason in 1521. 'Never glad, confident morning again', and later in the century the castle was sold to the family of Thynne, who held it for the king in 1645, after which it was demolished. The vill or township was planted beside the castle on the hill, evidently in one of the outer baileys or enclosures. It was granted a weekly market on Wednesdays in 1200, and an annual fair, on 6, 7 and 8 July, in 1248. Thomas Corbet established the 'chapel of St Margaret in the vill of Caurs' in 1272 for the greater convenience of the town, which was in the parish of Westbury. The chapel in the castle itself was dedicated to St Nicholas (usually an early Norman dedication).

Of all this almost nothing remains visible, as the result of decay, Parliamentary demolition, the stone-robbing of local depredators, and ever encroaching trees and undergrowth. The core of the castle was and is a great motte on the south side of the hill, rising 16 m from the bottom of its rock-cut inner ditch, with an (inner)

bailey to the east, with double ditches and itself forming a plateau well above the level of the remainder of the summit of the hill. The motte has vestiges of a shell keep, and the bailey of a curtain wall and a large square well. There were outer baileys and the whole came to be fortified in stone. Surviving accounts of 1399–1400 refer to a middle ward and an outer ward, with the lord's stables and kennels for his hounds in the latter. There were then an outer gate and an inner gate to the castle. In the inner ward the privies of both 'my lord and my lady' were glazed.

Chepstow, *Monmouthshire*

The castle of Chepstow high on its cliff above the Wye, the river on one side (north) and the future walled town on the other, was founded by William fitz Osbern, the Conqueror's earl of Hereford, as the gateway to South Wales. He, 'the bravest of all the Normans', was also the Conqueror's closest friend, 'whom of all his intimates he had loved the most since their childhood together' (William of

Poitiers). As a particular mark of trust he, like another close friend of the new Norman king, Roger of Montgomery, earl of Shrewsbury (see Arundel and Hen Domen) was given great lordship not only on the south-east invasion coast (i.e. Carisbrooke and the Isle of Wight) but also on the borders of the kingdom towards Wales with ample scope there for expansion. Both were made earls in England, William fitz Osbern as early as 1067, and both gladly and characteristically seized their opportunities. By the time of his tragic death in Flanders in 1071, fitz Osbern had penetrated deep into Gwent and had acquired from his base at Chepstow most of the modern county of Monmouth. His son and successor, Roger 'of Breteuil', foolishly rebelled in 1075, which brought the castle and lordship into royal hands until 1115; but after that the sequence of the lords of Chepstow or Striguil reads like a roll-call of chivalry – Clare, Marshal and Bigod, Mowbray and Herbert.

In consequence, architecturally there is something for everybody at Chepstow, and almost all of it of great interest and importance. It was fortified in stone from the beginning: the present Middle (east) and Upper (west) baileys on either side of the keep both have vestiges of walls of the fitz Osbern period (1067–71) in their later southern curtains, and the keep also, placed on the narrowest part of the ridge, is of his time and thus one of the earliest in the land. In its original form (it was heightened and otherwise altered in the thirteenth century) it was of two storeys only, i.e. the first-floor hall and chamber type of keep as opposed to the tower proper, such as is first found at Langeais and occurs again in England in the twelfth century at, e.g., Castle Rising and Middleham. The entrance, with a fine tympanum, was and is in the east wall, whence a straight stair led up to the *étage noble*. In *c.*1189 and the time of William the Marshal, then created earl of Pembroke, the wall dividing the present Middle and Lower baileys was built as what was then the eastern outer curtain of the castle, with a great drum tower guarding the gateway and another at the junction with the south curtain. In the time of the Marshal's sons and between *c.*1225 and 1245 new baileys were added to the castle east and west, respectively the present Lower Bailey with its twin-towered gatehouse (nearest the camera), and the so-called Barbican with its cylindrical south-west tower. Finally, the castle reached its maximum development in the time of Roger Bigod III, earl of Norfolk, between 1270 and 1306, when the Lower Bailey to the east received its splendid residential range – halls, chapel, chambers, kitchens – on the safe, north side and the enormous Marten's Tower (with its own accommodation) at the south-east angle, while, at the other end of the castle, the rectangular western gatehouse was added to the barbican. This Bigod earl also built the town walls.

Held for the king and twice besieged in the seventeenth-century civil wars, Chepstow nevertheless escaped Parliamentary slighting to be instead garrisoned, and 'modernized' as a fortress by the thickening of its southern curtain and the earthing up of towers (after the manner of Dover in the eighteenth and nineteenth centuries) until eventual 'dismantling' in 1690.

FURTHER READING

J. C. Perks, *Chepstow Castle*, Cadw Official Handbook, Cardiff.

Chilham, *Kent*

Some sort of time-warp exists at Chilham which enables at least local guide-books still to talk about the castle's foundation by Julius Caesar or Hengist and Horsa. In reality the foundation was soon after 1066 and presumably by Fulbert of Dover (d. 1121 × 1130: Douvres, Calvados), who held Chilham of Odo of Bayeux in Domesday and in chief after the bishop's fall, and whose descendants certainly held the castle as the *caput* of their barony. Further, the remains of a mid-eleventh-century hall incorporated in the forebuilding of the present keep must go back to

Fulbert's time. The most important feature of Chilham, and almost all that survives, is that keep (8 o'clock in the photograph), an example, comparatively rare in this country, of an octagonal or polygonal great tower (cf. Odiham, Richard's Castle, Tickhill, respectively), here with the addition of a forebuilding and one turret containing the vice, both of which bring it closest in plan to Henry II's keep at Orford which, however, is larger. Chilham too, which has been dated on architectural grounds to the third quarter of the twelfth century, may be attributed to Henry II, who is known to have spent over £400 upon works at the castle between 1171 and 1174 when it was in his hands. Internally the keep is now much altered but still stands within a rectangular walled enclosure close about it.

In the fourteenth century Chilham passed to the family of Ros (cf. Helmsley) who, being Lancastrians, lost it on the triumph of the Yorkist cause and the accession of Edward IV. In the sixteenth century Leland reported that 'Chilham castel is now almost doune', and Sir Thomas Cheney, to whom Henry VIII granted the manor, is said to have demolished much of it. The present great Jacobean house (centre) adjacent was built for Sir Thomas Digges and bears the date 1616 and the text, 'The Lord is my house of defence and my castle.'

Christchurch, *Hampshire*

Christchurch (Twyneham, a burgh in the Burghal Hidage) was royal demesne in Domesday but was granted by Henry I to Richard de Redvers (Reviers, Calvados), his loyal supporter in the struggle for the Conqueror's Anglo-Norman inheritance. To this Richard de Redvers, therefore, who died in 1107, the foundation of the castle is usually attributed, and it remained the possession of his family, earls of Devon from 1141, lords also of the castles of Plympton and Carisbrooke, until the end of the thirteenth century. The castle, with the priory (Augustinian, second founder Richard II de Redvers in *c.* 1150) and the town, occupy a promontory between the two rivers Avon and Stour which converge into the bay, the castle standing upon the bank of the Avon or, rather, the parallel Mill Stream. It was raised upon the motte-and-bailey plan, and has the ruins of an impressive rectangular tower keep, without buttresses, upon the motte – or, as perhaps one should say, within it, for conservation work in the 1950s revealed a window opening beneath the present surface of the mound. The most important part of the castle to survive, however, is the mid-twelfth-century hall beside the river, dated on architectural grounds to *c.* 1160. This is now cut off from the motte and keep, or donjon, by the gardens and bowling-green which occupy the rest of the bailey, and seems no longer recognized in popular local lore for what it is, part of the castle and the principal part of the lodgings of its lords. It is accordingly a building of very high quality, oblong and of two storeys, the *étage noble* at first-floor level above an undercroft and comprising the hall (north and nearest the camera) and chamber or solar (south) separated by timber partition walls now vanished. Entrance was by an external stair (cf. e.g. Boothby Pagnell) into the lower (south) end of the hall. While the ground-floor undercroft, presumably used for storage,

was lit only by narrow loops for security reasons, the *étage noble* has grand two-light windows, the window in the north wall, marking the high-table end of the hall, being particularly richly decorated. There is a fireplace in the east wall of the hall (the elegant and contemporary chimney of which is a notable feature) and a vice connecting hall, undercroft and wall-walk in the north-east angle. The garderobe turret by the south-east corner of the chamber over the river is evidently a thirteenth-century addition.

The castle of Christchurch has little recorded history after the wars of Stephen's reign. In the fourteenth century it passed to the Montagu earls of Salisbury, and in the earlier sixteenth century was held by the Lady Margaret Pole, founder of the magnificent Salisbury chantry in the priory church. It was slighted after the seventeenth-century Civil War.

Clare, *Suffolk*

'How are the mighty fallen!' – though in this case most honourably as well as tragically when, on 24 June 1314, the young Gilbert de Clare was slain at Bannockburn without heirs of his body. 'The greatest baronial family of medieval England' took its name from Clare in Suffolk where the founder of the line in England, Richard son of count Gilbert of Brionne, lord also of Tonbridge in Kent, raised the castle as the centre of his East Anglian honour in the first generation of the Norman Conquest and before his death (as a monk at St Neot's) in *c*. 1090. His descendants in the twelfth and thirteenth centuries were to become earls of Hertford and of Gloucester and lords of Glamorgan in Wales. Though after 1314 the lordship of this castle remained most distinguished in the hands first of the house of Mortimer and then of the Yorkist and Tudor monarchs, it never perhaps quite fulfilled its early potential to be among the finest in the land, as the Clare lords themselves in the thirteenth century developed Tonbridge on the one hand and built the mighty castle of Caerphilly in Glamorgan on the other. It is symptomatic

of shifting interests that whereas the twelfth-century earls were buried in their priory of Stoke-by-Clare their thirteenth-century successors chose Tewkesbury in the West Country. Nevertheless, after Bannockburn, the Clare heiress, the much-married lady Elizabeth de Burgh, often resided in state at Clare until her death in 1360, and the captains and the kings might still come a century later.

All splendour now has long departed. Save for the great motte – 260 m in circumference at the base, 30 m high, and with a fragment of shell keep still upon it – even the earthworks of the former castle have been mutilated almost beyond recognition by the encroachment of the town, more especially by the half-moon Station Road curving through both inner and outer baileys, and the railway which, having largely destroyed the former by its track and station, has now withdrawn again, too late. The original arrangement of the castle (here seen from the west) was of the motte with a main and inner bailey running due east of it, and, separated by an east–west ditch, a large outer bailey to the north, now bisected by Station Road. The main entrance to the castle from the town was into this outer court, evidently where the road now enters it (lined up on the old road to Stoke-by-Clare via Nethergate Street), and that same intruding road crosses the ditch into the inner bailey on the site of the medieval defended crossing and inner gate. A 'Norman' buttress was found here by excavation in 1848. Vestiges of the curtain wall which once descended the motte from the keep at two points and enclosed the inner bailey can still be seen. The inner bailey contained the main residential accommodation apart from that within the keep itself. There are further embankments to the east between the inner bailey and the Clinton stream. The castle was strongly sited in the angle between that stream and the river Stour, the course of the latter being diverted to defend it on the south side.

Clavering, *Essex*

If J. H. Round was right in identifying Clavering as the 'Robert's castle' north of London, i.e. the castle of Robert fitz Wimarc, to which some of Edward the Confessor's Norman friends fled in 1052 on the triumphant return of the exiled earl Godwin and his sons, then it joins Richard's Castle and Ewyas Harold as one of the very few known pre-Conquest castles in England, each raised by those Norman and French lords brought into the kingdom by the half-Norman Edward. Robert fitz Wimarc himself was certainly one of them, a kinsman, it is recorded, of both the Confessor and the Conqueror, made 'staller' or official of his household by the former, and also probably sheriff of Essex. He evidently remained in England after the Godwinson coup of 1052, to appear in the *Vita Edwardi* (and the Bayeux Tapestry) at the Confessor's death-bed in 1066 and in William of Poitiers' account of the Norman invasion of the same year to warn the duke, 'his lord and kinsman', of Harold's victory at Stamford Bridge. There seems no need to rob him of his *Normanitas,* for he is specifically called 'Norman' by William of Poitiers and by Florence of Worcester. The Normans of this age were ethnically mixed, and in any case the Breton name 'Wimarc' is the name of his *mother* (*Wimarca, Wimara,*

Guimara). He was sheriff of Essex under the Conqueror and in that office was succeeded by his son, Swein of Essex, the Domesday lord of Clavering after his father.

The castle site at Clavering, north of the church, consists of an oblong earthen platform some 90 m by 56 m, standing some 4 m or 5 m above the moat which surrounds it on all sides. On the north side, between it and the little river Stort, there is an impressive series of roughly parallel earthern banks which have been interpreted as hydraulic works to divert the stream and create an artificial lake and control the water in the moat – to make of the place a sort of early Caerphilly in miniature.

Though Morant, the county historian, wrote (1768) of walls 'not long since standing', the castle appears to have no known history nor to have been archaeologically investigated, in which case no doubt the less said the better. It is, however, an impeccably recorded fact that Robert's son and heir Swein raised the great motte-and-bailey castle at Rayleigh (Rayleigh Mount – which does have a history thereafter) – *In hoc manerio fecit Suenus suum castellum, D.B.* ii, 43b – on new lands acquired from the new régime, and perhaps the one replaced the other.

Clun, *Shropshire*

The castle of Clun was sited within the natural defence of a bend in the river, with the town it dominated to the east and south (the church of St George being across the bridge on the other side of the river). It consists of an oval motte, rising almost sheer from the river on the west, and two baileys to the east with further earthworks marking a pool or fishpond towards the north with a sluice to the river. About the summit of the motte there are the remains of a curtain wall or shell keep, including the entrance formed of two semi-circular and solid towers of uncertain date facing the river. But the donjon at Clun comprised not only a shell keep upon a motte but a tower keep also, and it is the latter which is the most interesting feature of the castle. Here, as at Guildford in Surrey, the great tower is dug into the motte (on the north side), with its foundations thus on the natural ground, to obviate the structural danger of placing so heavy a building upon an artificial mound. The south wall, which presumably contained the entrance from the motte top, has vanished, and the tower consisted of a basement and three residential floors above, each with a fireplace.

The foundation of the castle is presumed to have been by Picot (his nickname: *alias* Robert) de Say (Sai, dep. Orne, in Normandy), an important vassal of earl Roger of Montgomery, and the tenant of Clun in Domesday with some of his knights already enfeoffed in the manor which had belonged to Edric the Wild before 1066. After 1102 the lordship of Clun was held in chief, with its great forest and its knights owing guard at the castle. About the middle of the century it passed to William I fitz Alan, lord of Oswestry, in right of his wife Isabel, the Say heiress. To him the tower keep is usually attributed, though because structurally it appears to belong to the late twelfth century it may well be the work of William II fitz Alan. Although Isabel de Say was married twice more (to Geoffrey de Vere *c.* 1164 and to William Boterel before 1188) her fitz Alan son, i.e. William II, eventually succeeded *c.* 1200, and the castle and lordship remained with that increasingly eminent house (see Arundel) until the Howards succeeded them in the sixteenth century. Leland in the 1530s noted of Clun castle, 'longynge to the Erle of Arundel', that it was 'somewhat ruinus', though he added that: 'It hath bene bothe stronge and well builded.' It was slighted by Parliament in 1646.

Colchester, *Essex*

There is reason to suppose that the Normans moved into the Eastern Counties and East Anglia at once after the occupation of London and William's coronation on Christmas Day 1066. In Essex the single most impressive monument to their presence is the huge keep of the new royal castle at Colchester, planted near the centre of the former Roman town, north of the High Street diverted south to accommodate it, and on the site of a late Old English unfortified *villa regalis* of the tenth century. Here, then, is that continuity and overwhelming change characteristic of the Norman Conquest and settlement. The great rectangular keep, partly demolished, its top hamper (at least one storey plus battlements and turrets) removed in and after 1683, is shown on the accompanying photograph from the south-west, trees and landscaping to north, west and east marking the baileys, Upper and Nether, which formerly surrounded it on all sides. It is by far the largest Norman tower keep in England, which means it is the largest tower keep in Europe. It thus even exceeds the majestic dimensions of the White Tower of London, which measures merely 32 m by 36 m to Colchester's 33 m by 46 m. Quite why Colchester was singled out for this unique distinction remains something of a mystery whose solution must at least take us back to the immediate circumstances of the Conqueror's reign. Physically the scale and shape of Colchester keep – including the south-eastern apsidal projection, housing the chapel (as at the Tower of London), and the outsize south-western angle turret, housing the main staircase – were predetermined by the chosen site, built about the vaulted podium of the late Roman temple of Claudius. A royal presence in the rich and fertile eastern counties was deemed essential (cf. the great keep at Norwich, which may also go back, in its first phase, to the Conqueror's day). The south-east coast of England above the Thames, no less than below it, was also the invasion coast, and here the threat was Scandinavian, by no means ending in 1066. Yet one may well feel that what is being expressed at Colchester certainly no less than at London is majesty and regality rather than direct military strength. Both are very similar in a plan otherwise unique in surviving keeps, and both may go back to the long-vanished (1204) great tower in the ducal palace at Rouen, dating from the mid-tenth century and reaching back perhaps to late Carolingian precedents.

Colchester keep was probably begun in 1074 or 1076 – perhaps a little earlier than the Tower of London – though its first phase ended soon after 1080 at only one storey high, marked now by filled-in battlements, perhaps in response to the invasion threat from Denmark at that time. It was continued up to the three storeys (plus turrets and battlements) no doubt originally intended in the years following 1101 when Henry I granted to Eudo Dapifer 'the city of Colchester and the tower and the castle and all the fortifications of the city, as my father had them, and my brother and myself'.

After that, the rest seems anticlimax. Following Eudo's death in 1120 the castle remained royal until 1629. It was developed in the twelfth and thirteenth centuries (but never on the scale of its erstwhile rival in London), and maintained until the fourteenth. Thereafter it was neglected to fall into ruin, and in the sixteenth and seventeenth centuries shared with the Tower, though less notoriously, the indignity of being used as a state prison. After the siege of Colchester in the Second Civil War of 1648 the castle, which had played no other

part, was the scene of the unwarranted execution of the Royalist defenders, Sir Charles Lucas and Sir George Lisle. In 1683 the ruins were handed over for demolition to one John Wheeler who, it is good to report, went bankrupt in the process. He, plus some eighteenth-century 'restoration', accounts for the present appearance of the great keep, made worse internally by its housing of the Colchester Museum.

FURTHER READING

P. J. Drury, 'Aspects of the Origins and Development of Colchester Castle', *Archaeological Journal,* CXXXIX.

Conisborough, *Yorkshire*

The foundation of the castle at Conisborough is attributed to William de Warenne (Varenne, near Arques, Seine-Inf.), friend and close companion of the Conqueror, lord in Normandy of the castles of Bellencombre and Mortemer, enriched in England with lands in thirteen counties including his principal lordships of Lewes in Sussex, Castle Acre in Norfolk and Conisborough in Yorkshire, in each of which he placed a castle as the *caput* of the honour. Here then is Norman lordship, and trust rewarded, on a huge scale; and William de Warenne was also to receive, just before his death on 24 June 1088, the earldom of Surrey from Rufus, which accounts for another Warenne castle, at Reigate in Surrey, arising soon afterwards. Even so, nothing is known of the first castle of Conisborough beyond its site, which evidently had no motte, for the extant stone walls, towers and other buildings are attributed on architectural grounds to the fifth earl, Hamelin, between *c.*1180 and 1200. As the illegitimate son of Geoffrey count of Anjou (husband of the empress Maud, daughter of Henry I and would-be queen of England), earl Hamelin was half-brother to Henry II who had granted him the marriage of the sole Warenne heiress in 1164. He died in 1202 and Conisborough is his principal monument.

There are vestiges of an outer ward and barbican through which one still approaches from the west, but the castle otherwise consists of a strongly walled enclosure with a keep, upon a natural hill made steeper by scarping and its own deep ditches. Its chief claims to distinction are the solid, projecting, semi-circular turrets set about the curtain to give flanking cover on its outer face (two survive to west and south-west, and one to the east), and the splendid keep or donjon, with its sophisticated, fine-jointed masonry, set in the north-east quarter of the bailey – 'one of the finest surviving pieces of twelfth-century secular architecture in the country' (M. W. Thompson). Rising sheer from a splayed out plinth, this is cylindrical in the latest fashion of the age, modelled upon, or derived from, it is thought, the earl's cylindrical keep at Mortemer in Normandy, but here set about with six wedge-shaped buttresses on a scale to serve as the turrets which they are (cf. Orford), ascending above the wall head. Entrance is at first-floor level via a vaulted passage and vaulted stairways in the thickness of the walls to the two residential floors above, respectively hall and chamber (top), each with splendid fireplace, garderobe and recessed wash basin, and the chamber with a small but beautifully decorated chapel (with sacristy) contrived in the east-facing buttress turret. First floor and basement contained unlit rooms for storage, with the well in the centre of the latter. The roof of this lordly edifice was conical with wall-walk and parapet about it, and four of the six buttress-turrets were hollow to contain respectively a dove-cote, an oven and two water cisterns.

After the death of the eighth and last Warenne earl in 1347 the castle passed via Edmund of Langley, youngest son of Edward III, to the house of York and so to the Crown in the person of Edward IV in 1461. Nevertheless by the sixteenth century it was ruinous.

FURTHER READING

M. W. Thompson, *Conisborough Castle*, English Heritage Handbook, London.

Conway, *Caernarvonshire*

When king Edward's army reached Conway in the Second Welsh War and in the second week of March 1283, preparations were put in hand at once for the raising of the new castle and burgh. The only buildings of any consequence known to have been then on the site were a residence of the native princes, Llywelyn's Hall, and their Cistercian abbey of St Mary (Aberconway), the burial place of Llywelyn the Great and others of his line. The take-over of the former (eventually demolished in 1316, its timbers used to make a storehouse in the new castle at Caernarvon), and the removal of the latter at considerable expense (the church remaining to this day as the parish church of the new burgh) to Maenan eight miles away up river, were a forceful demonstration of the new régime henceforth imposed upon Gwynedd, quite apart from the massive symbolism of the royal castle about to be planted. That is one of the four greatest of Edward I's castles in North Wales and therefore one of the finest anywhere. The site chosen was impeccable, a high and narrow spine of rock, its furthest footings to the east washed by the waters of the Conway river and its tributory the Gyffin. Thus Conway like Caernarvon stood upon tidal waters, while its command of the crossing of the river estuary is shown only too clearly by the assortment of modern bridges which now detract from the majesty of the castle. Like Caernarvon also, Conway was conceived and planned in association with a fortified town, and the building of the two together went forward as one integrated operation. The rock site of the castle also imposed an overall plan (p. 19) very similar to that of Caernarvon, somewhat irregular, elongated east and west, with a narrow waist facilitating division into two wards. Here, of course, the (eight) mural towers were not polygonal but massively cylindrical, of the type most favoured at this period, and the Inner Ward, the inner sanctum of regality and effectively the donjon, was more markedly the smaller of the two, though architecturally no less the *pièce maîtresse* of the great building. It could be entered direct from outside via a (vanished) postern, which was in fact a water-gate, and the east barbican, which was laid out as a garden: and the four great drum towers at its corners were picked out by turrets from which, no doubt, the royal standards flew when the king was in residence. Within was the suite of royal lodgings built specifically by Master James of St George (p. 21) by contract and comprising, at first-floor level, the King's Hall, his (Privy) Chamber and his Presence Chamber, with sleeping chambers in the south-east tower (the King's Tower) and an elegant chapel in the north-east (the Chapel Tower). The Outer Ward contained the Great Hall, of eccentric shape because of the irregularity of the curtain and the site, the kitchens and stables, and the necessary accommodation of the permanent staff including the constable in a lodging incorporating the two western towers. It is to be noted that both the two principal gateways into the castle, the Main Gate at the west end (from the town) and the gateway into the Inner Ward at the east end (from the river and open country), are not the contemporary type of the great twin-towered gatehouses so splendidly represented at Caernarvon, Harlech or Beaumaris, but simply passages through the curtain walls, albeit very well defended. The reason is that such gateways at Conway were simply not required – or in effect were there already in the plan – for in each case the thrusting proximity of two great mural

The wards and mural towers
of Conway Castle, 1948

towers, one on either side, gave ample protection to the entrance, each of which in turn was further protected by its barbican. There was no weakness here.

Perhaps the most impressive single fact about Conway is the speed of its completion (unlike Caernarvon) within the five years between 1283 and 1287. The cost was some £14,000 and both that total and the time includes the walled town and the castle, between them forming 'one of the outstanding achievements of medieval military architecture in all Europe' (A. J. Taylor). The town walls with their three gates are themselves now outstanding for the completeness of their survival, the near-unity of their construction, the absence of later additions or modifications, and the remarkably full and detailed documentation which has survived of their building. As for the castle, the advent of the Welsh Tudors in 1485 brought increasing neglect until it was sold to the first lord Conway for £100 in 1627. In the Civil War it was held for the Crown until 1646. The Council of State ordered its slighting in 1655 and in 1665 the third lord Conway, having received back a great building beyond economic repair, dismantled and sold its lead, timbers and ironwork. So matters remained until Telford's road-bridge (1826) followed by the railway brought increasing appreciation and afterwards conservation.

FURTHER READING

A. J. Taylor, *Conway Castle and Town Walls,* Cadw Official Handbook, London.

100

Corfe, *Dorset*

Corfe, dramatically and beautifully sited on its natural hill (scarped to improve upon nature) was one of the great royal castles of the realm, which makes its vicious slighting by Parliament in 1646 particularly tragic. Whether or not the place is where Edward the Martyr was slain in 978, and whether or not the timber precursor of the early Norman hall in the west bailey was part of the royal residence where the deed was done, is irrelevant to the history of the castle, which was first placed here by William the Conqueror, who obtained the land for that purpose by exchange from the abbess of Shaftesbury. The Conqueror's castle may well have incorporated the whole of the present site and may well also have included some of the earliest stone fortification and castle-building in England (cf. e.g. Richmond and Ludlow, Chepstow and the Tower of London), for the massive curtain of the inner bailey about the summit of the hill dates back to the eleventh century, and so does the hall in the west bailey. The great rectangular tower keep in the inner bailey, though later than the curtain (and its forebuilding and southern annexe slightly later adjuncts), is also very early, best dated to *c.* 1100, and with it went a middle or south-west bailey below, again massively defended

Corfe in relation to its settlement, the earthwork siege castle of the twelfth century bottom right

by stone walls though later altered. The west bailey and the outer bailey one must assume to have been palisaded, but in 1139 when Stephen besieged but failed to take it (his siege-castle still exists 365 m to the south-west – bottom right on the photograph) Corfe could be described as one of the most secure castles in all England, and the fact that no major work is recorded here by Henry II is further testimony to its early strength. Subsequent development was largely confined to the thirteenth century, notably by John whose favourite castle and residence this was. Most notable among his works is the 'Gloriette', the supremely elegant, though now shattered, courtyard residence in the inner bailey. John is also responsible for the towered curtain of the west bailey with the octagonal 'Butavant' at the prow (nearest the camera: cf. Château-Gaillard), and for the great ditch across the waist of the castle beneath the keep, which greatly altered the disposition of the former middle bailey. The same king may also have begun the towered curtain of the present middle and outer baileys, which was completed by Edward I, who also heightened the keep. Corfe was first alienated from the crown by Elizabeth I, who sold it to Christopher Hatton for £4,761 18s. 7$\frac{1}{4}$d. in 1572. The seventeenth-century siege, when the castle was held for the king by Lady Banks, and was taken only by the treachery of the turncoat Colonel Pitman, lasted intermittently from 1643 to February 1646.

Denbigh

Denbigh, castle and fortified town, is another product of the Second Welsh War of 1282–3 and Edward I's conquest of Wales, but with the difference (not noticeable architecturally) that this was technically not a new royal castle and attendant borough but pertained to Henry de Lacy, earl of Lincoln, to whom the king granted the lordship on 16 October 1282. Nevertheless the operation (like those of Hawarden, Holt and Chirk which were also seigneurial castles) was part of Edward I's concerted programme of fortification in the north especially, and the works were begun with the royal resources and planned by the king's master mason, James of St George, king and earl both being at Denbigh for their launching in later October 1282. The castle was to be the new centre of the new lordship of the cantred of Rhufoniog (one of the disputed 'Four Cantreds'), assigned to Llywelyn by the Treaty of Montgomery in 1267 and regained ten years later in the First Welsh War, and it was deliberately and symbolically placed on the site of a former residence of the Welsh princes of Gwynedd. After the planning and initial preparations the earl was responsible for the works which are thought to have been effectively completed by his death in 1311.

The town walls were built first, to provide a general defence, with the result that in the castle, thereafter constructed in the south-west quarter, two phases of work can be seen, the west and south curtains which form also part of the town walls and were built with semi-cylindrical towers in and after 1282, and the stronger north and east curtains with their polygonal towers (cf. Caernarvon) and great triangular gatehouse built a few years later. The screen wall or mantlet about the west and south curtains to strengthen them, and which makes the castle semi-concentric, also belongs to a slightly later phase, and so do the residential buildings, hall, chambers, chapel and pigeon house within the bailey. A unique feature of the castle of Denbigh is the great gatehouse formed of three conjoined polygonal towers, two projecting forward (north) to flank the entrance and one behind. This arrangement afforded, amongst other things and other defences, the rare device of a bent entrance (cf. Pembroke, inner gatehouse) via a central lobby.

By the sixteenth century a large part of the castle had fallen into decay, though in Elizabeth I's time there was a brief revival through restorations and refurbishment by Robert Dudley, earl of Leicester, who also built a new church, now also ruined, in the town. By then most of the inhabitants had deserted the old, walled town to build more spaciously lower down the hill. Nevertheless, castle and town were put into a state of defence and held for the king in the seventeenth-century Civil War, and withstood a siege from April to October 1646. Deliberate slighting and then ruination followed until local conservation in the nineteenth century and official conservation in this.

FURTHER READING

L. A. S. Butler, *Denbigh Castle, Town Walls, and Friary*, Cadw Official Handbook, London.

Dover, *Kent*

From the battlefield of Hastings, after a rest of five days, the Conqueror made for Dover which, there is good reason to believe, he had been seeking to obtain from the 1050s as a base and surety for his succession to the English throne, now granted him by God. It was perhaps the strongest place on the south-east invasion coast, a former Iron Age fortress high on its cliff and hill, then serving as an Old English burgh, as witness the late tenth- or early eleventh-century church of St Mary-in-Castro still within it (centre: heavily restored) with an attendant Roman *pharos* or lighthouse as its bell-tower. Having taken the fortress without opposition, the duke raised a castle inside it – during eight days according to William of Poitiers – very much on the analogy of Hastings. Nothing is known of this first Norman castle of late October 1066 at Dover except that a glimpse of its ditch and bank hard by the south transept of the church was obtained in the 1950s during excavation of the so-called Harold's Earthwork which surrounds the church and which itself turned out to be of thirteenth-century date. If there was

ever a motte it has vanished, and it may be that the Conqueror's castle was simply an enclosure in the middle of the Iron Age fortress and Anglo-Saxon burgh, like Old Sarum.

The expansion of the castle to take in the whole site and to become one of the greatest in the realm ('the key of the kingdom' in Matthew Paris' phrase) was evidently begun by Henry II (1154–89). Enormous, and vastly expensive, works were carried out here in the second half of his reign and especially in the decade from 1180 (see plan p. 13). They comprised, to the north, the great rectangular tower keep, one of the largest and most sophisticated in Europe, and the curtain of the inner bailey all about it, notable for its systematic use of (rectangular) flanking towers, and its two twin-towered gateways (both originally with a barbican) north and south, the King's Gate and the Palace Gate respectively. They also comprised, on the north-east, the beginning of the outer curtain which surrounds the inner bailey and its keep, so that at Dover in the 1180s the principle of concentric fortification was already being applied, as at Château-Gaillard in the next decade. This outer curtain about the northern apex of the castle, with wing walls linking it to the southern face of the inner bailey, was completed by king John, while the walling-in of the whole position, with towered curtain walls running to the cliff's edge west and east (the latter just possibly the work of Henry II) and looping round St Mary-in-Castro and Harold's Earthwork (the latter also of this period), is the achievement of Henry III's masons, completed by c. 1260. In his time also a range of grand residential accommodation was built on the east side of the inner bailey to replace that of his father and grandfather and supplement the accommodation within the keep.

In the civil war which ended John's reign, and also produced Magna Carta (1215), Dover withstood, but only just, a siege by the king's enemies under command of prince Louis of France. The assailants undermined the main outer gate, which then stood at the northern apex of the castle, and brought down half of it. When the war was over, therefore, in the early years of the young Henry III, not only was the breach closed but the whole working plan of the castle was altered to ensure that nothing of that kind could happen again. King John's shattered gate was rebuilt solid and transformed into the formidable trinity of the Norfolk Towers, with other new towers adjacent. Further to deny to any future enemy the ground from which prince Louis had directed his attack, a great outwork was constructed in its place (visible on the photograph, top right, though cased in Napoleonic brick), linked to the main structure by underground passages and

Dover and its castle from the sea, the church of St. Mary and Roman *pharos* centre right

commanded by the St John Tower built in the ditch. To complete this expensive exercise in locking the stable door after the horse had been stolen, the FitzWilliam postern (1 o'clock on the photograph) was constructed at this time, with a covered passage-way again to give egress to the dangerous northern ground; and all this having been done, a new main gateway had to be constructed, which is the splendid Constable's Gate (*c.* 1227) opposite FitzWilliam on the north-west side.

Dover is thus a magnificent example of the typical history of so many English castles, i.e. of an early foundation at the time of the Norman Conquest and settlement, followed by continuous development upon the same site. As late as 1625 Charles I could lodge his betrothed bride, Henrietta Maria, in the royal apartments within the keep (though not without complaint from her courtiers). Such continuity of function, however, can do as much damage to an ancient secular building as neglect, as witness Arundel or Windsor. In the case of Dover, the revived military importance of its site *vis-à-vis* the threat of French invasion during the Napoleonic period and later in the nineteenth century led to a drastic 'modernization' of the fortress, and dire damage to its medieval fabric, above all by the cutting down of towers and by the earthing up of walls, the emplacement of gun-batteries, and the construction of brick casements, caponiers and vaults. The army finally withdrew only in 1956, and its lingering presence accounts for the robust barrack buildings so prominent in the foreground of the photograph. One adds mid-eighteenth-century barracks in the inner bailey where Henry III's hall, chambers, chapel and kitchens once stood. Such things, of course, are not without their interest, but yet must be regretted in this place.

FURTHER READING

R. Allen Brown, *Dover Castle*, English Heritage Handbook, London.

Durham, *County Durham*

There is no more dramatic site in all England or Britain than Durham, cathedral priory church and castle side by side upon their rock almost surrounded by a tight loop of the river Wear, and both set in a fortified city. Both are Norman, and mark the beginning of that long historical process whereby an English royal government, essentially southern (Wessex), penetrated and was imposed upon the far north of the kingdom, rival Scottish ambitions notwithstanding. The symbolism, too, is inescapable and deliberate. Church and castle, here on an imperial scale, evoke and concentrate the twin authorities of medieval society, Church and State, God and Caesar, the Two Swords, spiritual and secular. And here in Durham both swords were in the same hands, those of the bishop, the prince-bishop, to whom the Conqueror entrusted the government of what became until the nineteenth century the Palatinate of Durham.

The church, begun in 1093, is the *non-pareil* of Norman Romanesque. The castle necessarily came first, planted across the neck of the narrow peninsula to

protect the city and its church behind. Its construction, we are told by Symeon of Durham, was ordered by the Conqueror himself, returning from his expedition against the Scots in 1072. It was raised on the 'motte-and-bailey' plan, but amongst its sumptuous, mostly later, masonry the surviving crypt chapel (now its finest single feature) and perhaps the core of the present gatehouse date from the earliest period. Much thereafter is attributed to bishop Ranulf Flambard (1099–1128), though we are specifically told only that he fortified the city with a wall and cleared away the houses between the castle and the church (i.e. the present Palace Green). How far at least in general the castle had developed by the 1140s is shown by the tantalizing poem of prior Lawrence, written in such flowery Latin as almost to defy precise translation. But as former chaplain to the bishop, Lawrence knew the castle, and his description has great value. Thus the keep in his time evidently comprised a shell wall revetting the motte, and within this a timber tower rising much higher on four posts, the whole connected with the bailey by a sloping bridge. In the bailey the chapel stood near the foot of the motte and is said to have rested on six columns which are presumably those of its surviving crypt. The gatehouse was there, and there were already two 'palaces', i.e. hall and chamber blocks – no doubt precursors of the present north and west ranges, the bishop requiring two halls for his two functions. The castle still has two halls, indeed three, for bishop Hugh du Puiset ('Pudsey', 1153–95) built a palatial residential range along the north side of the bailey which is basically one hall upon another (originally with attendant chambers and service rooms, mostly gone), with the surviving stately entrance portal. All this is screened now by bishop Tunstall's (1530–59) gallery and turret, east of which is his chapel, i.e. Tunstall's Chapel. The other hall is the present great hall of the college in the west range, many times rebuilt but basically of bishop Bek (1283/4–1311). South of this are bishop Foxe's (1494–1501) splendid kitchens, created out of earlier buildings of Hugh du Puiset. Because of the continuity of occupation few castles emphasize their residential role more than Durham (where the bishop still has his suite and bedroom), and the fact that it is an episcopal castle does not affect the issue. The keep, however, though residential still, is mainly 1840, replacing – and as an irregular octagon more or less repeating – the fourteenth-century edifice of bishop Thomas Hatfield (1345–81), which evidently only then replaced the timber tower of prior Lawrence.

Edlingham, *Northumberland*

The small castle of Edlingham, lately the object of extensive and fruitful archaeological research, lies at the east end of an almost deserted medieval village still marked by its church and spread of ridged fields. The castle stands on low ground beside the Edlingham Burn to the south of it. It began as an unfortified manor house within a rather larger enclosure than the present one, the earliest and principal building revealed by recent excavations being a stone-built hall-house, running east and west, due north of the tower, which is later. This was a building of some sophistication, to be compared, perhaps, with Acton Burnell. It had

octagonal angle turrets, a first-floor hall (with external staircase and central hearth), service rooms on the two storeys west, and chambers on two storeys east, all integrated in one structure. It is dated to the close of the thirteenth century and attributed to William Felton, a man who had risen far in the service and wars of Edward I, was constable of Beaumaris from 1295 to 1301, was already lord of Nafferton in southern Northumberland, and who bought the manor from Thomas de Edlingham at this time. Some fifty years later the manor house was fortified by William's son and successor, William Felton II, who built a strong tower south of the hall on the edge of the burn and a walled bailey with an imposing gatehouse to the north, both altered and further strengthened later. The *pièce maîtresse* of the new castle was and still is the tower, comparatively small but quite formidable in strength, with diagonal buttresses rising into projecting bartizans at the four angles, and containing accommodation particularly ornate for what was, after all, the minor castle of a minor lord. Each of three floors comprised a good chamber with a fireplace. The ground floor was vaulted and formed a separate unit. The first floor, entered via a forebuilding or annexe direct from the screens passage of the hall-house, was elegantly vaulted and rose loftily through two stages of the tower with a third chamber above it and *en suite* with it.

110

Edlingham is thus, like so many of the lesser fortifications of the far north of England, including the so-called peles, to be numbered among the strong houses built or fortified in the fourteenth and fifteenth centuries in the circumstances of that endemic warfare with the Scots which was the *damnosa hereditas* of Edward I's failure to impose his will upon the northern kingdom. In 1402 it passed from the family of Felton to that of Hastings, and in 1514 was purchased by George Swinburne, constable of Prudhoe. In 1572 in the will of Thomas Swinburne it is still 'my castle of Edlingham' and an inventory of that date shows altered domestic arrangements but still within the medieval buildings. The end came evidently in the later seventeenth century, with a partial demolition recorded in 1661.

FURTHER READING

Graham Fairclough, 'Edlingham castle, Northumberland', *Transactions Ancient Monuments Society*, new series, XXVIII.

Ewyas Harold, *Herefordshire*

Like neighbouring Richard's Castle, Ewyas Harold can make claim to be a pre-Conquest castle, one of those pertaining to the group of Norman and French lords

whom king Edward established in Herefordshire under his nephew, earl Ralph of Mantes. Writing of the flight of the 'Frenchmen' from London in 1052 on the triumphant return of the banished earl Godwin, the 'E' version of the *Anglo-Saxon Chronicle* relates that 'they took horses and departed, some west to Pentecost's castle, and some north to Robert's castle'. The two castles specified have been reasonably identified as respectively Ewyas Harold, the castle of Osbern Pentecost, and Clavering in Essex, the castle of Robert fitz Wimarc. In Domesday the castle of Ewyas Harold was held by Alfred of Malmesbury of the king but had formerly been held by him of William fitz Osbern, the Conqueror's earl of Hereford, who had restored or refortified (*refirmare*) it and granted it to him. Alfred himself was the nephew of Osbern Pentecost, who had been banished in 1052 (he went to Scotland) and his castle presumably slighted. In the time of Rufus Ewyas Harold and other lands of Alfred were granted to Harold, the son of Edward the Confessor's earl Ralph, who has given his name to it and who founded *c.* 1100 the small Benedictine priory (a cell to Gloucester) which lay at the foot of the castle hill and is now marked only by the parish church of St Michael. Harold of Ewyas Harold was succeeded after 1100 by his son, Robert I, the founder of Dore abbey in 1147, and he by his son Robert II who died in 1198 leaving an heiress, Sibyl.

The castle thus became the centre of a considerable lordship, referred to as a *castelleria* in Domesday Book and returning a total of twenty-two fees to the feudal inquest of 1166. Yet not one stone remains of the masonry buildings it surely acquired, so effectively have they been robbed out (G. T. Clark surmised from robber trenches a shell keep and stone curtain with domestic buildings on the east side of the bailey). Its later history has therefore not been studied, and the site has not been archaeologically investigated in modern times in spite of its immense interest. What remains is the formidable motte cut off in classic fashion from the end of a promontory, with the bailey to south and east as a kind of platform before the ground drops on three sides to the confluence of the two streams and road at its foot.

Exeter, *Devon*

Exeter from the air is disappointing, the outline of the Roman city and Anglo Saxon burgh now largely obliterated and the site of the castle in the north-east corner (due north of the cathedral and at nine o'clock on the accompanying photograph) obscured by trees and post-medieval buildings. That site, we know, was chosen by the Conqueror himself early in 1068 after he had suppressed the defiance of the citizens by a siege of eighteen days, and was a promontory of natural reddish rock – hence the castle's name, 'Rougemont'. The king left Baldwin de Meules (cf. Okehampton) and other distinguished knights to carry out the work of the new castle and hold it, while he himself with his army rode on into Cornwall. The result, like the royal castle and future Tower of London, was a roughly quadrangular ditched and banked enclosure within the angle of the former Roman city walls, though here there is evidence of an outer enclosure to the

south and no great tower or keep appears ever to have been added. The principal claim to fame of Exeter castle now is the very early gatehouse (long since blocked and presumably once the inner gate) very probably dating back to the first castle of the Conqueror and Baldwin de Meules. Facing south near the south-east angle of the main, inner enclosure, it is a stone tower pierced by the entrance passage (cf. Richmond and Ludlow) with two storeys above and striking triangular-headed window openings. The curtain abuts it on either side and is presumably later, replacing an original palisade. The most dramatic event known in the subsequent history of the castle is Stephen's successful siege in 1136, against Baldwin de Redvers who had seized it. By that time it is clear that the main enclosure at least was walled all round. Thereafter continuous maintenance of what remained a royal castle seems, in the later Middle Ages at least, to have been concentrated chiefly upon the shire hall and gaol within it, so that as early as 1311 a survey of dilapidations shows much of the castle ruinous, and there is no record of any substantial work after 1325.

Eye, *Suffolk*

The castle of Eye was one of the first to be raised in Suffolk, by William Malet, known companion of the Conqueror at Hastings, before his untimely death in action, probably at the siege of Ely in 1070–1. Thenceforth it was the *caput* of the great honour to which it gave its name, conferred upon William Malet and Robert his son and heir by the first Norman king. Domesday refers to the castle and the borough, the park and the market, the last as adversely affecting the old-established market of the bishop at nearby Hoxne. Robert Malet founded Eye priory (as a cell to the abbey of Bernay in Normandy) for the salvation of his father's soul amongst others, and no doubt in accordance with his intention. Here, in short, is a perfect example of the Norman settlement, of aristocratic colonization, of the creation and imposition of new lordships.

But 'never glad confident morning again'. Robert Malet evidently died about 1106, and no heir was accepted in England. Honour and castle reverted to the Crown in the person of Henry I, who subsequently granted them to his nephew Stephen of Blois, count of Boulogne and Mortain and future king. This turns out to be the pattern of the future. Eye was to be held by many great lords of the first rank – Stephen, William his son, Henry duke of Brabant, Richard earl of Cornwall, 'King of the Romans' and brother of Henry III, the Ufford and de la Pole earls of Suffolk – but too often, especially in the earlier centuries, as but one unit in a great accumulation of lordships, held by men whose patrimony or principal interests were elsewhere. In consequence, it would seem, Eye never fulfilled its initial potential as one of the great castles of the realm, and has in fact very little 'history'. Thus throughout the reign of Henry II when it was in the king's hand only minor works and maintenance are recorded; though one item in 1179 for the repair of buildings in the castle damaged 'in time of war' certainly suggests that it saw action in the rebellion of the Young King in 1173–4.

The castle, due west of the fine church of St Peter, was once an impressive motte-and-bailey. As early as 1911 the *Victoria County History* spoke scathingly of 'the violent usage meted out to this strong fortification'. The whole site is much built over and encroached upon, the ditches and banks have gone, a derelict school presses against the motte, and most recently a housing estate, or group of 'Executive Homes', has been thrust into and onto the former bailey. The motte, however, some 12 m or 15 m high in accordance with the slope of the ground to the east, still recognizably survives, albeit crowned by a bogus nineteenth-century shell keep (there was a windmill there in the eighteenth century), and the line of the adjacent streets (*e.g.* Castle Street and Church Street) still marks the castle's former shape and dominance.

Farnham, *Surrey*

Farnham may be archaeologically described as a motte-and-bailey within a large D-shaped outer enclosure, although that is not very revealing. Its two particular

interests are (a) that like Durham it has always been throughout its history an episcopal castle, in this case pertaining to the bishop of Winchester, and (b) the complexity of its motte as shown especially by the excavations of 1958–9. We are told by the Winchester Annals that the castle was founded in 1138, in what was then merely an episcopal manor (Farnham was subsequently developed and granted borough status in 1248), by the great bishop Henry of Blois, who ruled the see from 1129 to his death in 1171 and was also papal legate and the brother of king Stephen (cf. Wolvesey). We know also that in 1155, soon after his accession, Henry II demolished this and other castles of the bishop, though it was soon afterwards restored. The excavations of 1958–9 showed that Henry of Blois' motte encased the foundations of a rectangular stone tower keep which were set upon the natural ground level and carried up with the mound so that the two formed one integrated donjon. This tower was evidently demolished in 1155, whereafter the motte was refortified by the present shell keep, the circular wall of which is again built up from the natural ground level so as to revet rather than crown the mound (cf. Berkeley). It was strengthened by the four rectangular turrets set at intervals about it, and entered through a shallow rectangular gate-tower (south) three storeys high which contained the bishop's chamber in 1299. Buildings within the keep included hall, chambers, chapel and kitchen and it thus served as a separate and seigneurial residential unit, doubtless for the bishop when he wanted it, at least until the fifteenth century.

The triangular domestic complex of the inner bailey, which forms a forecourt south of the keep with which it communicates, though obviously much altered, enlarged and modernized, also has a twelfth-century core which included great hall, kitchen, chambers and chapel. The most important and impressive medieval addition is the entrance tower to this, the mis-named Foxe's Tower, built by bishop Waynfleet (founder of Magdalen College, Oxford) between 1470 and 1475. The outer bailey is enclosed by ditch and bank and by a curtain wall of twelfth-century appearance but no great strength, set with rectangular mural towers and a fourteenth-century outer gate (south-west).

FURTHER READING

M. W. Thompson, 'Recent Excavations in the Keep of Farnham Castle, Surrey', *Medieval Archaeology*, IV.

Flint

Flint is the most ruined of Edward I's new castles in North Wales but not the least interesting. After an honourable role in the seventeenth-century Civil War and eventual surrender to the Parliamentary forces in 1646, it was ordered to be dismantled, and the job was so brutally done that in 1652 it was reported as almost buried in its own ruins. In the eighteenth and nineteenth centuries the site was encroached upon, with factories in the Inner Ward, and only since 1915 has it been looked after and conserved by the good offices of the Office of Works and its latter-day successors.

Flint, with Rhuddlan, was the product of the First Welsh War in 1277, and the works there initially an integral part of the campaign, the whole army, with large contingents of craftsmen and labourers and under the king's command, moving forward on or about July from Chester, a fleet accompanying them along the coast. Flint, where everything was new including the name, was their first base before they moved on to Rhuddlan, and at both a new town was planned as well as a castle, with direct access to sea-going shipping, that merchants and civilians as well as soldiers should be settled in the hitherto disputed territory of Englefield, the future Flintshire.

The new fortified borough never received more than ditch, banks and palisade for its defences, which were evidently constructed first, but the castle was splendidly completed in stone by 1286, at a combined cost with the town of some £7,000, mostly under the direction of Master James of St George and the repeated personal supervision of the king. After a large and semi-rectangular Outer Ward (south) behind its own great ditch, the principal strength of the castle lies in the Inner Ward and keep, built on the plan familiar in thirteenth-century France, Savoy and elsewhere (Dourdan, Yverdon) of a rectangular enclosure with angle towers, one of which is greatly enlarged, and here off-set (south-east), to be the donjon. In short, Flint had a tower keep as its donjon, a type often but erroneously said to be obsolete at this date in England (cf. Cambridge, also by Edward I). It was cylindrical and free-standing in the waters of its moat and the estuary of the river Dee, guarding the harbour and the castle's inner gate into the Inner Ward, and

externally may remind one of the Tour de Constance at Aigues Mortes. Internally, however, it was, to use a dangerous word, unique among known great towers, though in some ways reminiscent of the castles of Frederick II at Castel del Monte in Apulia and Edward II at Queenborough in Kent. There were a basement and probably two residential floors, the second entirely vanished.

The basement comprised a large, circular room, intended for heavy stores, entirely surrounded by a wide mural gallery with which it communicated by three broad openings. Above this level, however, the residential apartments (which at first-floor level included a chapel) stood over the gallery as a series of wedge-shaped rooms, and did not occupy the central space, which here became a spacious and octagonal lighting shaft bringing them both light and air. The great tower thus provided some of the best residential accommodation, which may have been intended for the constable or for the justiciar of Chester or for both. We are free to conjecture at least one further suite of more ample accommodation – hall, chambers, chapel, kitchens – of which no trace remains within the Inner Ward, while the three angle towers (of which the north-east is the best preserved) also contained residential chambers.

The best preserved section of the curtain of the Inner Ward is the southern, where the embrasures for arrow loops are to be noted (cf. the surviving north-west section). Helpless at Flint, Richard II submitted to the triumphant Bolingbroke on 22 August 1399.

Framlingham, *Suffolk*

As for Bungay, the earliest history of Framlingham is ill served. The first known reference to the castle occurs only in 1148 when earl Hugh Bigod entertained Theobald, archbishop of Canterbury, within it. The confident and reiterated statement that the place was granted to the first Roger Bigod by Henry I in 1101 seems to go back only to Dugdale on the authority of Matthew Paris. However there is nothing against the traditional ascription of the first castle to the same Roger (d. 1107), and its foundation may well date from the eleventh century and the early years of the Norman settlement. Roger was already in possession of Framlingham at the time of the Domesday survey, albeit as a tenant of Hugh, earl of Chester; the fact that by 1086 the manor had more than doubled in value since the

The towered curtain wall of the inner ward at Framlingham

Confessor's day may suggest that the castle was planted here soon after the Conquest; as may perhaps the fact that in the beginning it is now known to have had a motte, subsequently levelled, in the north part of what is now the walled inner enclosure. Thereafter the descent of Framlingham follows that of Bungay and its twelfth-century history is similarly dramatic, being confiscated from earl Hugh from 1157 to 1165, restored in the latter year, demolished in 1175, and restored by Richard I to earl Roger Bigod in 1189, thereafter certainly to be rebuilt in its present form by him. Moreover the new castle was besieged and taken by king John in 1216 in the civil war that closed his reign.

The castle, whose earthworks are at least as impressive as its towered curtain walls, presently consists of three enclosures, an inner ward (often thought of as the castle proper), a great horse-shoe shaped outer bailey to east, south and west, and the Lower Court, north-west of the Inner, at ten o'clock on the aerial photograph. North and east of the castle there is, in addition, a surviving section of the Town Ditch which enclosed the township which developed south of the castle where the church can be seen. Excavations in 1969–70 revealed that the first castle had a motte and (inner?) bailey, but the towered wall of c. 1190 which now surrounds the whole of that area has, on its east inner face, opposite the modern Poorhouse, clear traces of a former hall and chapel, older than itself yet subsequent to the motte. This must mean that there was a drastic remodelling of the castle, involving both the levelling of the motte and the construction of at least some stone buildings, at a date which rather slender archaeological and architectural evidence suggests was mid- to late twelfth-century. One might perhaps suggest that this may have followed and marked Hugh Bigod's elevation to the earldom in 1141, or that it may be the work of the same Hugh in the years between 1165 and 1173 when important works are thought to have been going forward at Bungay and the king was building Orford. However that may be, the present curtain walls of the inner enclosure with their thirteen towers, one of which is the gateway to the south, mark the rebuilding of the slighted castle by earl Roger Bigod in the time of Richard I. He also built a new great hall, on the site of the Poorhouse (which incorporates part of it) and opposite the old one. It had a chamber block or solar north of it, and there was a postern to the south which led, via the walled passage and defensive tower still standing, into or out of the Lower Court which is also thought to be earl Roger's work. Beyond the Lower Court the ground falls quite sharply to the river, which was dammed further to protect the castle on this western side by an artificial lake which also provided the amenities of fish and pleasure. In Tudor and Howard times this Lower Court became a garden, while the present chimneys were raised about the inner court somewhat to spoil the majesty of the castle's profile. There is no evidence that the great outer bailey was ever walled, and there is reference to the repair of palisades about it as late as 1295. North of the castle the deer park extended far into the countryside.

Mary Tudor was in possession and in residence when proclaimed queen here in 1553. Thereafter, though restored to the Howards, the castle evidently declined in importance. In 1635 Theophilus Howard, earl of Suffolk, sold it to one Sir Robert Hitcham, who in turn bequeathed it to Pembroke College, Cambridge. That institution, in accordance with Sir Robert's will, is responsible for the gutting of the castle's interior and the construction of the inappropriate Poorhouse.

Goodrich, *Herefordshire*

The early history of Goodrich, before king John's grant of it to William Marshall, earl of Pembroke, in 1204, is surprisingly obscure. Because of early references to *castellum Godrici*, its foundation has been attributed to one Godric Mappesone, an English minor tenant of the king's demesne who in Domesday held Howle in Walford on the other side of the river, but this seems very unlikely. The castle may have taken its name from 'the land of Godric' on which it stood, but its association in the eleventh and twelfth centuries from charter evidence is with the lordship of Monmouth until *c.* 1144. Thereafter it may have been held by the Clare earl of Pembroke, which would account both for the reappearance of the place as royal demesne in 1177 (i.e. after the death of Richard fitz Gilbert in 1176) and for the grant of castle and lordship to William Marshal in 1204. Thence forward all is clear except that the early tower keep, retained by the Marshal and his successors in their rebuilding of the castle, thus remains embarrassingly anonymous. On architectural grounds it is usually dated to the mid-twelfth century, but may be earlier.

The castle stands on a rocky spur above the west bank of the Wye, where it commands an ancient ford (hence Walford). That William Marshal and his sons carried out extensive works, probably comprising a rectangular enclosure with angle towers about the early keep, is clear from the lower levels of the east curtain,

foundations of a predecessor beneath the south-west tower, and a reset sedile in the chapel, all dated archaeologically to the early thirteenth century. Otherwise the present castle is almost entirely the product of a nearly complete rebuilding by Aymer de Valence, earl of Pembroke and uncle of Edward I, in *c.* 1300. The result of his labours and expense was a very fine castle in the latest mode, quadrangular with great, spurred angle towers, formidable rock-cut ditches on two sides, east and south, and an outer ward on the other two with an impressive, half-moon barbican on the north-east, clearly derived from the very similar barbican (the 'Lions Tower') built by his nephew Edward at the Tower of London. Analysis of the lavish residential accommodation shows four separate establishments, each of high quality for people of high quality, based upon three halls (west, east and north-west, the last mislabelled 'solar' on most plans), with subsidiary chambers in the angle towers, all served by a common kitchen (west of the keep) and chapel (in the Chapel Tower which is part of the formidable gatehouse at the north-east).

In the fourteenth century the castle passed to the Talbots, later earls of Shrewsbury. In the seventeenth century Civil War it was held for the king, besieged and damaged in 1646, and thereafter slighted.

Guildford, *Surrey*

Our knowledge of the castle of Guildford scarcely matches its interest and former importance. No documentary reference is known earlier than 1173 and almost nothing of medieval date remains upstanding save the donjon – i.e. the tower keep and fragmentary shell keep upon the motte – though the site is thought to cover some six acres and contained a royal residence so impressive at least in the thirteenth century as to be given the rare description of 'palace' thereafter.

As basically a motte-and-bailey, the castle's foundation not long after the Conquest is assumed. The rectangular tower keep is attributed on architectural grounds to the first half or second quarter of the twelfth century, while the polygonal shell keep about it, of which only fragments remain, is thought to be earlier. If, as is generally supposed, the shell replaced a palisade, then the latter is likely to reach back to the eleventh century. The tower is comparatively small, 13 m square, with no cross-wall, and had two floors above a basement. The entrance was at first-floor level, and this, the principal residential floor, had mural chambers including a chapel. When built, this keep had the rare embellishment of polychrome masonry (cf. Château-Gaillard), and its particular archaeological interest is that its east face and footings went down the side of the motte to rest on the natural ground (a chalk spur) after the manner of Clun. The principal bailey evidently lay south and south-east of the donjon and contained the royal lodgings which Henry III developed and extended as one of his favourite residences. In all, he lavished some £1,800 upon Guildford (£770 between 1253 and 1256) and we hear of the aisled hall, the two chapels of St Stephen and St Katherine, the chambers of the king, the queen and their son the lord Edward, the Chancellor's chamber, the great chamber which in 1256 was to be whitewashed and diapered and its ceiling painted green spangled with gold and silver, and of the cloister with marble columns in the garden. Yet after Henry III's time all this, now the 'palace', was increasingly neglected in spite of Edward III's attempt to restore it, and after 1366 was evidently abandoned. In the 1380s materials from the decayed building were being collected and stored, and lead was sent to the works at the castles of Southampton and Portchester. In 1611 the ruined castle, which had been royal throughout its recorded history, was alienated to one Francis Carter, which evidently accounts for the seventeenth-century house now in the castle grounds. In 1886 the site was bought by the Corporation and laid out as a municipal garden.

Harlech, *Merionethshire*

Harlech is the most dramatically sited of all Edward I's castles in North Wales, and this combined with its spectacular mountainous context and the austere might of its plan and architectural appearance, make it surely the *non pareil* among them, though only Caernarvon can be the greatest. It was begun in the early summer of 1283, after Conway but just before Caernarvon, and was finished by December 1290, the majestic result of some seven and a half years' labour and an expenditure of some £9,500. It is the creation above all of Master James of St George, who translated into stunning achievement the king's will, desires and knowledge. In July 1290 Master James was appointed constable of the new castle as a special reward for his services.

On its rock then high above the sea and the estuary of the river Dwyryd (with the castle dock where the railways goods yard is now), the castle stands within the further protection of a great rock-cut ditch made on the only accessible sides to east and south. It is built of the stone on which it stands, and is concentric in plan though the narrow outer ward is little more than a revetted platform, its largely destroyed low curtain having no towers or turrets save those of the postern (north), the outer gate (east) and the large garderobe and rubbish shoot (south). It suffices to keep an enemy at his distance and is more than adequately covered by the towering curtain of the inner ward behind. Nine-tenths of the strength of the castle is in the Inner Ward with its four great drum towers at the angles, almost a rectangle but its north and south walls splayed out to accommodate the massive Gatehouse thrusting out, with the outer gate and ditch beyond it, eastward in the only direction from which attack can come. It is the *pièce maîtresse* of Harlech, sometimes called a keep-gatehouse, certainly the strongest single unit of the whole castle and containing the best residential accommodation. Basically it is formed of two projecting towers, here semi-cylindrical, facing the field one on either side of the entrance passage (defended by three gates, three portcullises, loops and

guardrooms), but the whole is brought back deep and rectangular into the Inner Ward, where it is finished off with a tall cylindrical staircase turret at each of its two angles, and a broad and sweeping external staircase to the first floor – the 'stately stayre' of a sixteenth-century survey and almost an *escalier d'honneur*. The upper levels, first and second, contain two stately suites of accommodation, each comprising hall (south) and chamber (north) end to end in the rear part of the gatehouse, with a bedchamber in each of the forward projecting towers and a chapel with a pair of little vestibules or vestries in between. The lower suite is thought to have been for the constable, and the upper presumably for the king, prince or visiting and privileged magnate, there being no other comparable set of apartments in the castle. The great angle towers of course contain residential chambers, and the more communal or public rooms and offices, now fragmentary, were ranged along three sides of the Inner Ward – great hall in pride of place, with buttery, pantry and kitchens, along the west side opposite the gateway, lesser hall and granary on the south side, and chapel plus bakehouse etc. along the north. From the start there was a defended 'Way from the Sea' up the west side of the rock to the vicinity of the north-west tower, and in *c.* 1295 a new water-gate was built at its start (north-west, near the station) and a stone wall thence round the base and north side of the rock up to the north-east angle tower (clearly shown on the photograph). Finally in 1323–4 the bridge approach to the castle from the east was strongly fortified by two towers in line beyond the outer gate and built up from the bottom of the ditch where their stumps can still be seen. There was a drawbridge at either end of this structure (itself a miniature version of some fortified road bridges still to be seen in France) and a stone-arched bridge between the two towers.

Harlech played an active part in the Welsh rebellion of Owen Glendower in the early fifteenth century and subsequently in the wars between York and Lancaster. There is no record of any repairs after the great siege of 1468 and much reference to decay in the sixteenth century. Nevertheless the castle was held for the king in the seventeenth-century Civil War and was the last castle in the realm to fall on 15 March 1647. Thereafter it was slighted, though not fundamentally, and an order to demolish it was mercifully not proceeded with.

FURTHER READING

A. J. Taylor, *Harlech Castle*, Cadw Official Handbook, Cardiff.

Hastings, *Sussex*

Both William of Jumièges and William of Poitiers inform us that after the occupation of Pevensey (on 28 September) and the raising of a castle there the Conqueror moved on to Hastings and raised another, while the Bayeux Tapestry in a well-known scene shows the raising of a motte at 'Hesteng ceastra'. There is really no doubt that the site of the Conqueror's castle is the present one on Castle Hill nor that his motte, much mutilated, is the core of the present castle mound to the east over which the later curtain wall now runs. Further, there is evidence both documentary and structural to show that the collegiate church of St Mary-in-the-Castle hard west of the motte (like the church within Pevensey castle, q.v.) pre-dates the castle, and was founded by or in memory of the aethling Alfred, younger brother of Edward the Confessor and murdered in 1037. This church, shown twice on the tapestry (Thames and Hudson, 1985, pls. 50, 51), thus became in October 1066 the headquarters of duke William from which he rode off to win his victory over Harold. Hastings is certainly listed as an Anglo-Saxon burgh in the Burghal Hidage of the early tenth century, and, the whole hill-top position into which the Conqueror thrust his castle having been in origin an Iron Age fortress, Dover becomes an even closer analogy than Pevensey. In 1066 (and long after) the harbour needed by duke William for his ships lay to the west at the foot of Castle Hill, which itself presumably jutted out into the sea, and a new Norman town was developed to the east. The new castle became the *caput* and administrative centre of the new Norman lordship, the rape of Hastings; an elaborate castle-guard provision of knights was organized for it; and castle and lordship were given by the Conqueror, first to Humphrey de Tilleul, and then, after his return to Normandy and his protesting wife (Orderic Vitalis), to Robert, count of Eu.

As may be seen from the aerial photograph, the sea, before it withdrew, took away much of Castle Hill and with it much of the castle. In the fourteenth century there is reference to 'the daily encroachment of the sea' as from the previous century at least, and with it came the decay and neglect of the castle. The encroachment and consequent decline were cumulative: in the reign of Elizabeth I one Edmond Saunders, an elderly fisherman deposed 'that yn his tyme the mayne sea did breake upon the cliffe, Whereby parte of the Castell was fallen and decayed'.

FURTHER READING

A. J. Taylor, 'Evidence for a Pre-Conquest Origin for the Chapels in Hastings and Pevensey Castles', *Château-Gaillard*, III.

Haughley, *Suffolk*

The great motte-and-bailey castle at Haughley is at once one of the most important and most neglected sites in East Anglia. In the photograph the motte is centre foreground and almost totally hidden by trees and undergrowth; the bailey or inner bailey, a little less so because of the modern house within it, runs south to the church yard. The *Victoria County History* of 1911, which contains what is still the only respectable account of the castle albeit exclusively archaeological, speaks of it as 'the most perfect earthwork of this type in the county' and of its 'stupendous artificial conical mount', 24 m high with a diameter of 64 m at the base and 24 m at its flat summit. The water-filled ditches and the banks surrounding the motte and the large rectangular bailey (88 m by 91 m) to the south are no less impressive, and there may have been an outer enclosure all the way round, thus enclosing the church (mentioned in Domesday and with fragments of early Norman work in the north wall of the nave). The present entrance into the bailey on the west may well be original; further inviting investigation are the reported traces of a shell keep upon the motte; and the whole site appears to be sealed as from 1173, after which no references to the castle have been found.

In Domesday the lord of Haughley was Hugh de Montfort (Montfort-sur-Risle, Eure), the duke's constable in Normandy, who had fought with him at Mortemer (1054) and Hastings and was by 1086 a great tenant-in-chief in Suffolk. Haughley or 'Hagenet' became the *caput* of his honour, *alias* the Honour of the Constable, originally set up to provide amongst other services knights for the castle-guard of Dover, of which he had the custody as early as 1067. It is he who in default of other evidence must be regarded as the founder of Haughley castle. He became a monk in 1088 and was succeeded by his son, Hugh (II by English reckoning), and he by Robert de Montfort who was banished by Henry I in 1107. Robert's sister, Alice, evidently took the honour by marriage successively to Simon de Moulins and Robert de Vere. Late in his reign Stephen granted the honour and castle to his close supporter, the ill-fated Henry of Essex, lord of Rayleigh. Henry in 1163 was 'appealed' by Robert de Montfort (scion of the displaced family) of treachery and cowardice in that he, though constable, had abandoned the royal standard and fled the field in an engagement with the Welsh near Basingwerk in 1157, and, being defeated in the ensuing judicial combat, was disinherited and became a monk at Reading. His possessions then escheated to the king and it was as a royal castle that Haughley was taken and destroyed by Robert, earl of Leicester, leader, with Hugh Bigod, earl of Norfolk, of the unsuccessful rebellion against Henry II, in 1173. After that the rest is silence, though one would love to break it.

Helmsley, *Yorkshire, North Riding*

Helmsley is sometimes attributed to Robert 'Fursan' de Ros (Roos in Holderness), lord of Helmsley from *c.* 1190 to his death in 1226, because of the earliest masonry visible on the site – i.e. the curtain, towers and keep of the inner ward all datable to *c.* 1200 – and a statement in the cartulary of Rievaulx abbey that the said Robert Fursan *levavit castra de Helmisley et de Warke*. The verb *levare*, however, does not necessarily imply foundation but can mean to build or even strengthen, and Robert certainly did not found Wark. The most outstanding feature of Helmsley is its double ditches which, there is reason to think, are a sign of particular regality (p. 23). A rare analogy is Berkhamsted in Hertfordshire, where the castle was first raised by Robert count of Mortain, half-brother to the Conqueror himself, no less. In Domesday, the same Robert count of Mortain was lord of Helmsley (where there was already some sort of vill with a church) and therefore one may at least suggest that he founded this castle also. Further, it seems not unlikely that there was a castle here in the time of Walter l'Espec, to whom Henry I granted both Wark and Helmsley, and who in founding neighbouring Rievaulx, where he died a monk in 1155, was clearly making of this place a principal centre of his lordship.

The castle sits on a ridge of rock running more or less north and south, and consists of an irregular rectangular enclosure within formidable rock-cut ditches, apparently with an outer enclosure both north and south. There is an elaborate barbican thrust out in front of the south or south-east gate, and another, less elaborate, protecting the north gate. On the west side there is something of a cliff

and here therefore the principal residential buildings, including the almost vanished hall (south-west) have always been. The curtain wall, with its three angle towers, the west tower, gates and keep, are all dated on architectural grounds to c. 1200 and the time of Robert II (Fursan) de Ros, who clearly rebuilt the castle (and was married to a daughter of the king of Scots). The curtain has been heightened in c. 1300 (William II de Ros, d. 1316?) and so has the keep on the east curtain, unusual in its design, half rectangular and half cylindrical. The southern barbican was added in the mid-thirteenth century, and the northern at about the same time. The castle chapel, west of the keep, was consecrated in 1246.

The township east of the castle was granted the liberties and customs of York by Robert II de Ros in c. 1200. The lordship of Helmsley remained with the family of Ros from 1157 to 1478. In the later sixteenth century the residential buildings were much altered or rebuilt by Edward Manners, third earl of Rutland. In the seventeenth century the castle was held for the king, besieged by Fairfax in 1644 and afterwards slighted. It was not finally abandoned as a residence, however, until the building of Duncombe Park in 1713.

FURTHER READING

Sir Charles Peers, *Helmsley Castle*, English Heritage Handbook, London.

Hen Domen, *Montgomeryshire*

Hen Domen, 'the old mound', is the local Welsh name long since given to the abandoned site of what was the first castle of Montgomery, planted here in then open country by Roger II of Montgomery, first Norman earl of Shrewsbury in or soon after 1071. Roger was a close friend, counsellor and contemporary of the Conqueror, who gave him first the lordship or rape of Arundel in 1067, and then, in 1071, the county and earldom of Shrewsbury. 'The earl himself built the castle called Montgomery', states the Shropshire Domesday unequivocally. It was placed, on the Welsh side of Offa's Dyke, on the highest point of a ridge commanding the ford across the Severn, henceforth 'the Ford of Montgomery', and was intended to serve both as a subsidiary centre of new lordship and, more particularly, as a base for Norman penetration of central Wales. Destroyed by the Welsh in 1095 and subsequently restored, it was lost to the house of Montgomery when Robert de Bellême forfeited all his English lands and castles following his rebellion in 1102. Thereafter Henry I granted the castle to Baldwin de Bollers, whose family continued to hold it until 1207 when its descent was disputed. In 1216 king John granted it to the Welsh prince Gwenwynwyn of Powys for his alliance but he was almost immediately driven out by Llywelyn the Great. The castle's decline must date from these events, and though it was evidently occupied until the late thirteenth century it became increasingly redundant after the foundation of 'the new castle of Montgomery' by Henry III in 1223.

The site at Hen Domen is a good example of a motte-and-bailey, quite small in relation to its importance, but of great strength with double ditches (a rare and perhaps regalian feature – cf. e.g. Helmsley). It runs almost due east and west, with the motte at the west end and the entrance to the bailey at the east. Prolonged and near comprehensive archaeological research principally of the bailey (the north-east section stripped bare in the photograph) has recently revealed not only successive phases of timber buildings – hall, chapel etc. – but more detail than usual of the strength of the castle's timber defences. Thus the palisades of the bailey had parapets and projecting towers, the motte was surrounded at the base by a palisade as well as a ditch, and at the foot of the bridge from the bailey to the motte top there was evidently a formidable forebuilding.

FURTHER READING

Philip Barker, 'Hen Domen, Montgomery: Excavations, 1960–7', *Château-Gaillard*, III.

Kenilworth, *Warwickshire*

Kenilworth, one of the great castles of the realm, stands representative of many things, including the second generation of the Norman settlement, the efficacy of extensive water defences (cf. Caerphilly; Leeds), and the continuing tradition of the castle as the ultimate noble residence into the sixteenth century and beyond. The land, formerly pertaining to the royal manor of Stoneleigh, was given some time before 1125 by Henry I to Geoffrey de Clinton his chamberlain (from St-Pierre-de-Semilly, Manche; the archtypal 'new man' of the text-books), who at once set about to found his castle and his priory (due east of the castle beyond the Abbey Pool) as the centre of his new lordship and the symbols of his new status. The first castle is thought to have comprised only the present inner bailey, perhaps with a motte where the keep with its earth-filled base now stands (cf. plan p. 8). The rectangular tower keep itself, however, is early. Certainly dating from the Clinton period, before 1174, it stands only two storeys high and is in that respect at least to be compared with Castle Rising (c. 1140). On the death of Geoffrey de Clinton II, son of the founder, in c. 1174, Henry II kept the castle in his hand, and it is very likely that the next major phase of development – the addition of the outer ward and the great extension of the Mere to the west – took place in the reign of John who spent the large sum of over £1,100 upon the castle. In 1253 Henry III granted Kenilworth to Simon de Montfort, earl of Leicester, which led on to the famous siege of 1266, when the desperate supporters of earl Simon, slain at Evesham, held out for six months against the whole force of the kingdom, then only yielding with the honours of war. After that the castle passed to the earls and

dukes of Lancaster, thereafter remaining a possession of that duchy. Thomas earl of Lancaster, executed in 1322, began to found the collegiate chapel of St Mary, never finished, in the outer ward (east), and his successor, John of Gaunt, son of Edward III, rebuilt in its present form the great range of palatial accommodation about the inner court and centred upon the splendid great hall. The last phase of Kenilworth's splendour occurred as late as the second half of the sixteenth century, when Elizabeth I granted the castle to her favourite, Robert Dudley, earl of Leicester. He made a new entrance from the north (Leicester's Gatehouse), as opposed to the original southern entrance via the Tiltyard and Mortimer's Tower, 'modernized' the keep (which accounts for its dreadfully inappropriate windows), and built Leicester's Buildings, breaking through the inner curtain to the south, for his noble guests. He also created the large, Elizabethan formal garden in the northern section of the outer bailey, now recently restored. In the seventeenth-century Civil War the castle was occupied by Parliamentary forces, yet it was slighted afterwards, which accounts for the absence of the keep's north wall and the draining away of the waters in which Kenilworth once stood. From then on only Leicester's Gatehouse, converted, continued as a residence and the whole great structure was left to decay, high and dry.

FURTHER READING

M. W. Thompson, *Kenilworth Castle*, English Heritage Handbook, London.

Kidwelly, *Carmarthenshire*

It is impossible not to treat Kidwelly as a splendid example of the later and perfected castle of the turn of the thirteenth and fourteenth centuries, when military architecture in England and Wales reached its apogee. Strictly, however, it stands as the entire rebuilding of a castle founded on this site with attendant fortified town in the earlier twelfth century by Roger, bishop of Salisbury, to whom Henry I granted this lordship in the South Wales coastal plain. It stood and stands on a cliff high above the river Gwendraeth on its east, and the town, marked by its banks and ditches, surrounded it on the other three sides. A traverse ditch, however, running west from the castle divides the town area into two, and it is possible that only the southern part was walled in the fourteenth century (the southern gatehouse almost alone survives – extreme left on the photograph). Bishop Roger also founded the Benedictine priory of St Mary on the other, east, side of the river, and there too a town developed.

The present castle was begun *c.* 1275 by Payn de Chaworth, friend and companion of Edward I on the latter's crusade, and completed (save for certain later developments) by Henry of Lancaster, his successor after his early death in 1279. To him is attributed the Inner Ward, a rectangular enclosure with great drum towers at the angles and two gateways, north and south, sufficiently

defended by them; the whole designed to accommodate the principal residential apartments along the east side above the river and integrated with the north-east and south-east towers. That range, however, of hall, solar and dramatically projecting chapel built up from the river on great spurs, is attributed to Henry of Lancaster immediately after his marriage to the Chaworth heiress in 1298. He is responsible also for the sweeping arc of the outer curtain which makes Kidwelly, so to speak, half a concentric fortress, and the banks and ditches of which mark the line of bishop Roger's castle. It is or was defended by semi-circular mural towers and had two gatehouses, one north and one south. The latter, the great southern gatehouse, is the finest single feature of the castle, though now known to have been remodelled and substantially rebuilt by the Lancastrian king Henry IV in the early fifteenth century (the work may have been previously begun by John of Gaunt), which accounts for the machicolation. It comprised self-contained accommodation for the constable on the first and second floors. The last addition to the castle was the provision in the late fifteenth century of more spacious residential buildings in the outer ward, notably a new hall on the west side, probably by Sir Rhys ap Tudor, to whom Henry VII granted the lordship.

FURTHER READING

C. A. Ralegh Radford, *Kidwelly Castle*, Cadw Official Handbook, Cardiff.

Kilpeck, *Herefordshire*

That so little is known of the history of Kilpeck seems surprising in view of the fame among art historians of its church and the importance of the site as a classic example of (surely) Norman aristocratic settlement. The interest of the site is threefold, not just the church but the planned vill or township in which it stands, clearly demarcated and now a 'deserted village', and the castle which dominates the whole. The present church is dated, purely on the artistic evidence of its sculpture, to *c.* 1150 or, more recently, *c.* 1140, and incorporates in the north-east corner of its nave a fragment of walling from an earlier church, dated purely on architectural grounds to the pre-Conquest period. Reference to such documentary evidence as survives, however, provides a significantly different pattern. First, the *Liber Landavensis* shows that at Llandaff cathedral in the twelfth century the tradition, and presumably the record, was that a church here was dedicated in the time of William the Conqueror by bishop Herwald, which suggests a Norman foundation as part of a new seigneurial complex of castle and attendant township. Second, charter evidence from the abbey of St Peter at Gloucester shows that in 1134 Hugh (I), son of William, the lord of Kilpeck and founder in that year of the small priory there as a cell to Gloucester, granted the church of St David at Kilpeck to that house. Clearly therefore, if the church of Hugh I's grant was the present one newly built, as seems most likely, then that church with its sculpture must be put

back to before 1134 (which would fit very well the documentary bracket for the artistically closely related church of Shobdon which is 1131 × 1143), or, if one can really believe that the monks accepted a derelict church which they were obliged to rebuild, then this Kilpeck product of the Herefordshire school of sculpture does not stem from the patronage of a minor secular lord but of the major abbey of Gloucester.

The castle is first mentioned in 1134 when, in the same charter, Hugh I granted 'the chapel of St Mary of the castle' to Gloucester as well as the church of St David. In Domesday Hugh's father, William son of Norman (royal forester of Haywood Hereford), held Kilpeck, then a parcel of the *terra regis* of Archenfield and valued at £4. The foundation of the castle (and vill?) has been attributed to him by no less an authority than Round. It may be so, since his descendants certainly held Kilpeck by knight-service and he and they were men of substance holding many estates elsewhere, including Little Taynton in Gloucestershire, held by the sergeanty service of the forestership of Haywood. In the thirteenth century we read of the honour of Kilpeck, though the estate itself was assessed at only $1\frac{1}{2}$ knights' fees. In that case one should perhaps attribute the shell keep, of which there are remains upon the castle motte, to Hugh I, William fitz Norman's son, to whom as the founder of the priory, were it not for the Llandaff evidence of the foundation of the earlier church, one might be tempted to attribute the whole complex in its present form.

In the absence of any modern archaeological investigation of the site it does not seem possible to go further. Hugh I, son of William died *c.* 1169 (his father, William fitz Norman, must have been a young man in 1086 and possibly therefore preceded at Kilpeck by *his* father, Norman) and was succeeded by his son Henry who, perhaps significantly, first regularly adopted the name 'de Kilpeck'. He died *c.* 1183 to be succeeded by his son John, who in 1193 acquired also the castle and 'barony' of Pulverbatch. When he died in 1205 his son, Hugh II de Kilpeck, was a minor, coming of age into his inheritance sometime between 1212 and 1216 and dying in 1244 leaving only daughters as heirs. There are fourteenth-century references to the castle and to guard-duty owed at it, and, indeed, it continues to be referred to in the descent of the manor or honour until the seventeenth century and beyond, though nothing of its condition appears to be known. The remains now are of a motte-and-bailey with the bailey immediately west of the church, between it and the motte, its entrance probably in the south-west quarter. South of this is an outer enclosure, and there were evidently two others, one west of the motte and one north. In the vicinity of the western outer work the neighbouring stream has been dammed to provide water defences. The remains of the polygonal shell keep on the motte contain vestiges of a fire-place, oven, drain-holes and a cross-wall. There are no obvious traces of the chapel but it is pleasing to note that the parish church is now dedicated to both St Mary and St David.

Kirby Muxloe, *Leicestershire*

Kirby Muxloe is one of the saddest sites in England, proclaiming the unfulfilled intentions of its executed lord. Begun in October 1480 by William lord Hastings, it was more of a fortified manor than a strong castle, built on the fashionable quadrangular plan (cf. Bodiam, Bolton), entirely symmetrical within a broad, wet moat, with a rectangular tower at each angle, an imposing twin-towered gatehouse, its principal display, in the centre of the north-west face, and a rectangular tower or turret in the centre of each of the other sides. It was built also of a fashionable brick (with dressed stone where necessary), though that is no weakness and nor are the gun-ports liberally inserted in the bases of its one remaining angle tower and gatehouse. Lord Hastings stood high in the favour and service in England and France of Edward IV who richly rewarded him: Chamberlain of the Household and of North Wales, Master of the Mint, peer of the realm and Knight of the Garter, his wife was a Neville and his daughter married a

Talbot earl of Shrewsbury. All this was expressed at Ashby-de-la-Zouche, his principal seat, where his rebuilding and embellishments included the splendid Hastings Tower. He then embarked upon the rebuilding of his family manor house at Kirby Muxloe, the foundations of the old house still visible within the enclosure of the new but unfinished castle. The accounts survive, from October 1480 to December 1484, to show the details and the progress of the work (more was done than now survives), and to show also their tragic cessation. On 9 April 1483 Edward IV died. On 14 June lord Hastings, his principal supporter, was arbitrarily executed without trial by Richard, duke of York, before the deposition of the young Edward V on the 25th and Richard's usurpation of the throne the following day. Minor works, presumably making good what had been done, were continued by the widowed lady Hastings until December, and the rest is silence.

FURTHER READING

Sir Charles Peers, *Kirby Muxloe Castle*, English Heritage Handbook, London.

Launceston, *Cornwall*

The imprint of the Norman Conquest is shown at Launceston, albeit in the far west of the kingdom, as early and dramatically as anywhere in England. The castle of 'Dunheved' was already here by 1086, evidently founded by Robert, count of Mortain, the Conqueror's half-brother, who, Domesday also tells us, had exchanged two manors with the bishop of Exeter for its dominating site. Count Robert in effect also founded 'the new town by the castle of Dunheved' (as a twelfth-century charter calls it) which was developed north and east of the castle, eventually to replace the ancient town of St Stephen's Launceston and to take its name. Fragments of the later town walls and one gate (south-east) survive, while the new town of Launceston remained the county town until 1835. Throughout the Middle Ages Launceston pertained to the earldom and (since 1337) the duchy of Cornwall, and the castle at least still does, though placed in 'Guardianship' of the Ministry of Works (and thereafter its successors) in 1951.

140

The first castle comprised a massive motte, largely artificial, at the north end of a ridge, with a large bailey to the south, the ramparts of which were evidently as formidable as the motte save on the west where the natural level falls steeply. Excavations since 1961 have shown or confirmed that the castle was being rebuilt and fortified in stone from the twelfth century, to which period the shell keep upon the motte is assigned. The principal period of development, however, was evidently in the thirteenth century during the lordship of Richard, earl of Cornwall, brother of Henry III. Then, especially, the cylindrical, two-storeyed great tower was raised on the motte within the shell keep, and the mantlet was built round the outside of it. The narrow space between the shell wall and the great tower was roofed over, and the whole complex of motte and multiple superstructure thus became one of the most impressive donjons to be found anywhere, reached by a covered flight of steps from the bailey (after the manner of present-day Windsor) with the Guard-Tower at the bottom. A survey made in 1337 for the young Edward, first duke of Cornwall, son of Edward III and the future 'Black Prince', having referred to ruinous walls which ought to be maintained by the knights holding by castleguard tenure of the castle (what are probably their several 'houses' have been revealed in recent excavations), goes on to list not only the donjon with its covered approach but also, in the bailey, the two gates north and south, the duke's hall and lodgings, the chapel, the constable's hall and lodging, kitchens and two stables for ten horses. Defects noted were thereafter made good and the castle was adequately maintained throughout the fourteenth and fifteenth centuries. Decay set in during the sixteenth century and was far advanced by the seventeenth, though certain public buildings required for the administration of the county were kept up until 1840 when the assizes were moved to Bodmin and the goals were demolished. Later the bailey was landscaped and turned into public gardens.

Leeds, *Kent*

Local tradition enshrined in the older books as to its remote antiquity notwithstanding, Leeds is in origin an early Norman castle, a kind of motte-and-bailey set in the most extensive water defences. In the Domesday Survey of 1086 'Esledes' is listed among the vast lands of the disgraced Odo, bishop of Bayeux (held of him by one Ethelwold), but was soon afterwards granted to the family of Crevequer (Crèvecoeur, Calvados, arr. Lisieux), the castle being founded presumably by Haimo I, *alias* Haimo dapifer, d. *ante* 1119 when his son Robert founded the Augustinian priory of Leeds at first within it. It remained in the hands of the Crevequers as part of their barony of Chatham until 1268 when it passed to William de Leybourne who, on account of his debts, was obliged to sell the manor and the castle of Leeds called 'la Mote' to Edward I in 1298. From then until the mid-sixteenth century almost without a break, Leeds was a royal castle, often assigned to the queen in dower though evidently avoiding the inadequate maintenance usually the lot of such buildings. It became in fact a favoured

residence of at least three kings, Edward I, Edward III and Henry VIII, all of whom spent considerable sums upon it. The first Edward added the towered outer curtain or revetment of the main island, i.e. the bailey, necessarily extended and altered the gatehouse and adjacent buildings to accommodate this, and built or rebuilt the 'Old Castle' or 'Gloriette', i.e. the inner sanctum of royal lodgings upon the small northern island at least once referred to in the building accounts as *parva mota*. Edward and Eleanor his queen were often here, and the king established a chantry in the castle for her after her death. The works of Edward III between 1359 and 1377 were also concentrated especially on the royal apartments in the Gloriette, and the castle, set in its greatly extended park, became one of those royal residences up and down the Thames valley where the king spent much of his time when in England – Windsor, Sheen, London, Gravesend and Rotherhithe, Hadleigh, Queenborough and Leeds ('Sweet Thames, run softly, till I end my song'). Henry VIII also spent most upon the 'modernization' and amendment of the Gloriette. Edward VI, however, alienated Leeds in 1552 to Sir Anthony St Leger, and it has remained private ever since, though one more king and queen were to be entertained here in the persons of George III and Charlotte by Lord Fairfax in 1778.

The castle has an elaborate barbican and approach across the water (cf. Bodiam) to the main gate on the south-west, and a water-gate (*not* Edward I's bath) on the east side. The principal lodgings and domestic quarters apart from those in the Gloriette were adjacent at the north end of the bailey, where the nineteenth-century residence now stands. The one dramatic incident in the history of Leeds castle was the siege of 1321, waged by the outraged Edward II pursuant upon the refusal of the constable of Bartholomew de Badlesmere (to whom the king had granted the castle), to admit queen Isabella; but principally it stands as an evocative reminder that castles were noble and royal residences in which the *dolce vita* could be lived as well, or better, than elsewhere.

Lewes, *Sussex*

Soon after Hastings, at which he was present, William of Warenne (Varenne, Seine-Inf.) was given the rape of Lewes and founded the castle in the Old English burgh. He also received from the Conqueror a great honour in East Anglia, centred upon his castle at Castle Acre in Norfolk, and another in Yorkshire where he planted the castle of Conisborough. He was created earl of Surrey (hence his castle at Reigate) by William Rufus shortly before his death in June 1088. This is lordship on a vast scale, and at Lewes and Castle Acre it was marked in Norman fashion by the foundation not only of the new castles but also of new religious houses, in each case a Cluniac priory (at Lewes almost obliterated by the Reformation and the railway). The particular claim to fame of William of Warenne's castle at Lewes is that it has two mottes, one to the south, with extant and well-known fortifications upon it, and the other (locally the Brack Mount) to the north of the oval bailey, now cut off and half hidden by encroaching modern buildings and therefore half forgotten. The only other known instance of two mottes in England is at Lincoln,

though there are some few cases of 'twin' donjons in France. The motte with its superstructure was at this date, and certainly in England, the most favoured form of donjon, and the donjon everywhere was the ultimate symbol of lordship (p. 5 above). A double donjon therefore requires an explanation, most likely to be found in dual lordship. At Lewes it may be suggested that the second motte represents the distinction of the first William of Warenne's wife Gundreda, whom, it is worth noting, he associated with him in unusual fashion in his foundation charter for Lewes Priory, and who was clearly very much a lady in her own right in a man's world, though there is no truth in the ancient and lingering legend that she was the daughter of duke William and/or his duchess Mathilda.

The lost northern motte still has traces of an early shell keep upon its summit, and the southern motte, of course, has the substantial remains of another, late eleventh- or early twelfth-century, with herring-bone work in it, and now strengthened by two later and semi-octagonal towers. It seems likely that it was similarly complex from the beginning, for there are foundations of an early square tower at the head of the present (and modern) steps and some other rectangular building adjacent to the north was excavated in 1884. There are clear traces (e.g. corbels) of the residential apartments that formerly stood round the inside of this keep (cf. Restormel, Tamworth, Windsor) to form a small courtyard, and the present two towers, facing respectively south and west, are thirteenth-century additions.

Though the bailey between the two mottes is now built upon and no longer maintained, substantial sections of its curtain wall survive on the south toward the High Street, again early and showing herring-bone courses, partly revetting its earthern bank. Moreover, this is strengthened by a contemporary rectangular tower, inwardly projecting (an early sign), in the motte ditch, and a stone gatehouse, again with herring-bone work and of inward projection, generally attributed to the late eleventh century. The gatehouse, partly ruined on its north or inner side, is masked by a very fine and heavily machicolated barbican projecting to the south, but was originally a two-storeyed rectangular gate-tower, with an entrance passage of two bays, of an early type such as is found also at Exeter (1068?) or Le Plessis Grimoult in Normandy (*ante* 1047) – or at Bramber. The later barbican is dated to the early fourteenth century and attributed to John, eighth and last of the Warenne earls of Surrey, who died in 1347.

1347 marks the end of the Warenne lordship in default of legitimate male heirs, Lewes passing to the fitz Alan earls of Sussex. It is possible that the decline of the castle began then, as it certainly did after the three-fold division of the combined Warenne and fitz Alan inheritance in 1439. It was partially dismantled in the seventeenth century. The splendid tomb-slab of the countess Gundreda, of black Tournai marble, has survived all such indignities and, with her and her husband, is now to be found in the local church of St John the Baptist, Southover.

Lidgate, *Suffolk*

The somewhat enigmatic earthworks at Lidgate, here seen from the north, are of considerable interest although neglected by historians and archaeologists. Though Lidgate is included in the motte-and-bailey category of early castles by the *Victoria County History*, and referred to as a castle in Gervase of Canterbury's 'Mappa Mundi' of *c.* 1200 and (once) in the Hundred Rolls of the late thirteenth century, it is probably best regarded as a *maison forte* or strong house of early date. Certainly it is atypical as a motte-and-bailey site in that the 'mound' is a rectangle, of no great height, and looks like a platform with strong ditches. The bailey enclosed the church (with Norman nave) but has lost its southern part, evidently encroached upon by the roadway and cottages. There is a further and narrow oblong enclosure on the north side (nearest the camera) of the mound or platform, and what appears to be a semi-circular outer court to the east, now with farm buildings in it. It has been suggested, though without evidence, that both these outer enclosures may be later additions.

Though we have no date of its foundation, and, indeed, almost no history of it at all, Lidgate is undoubtedly early, and what is known of its lordship and of the

manor to which it pertained gives it an additional interest as the castle or *maison forte* of an under-tenant and, what is more, the under-tenant of an abbot. According to a good Bury tradition the manor was given by the Conqueror to Reginald Sanceler, 'Denasez', so-called because he had lost his nose in the wars of king William I; and he in turn, wishing to make a pilgrimage to Jerusalem for his soul's health, gave it to St Edmund in the time of abbot Baldwin. The Conqueror's grant can only have been in late 1086 or 1087 since neither Reginald nor Bury possess Lidgate in Domesday (1086), and Reginald's gift must have been before 1097 when abbot Baldwin died. A charter of Rufus addressed to abbot Baldwin, i.e. again before 1097, shows that it was then held of St Edmund by Ralph, the abbot's steward. To that hereditary office the manor thereafter pertained, the family taking the name of Hastings in the twelfth century, and Lidgate serving as their official residence, presumably from the late eleventh century. The stewards of Bury St Edmunds, which ruled over the eight-and-a-half hundreds of West Suffolk, were men of standing and substance. They held Lidgate by military tenure, owing the service of one knight to the abbot, while in an inquisition of 1219 a total of eight knights' fees are said to be held of them.

Lincoln

One of the many virtues of aerial photographs is that they emphasize the common juxtaposition of castle and church, the twin pillars of feudal lordship. Sometimes, as at Durham, Rochester or here at Lincoln, this is on the grand scale, so that one thinks, as one was meant to think, of God and Caesar, Church and State, and the Two Swords of lay and ecclesiastical authority. In spite of the Gregorian reformers the two authorities remained integrated: at Durham they were combined in the bishop, and at Lincoln the bishop's knights rendered guard service in the royal castle which he himself found it convenient to pass through on the way to his residence on the other (west) side, until the present (ruined) palace was built south of the cathedral in the latter half of the twelfth century.

The Norman Conquest, of course, brought both castle and cathedral to then half-Scandinavian Lincoln, the latter from Dorchester-on-Thames by bishop Remigius in 1072. The castle was founded by the Conqueror himself, returning from his first expedition to York and the north in 1068, and was placed in the south-west quarter of the Roman walled city (on a site which was thereafter hard west of bishop Remigius' new church), 166 houses or messuages being destroyed to make room for it. It owes its present gloomy appearance to the fact that as early as the fourteenth century it sank to the level of mere gaol and so remained until

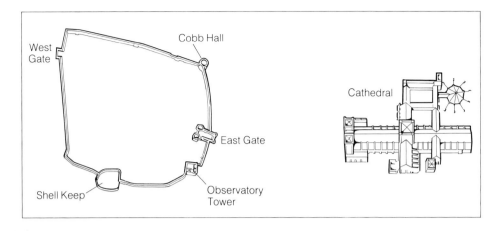

yesterday, hence the modern prison building and Assize Courts now within it. Hence also no doubt its comparative neglect by scholars; yet it is amongst the most interesting castles in the kingdom, and of its importance in Norman and Angevin England there can be no doubt. In Stephen's reign especially it was a bone of contention between the king and Ranulf II, earl of Chester, who evidently claimed it in right of his mother, the countess Lucy (d. 1136), seized it in 1140 and lost it in 1146. It was in the course of his siege of the castle in 1141 that the king was defeated and captured by his enemies in the Battle of Lincoln. By then certainly the ample castle site of nearly six acres was walled in stone, and had been since before 1115 at the latest, with two gateways, east and west, but no known mural towers save the twin keeps on the south side (the present 'Cobb Hall' at the north-east angle being a later addition). The east gate has a Norman core and is no doubt roughly contemporary with the wall in which it stands, though later rebuilt and altered to produce its present external pointed arch, with bartizans above which look fourteenth-century, and a twin-towered barbican demolished in 1791. The west gate, thought from recent archaeological investigation to stand on earlier foundations and which had a projecting barbican from the beginning, is an early insertion in a wall already existing, built by bishop Robert Bloet for access to his house beyond by licence of Henry I dated between 1101 and 1115. But the principal claim to fame of Lincoln is its twin mottes, in England to be compared only with Lewes. Both are on the south front, that to the west, placed centrally, bearing a polygonal shell keep of twelfth-century date, and the other, smaller, at the south-east angle of the castle, bearing what is now the Observatory Tower but with a rectangular twelfth-century base. Again we must surely look for dual lordship, and at Lincoln perhaps have some glimpse of it in the fourteenth-century summary of a charter of 1146 (the original is lost). In it king Stephen granted the castle and city of Lincoln to Ranulf earl of Chester until he should recover for him his Norman lands and castles. Then the castle would be restored except that the earl might fortify 'one of his towers of the castle of Lincoln' and have the lordship of it, until the king could grant him the castle of Tickhill. Whereupon the king would have both 'tower and city', but the earl would retain 'his tower which his mother had fortified' and the constableship of the castle by hereditary right. The shell keep on the larger motte to this day is known as Lucy's Tower and may have been raised by her before 1136.

The Tower of London

It was probably December in 1066 before the Normans entered London from the north, after a long, circuitous and intimidating march from Hastings via Dover, Canterbury, Winchester, Wallingford (where the Thames was crossed) and Little Berkhamsted. We are told specifically by William of Poitiers that before the Conqueror himself entered the city he sent an advance-party ahead to raise a castle in it, and, again, that after his triumphal coronation in Westminster Abbey on Christmas Day the new king withdrew to Barking while fortifications were completed to contain the restless Londoners. It seems certain that in these events we have the foundation of what became the Tower of London, and probably of the other two early Norman castles in London also, i.e. Baynard's Castle in the south-

west angle of the walled city, and the castle of Montfichet north of the former, near Ludgate Circus.

The Conqueror's royal castle was planted in the south-east, within the angle of the Roman walls, and consisted of a great entrenchment thus on two sides (north and west) with the river immediately to the south (p. 12, top left). There is no trace or record of any motte, but before the first Norman reign was far advanced (traditionally in 1078) a huge donjon in the form of the great White Tower began to rise within the enclosure to provide palatial accommodation for the new king. In all feudal Europe, save only Colchester which is also the Conqueror's and even larger, there is nothing like the rectangular tower keep of London, in scale and therefore majesty, and in the apsidal projection at its south-east angle which houses the apses of the chapels within. It is thought that both may have been based upon the tenth-century great tower of the ducal castle at Rouen, vanished since 1204. The accommodation the White Tower provided was a basement for provisions and two residential floors (not three as now), each of hall, chamber and chapel, the upper the grander, rising through two stages with a mural gallery, served by the splendid chapel of St John, and intended for the king himself. Almost from its completion until now men have spoken not of the castle but of the Tower of London.

From then on all is continuity after the manner of Dover, with concomitant damage to the fabric after the castle became obsolete as both residence and fortress in the sixteenth century. Here, following the notorious phase as state prison in the Tudor and early Stuart period, there was little 'modernization' for direct military purposes, but comparable demolition and disfigurement as an expanding Ordnance Office within made of it little more than an armament factory until restoration in the later nineteenth century. The three major phases of medieval development, after Rufus (in all probability) had walled in the Conqueror's enclosure, each involved a great expansion of the site, and occurred in the late twelfth century in the reign of Richard I, and in the reigns of Henry III and Edward I in the course of the thirteenth century.

The first phase was put in hand in or about 1190 by William Longchamp, bishop of Ely, left in charge of the kingdom by Richard the Lionheart on his departure on the Third Crusade. The result was almost to double the area of the Tower by expansion westward (p. 12, lower left), with a new water-filled moat (which did not work) and a towered curtain wall which survives only in the present Bell Tower (at the south-west angle of what is now the inner curtain) and (partially) in the southern stretch between that and the Bloody Tower. The second phase occupied almost the whole of the long reign of Henry III (1216–72) and involved a great extension of the whole area of the castle north and east, thus breaking through the confinement of the eastern city wall, hitherto close by the White Tower itself (p. 12, top right), and engulfing the former city parish church of St Peter-ad-Vincula which ever since has stood within the fortress in the north-west corner. The result was a great castle represented today by the present inner curtain, most of whose towers are Henry III's, with a land-gate in the middle of the west front, a water-gate, on the site of the present Bloody Tower, guarded by the great cylindrical Wakefield Tower, and a further development of spacious residential accommodation for king and court south of the White Tower and now all gone. There were, however, setbacks, not least the collapse of the new land-gate and its attendant curtain, and this, occurring in 1240, is the starting point of Edward I's great works of 1275–85 (p. 12, lower right). These may be summarized as the rebuilding of the western curtain, with the huge Beauchamp Tower on the site of Henry III's land-gate; the filling in of Henry III's moat and the construction of a lower outer curtain entirely to surround the castle, thus pushing back the river which had hitherto washed the foot of what now becomes the innner curtain on the south; and the digging of the present huge moat, then water-filled, round the three landward sides. All this required new entrances, and so Edward provided St Thomas' Tower (the appellation 'Traitor's Gate' is a modern misnomer) as a water-gate on the south, and an elaborate, triple, landward entrance on the south-west via the barbican called the Lions Tower (almost vanished), the Middle Tower and the Byward Tower.

Thus by about 1300 a majestic concentric castle had evolved, one of the strongest castles in the realm, with the Conqueror's White Tower still dominant at the centre. Little more needed to be done thereafter though some was, e.g. the Cradle Tower added as a supplementary water-gate east of St Thomas by Edward III. A survey made in 1597, almost like a Tudor aerial photograph (pp. 28–9), shows all this for the last time, with the rot of decay and the Ordnance Office (north) beginning to set in.

FURTHER READING

R. Allen Brown and P. E. Curnow, *Tower of London*, Department of Environment, Official Handbook, HMSO, London.

Ludlow, *Shropshire*

At Ludlow, like Chepstow, there is something for everybody. The situation here is of an early Norman foundation on a naturally strong site, with attendant new town laid out on the grid or chequer pattern to the east, the castle cut off in classic fashion on the highest and ultimate part of the promontory by deep ditches (the outer now largely filled up), and thereafter continuously developed and occupied through to the late seventeenth century. The whole was a new centre of new lordship carved out of their great manor of Stanton Lacy by the Lacy family (Lassy, Calvados). There is no reference to Ludlow in Domesday where Roger de Lacy held Stanton in chief (with much else), and therefore the foundation of the castle (and town) is usually attributed to him, but after 1086 (c. 1090?), though the possibility that his father, Walter de Lacy, d. 1084/5, began it should perhaps not be discounted. Thereafter, with political breaks under king Stephen (who besieged the castle in 1139) and the Angevins, the house of Lacy held Ludlow until 1241 when the heiress Mathilda took it by marriage first to Peter of Geneva (d. 1249) and then to Geoffrey de Geneville, whose son by her, Peter, held it until his death in 1292. In 1316 the heiress Joan took her inheritance in marriage to Roger Mortimer of Wigmore (paramour of Isabella, queen of Edward II), and his successors remained lords of Ludlow (and earls of March) until succeeded in turn by Richard, duke of York, whose son Edward became the Yorkist king in 1461. Thereafter the castle was royal, and as such became the headquarters of the Council of Wales in the late fifteenth century, which accounts for the extensive Tudor buildings and remodellings, notably in the inner bailey north and south (by the keep) and in the outer bailey by the gate. Not until after the final dissolution of the Council in 1689 was the place partly dismantled and left to decay.

Architecturally the castle has many claims to fame. Clearly it was built in stone from the beginning (cf. Richmond) with no motte or other known keep, not only the curtain of the inner ward being basically of the late eleventh century but also its rectangular projecting mural towers (save for the fourteenth-century Garde-robe Tower). With the exception of the Postern Tower (west) these towers were originally open to the gorge. The very large outer bailey is thought to be a later addition and its curtain and gatehouse (east) were dated by St John Hope to the late twelfth century, though the presence of another 'early', open-backed, rectangular

mural tower on the east front north of the gatehouse – and another now gone but recorded in 1811 to the south – may be noted. Another feature of particular interest at Ludlow is the eleventh-century gatehouse to the inner ward, subsequently converted into the present tower keep, the entrance passage being blocked (cf. Richmond again). Hope made the reasonable suggestion that this conversion was contemporary with the addition of the outer ward. This keep was then cut back from the north to its present dimensions in the fifteenth century when also two extra floors were inserted (without heightening the structure). Also at Ludlow is a rare example, unique in an English castle, of a 'round church', modelled on the Temple at Jerusalem, the headquarters of the Military Order of the Templars – i.e. the castle chapel of St Mary Magdalene in the Inner Bailey, with its circular and richly decorated nave (the rectangular chancel with semi-octagonal apse is ruined), surely dating from the earlier twelfth century though thought to have been built in two phases. Lastly there is the splendid residential complex on the north side of the Inner Ward, consisting of a first-floor hall with a chamber block on either side, perhaps begun by Peter de Geneville in the late thirteenth century but dating mainly from the fourteenth and completed in the early Mortimer period.

Mettingham, *Suffolk*

Mettingham shows the sad and shattered remains of a fourteenth-century castle, early converted into a college of secular priests itself suppressed at the Reformation, and by the eighteenth century sunk to farmyard status. The present house (1880) in what was once the southern court bears no other relation to the medieval plan and arrangements. A licence to crenellate issued by Edward III in 1342 to Sir John de Norwich, one of his successful captains in the wars with France, must give us an approximate date for the foundation of the castle. Sir John, who died in 1361, also founded a college for secular priests at Raveningham in Norfolk. His grandson, another Sir John, died at Mettingham in 1373 without heirs of his body, whereupon the property passed to his cousin Catherine de Brews. Catherine, being a nun at Dartford in Kent, conveyed Mettingham in turn to the family college at Raveningham which eventually moved here in 1394. The college was suppressed in 1542 by Henry VIII who immediately granted the property to one Sir Anthony Denny.

It is not easy now to get back to the original castle, which was evidently a typical 'fortified manor' of the age (cf. neighbouring Wingfield), basically consisting of a moated quadrangular enclosure, not heavily fortified but with a (rectangular) tower at each corner, and an impressive gatehouse, here in the middle of the north front. At Mettingham there were two courtyards, north and south with an east–west moat between them, the castle proper occupying the northern of the two, where the gatehouse (top) and fragments of curtain wall still stand. A survey of 1562 made for Sir Nicholas Bacon makes it clear that the principal domestic range then at least lay along the south side of this main

courtyard, opposite the gatehouse, and comprised a ground-floor hall and two-storeyed chamber block, with the ancillary domestic offices of buttery, pantry, kitchen, bakery, brewhouse, etc. (It is worth noting that the window openings in the north curtain wall west of the gatehouse are thus *not* those of the hall though traditionally said to be so.) At Mettingham there is and was also a small inner quadrangular enclosure on the east side of the castle, with access from the main, northern, court though lying in the north-east corner of the outer, southern, court. It is to the right of the modern house on the photograph and was marked by the broadest moats and by 'Kate's Tower' (after Catherine de Brews) which Suckling (*History of Suffolk*, 1846) says fell in the late 1830s. This inner enclosure, though of course afterwards occupied by the college in common with the rest of the buildings, must have been the inner sanctum or donjon of Sir John de Norwich's castle and is presumably 'the olde castell', standing ruined within its own moat, of the 1562 survey.

Middleham, *Yorkshire*

The manor of Middleham, 'one league long and one league wide' but 'waste' in Domesday, was after the Norman Conquest part of the great honour of Richmond and was given by the first Breton lord, count Alan the Red, to his brother Ribald before 1086. The first castle of Middleham is attributed to him in the early years of the Norman settlement of Yorkshire, and is identified as the small but powerful motte-and-bailey earthwork, known as William's Hill, still very much surviving on higher ground some 460 m south-west of the present castle.

At Middleham we thus have a good example of the moving of the site of a castle in accordance with changing circumstances and standards, as we also later have architectural development accompanying the rising social eminence of its lords. It is also worth noting that in the first phase of its history it is a potent example of a castle held not in chief but of some other lord than the king, in this case the lord of Richmond. Indeed, we may wonder at the status, power and wealth of Ribald's descendants, mesne tenants who, in moving the site of their castle, could build one of the largest keeps in all Norman England (and thus in Western Europe), still literally fit for a king more than three hundred years later, towards the end of the fifteenth century. Of two storeys only, like Castle Rising, it is usually dated on architectural grounds to *c.* 1170 and the time of Ribald's grandson, Robert, who died in 1184 or '5, but may well go back a generation to the lordship of Ralph the son of Ribald, who succeeded his father before 1130 and died in 1168 or after. Yet the great days of Middleham were undoubtedly yet to come. In 1270 it passed, by the marriage of an heiress (Mary, 'the lady of Middleham') to a branch of the future great Neville family who were to dominate the north, and even for a time the

The motte-and-bailey castle of the late eleventh century at William's Hill

history of England, in the later Middle Ages. The last Neville lord of Middleham was Warwick the King-Maker, no less, who being slain at Barnet in 1470, the castle escheated to the Yorkist king Edward IV, who granted it to his brother, Richard duke of Gloucester, subsequently Richard III. Richard married Anne, Warwick's daughter, and loved this place, where his only son was born and died. After Richard came the anti-climax of the Tudors with the usual ruin and decay.

Though there was once an outer ward to the east now almost vanished, the present castle consists overwhelmingly of the keep, close wrapt about with ditch and late thirteenth-century curtain, the latter developed throughout the fourteenth and fifteenth centuries with ranges of lodgings and offices, to make of the whole a quadrangular castle of northern type like Bolton-in-Wensleydale but here with the keep its heart and soul and centre. The machicolated gatehouse in the north-east angle is fourteenth-century. From start to finish the rectangular keep, of first-floor hall and chamber type like Rising, 'modernized' in the fifteenth century (cf. Dover) and its chapel on the east side added to it in the thirteenth, contained the best and grandest residential accommodation, joined in the end by timber galleries to the lodgings south and west.

FURTHER READING

Sir Charles Peers, *Middleham Castle*, English Heritage Handbook, London.

Mileham, *Norfolk*

A flat-topped motte in association with an almost circular earthwork which resolves itself into two baileys, an inner and an outer, towards the north and the road; the stump of a small, rectangular tower keep on the motte; also a rectangular earthwork enclosure mostly on the other side of the road, suspected as possibly Roman but revealing pottery only of twelfth–thirteenth-century date in trial excavations in 1968 – clearly there was a castle of some consequence here though almost nothing is at present known about it. The importance of the castle as well as the value of the manor in which it stood is presumably reflected in the amount of property Stephen gave to his loyal supporter, William de Chesney, in exchange for both in *c.* 1154 – Hingham, Stow Bedon and Kirby Bedon, Rackheath and Raynham, all in Norfolk, together with the hundred-and-a-half of Hingham and the hundred of Taverham. These properties were to revert to the king if either William or his son were able to regain Mileham, their land and their castle. Round interpreted this transaction as implying that Stephen had taken Mileham from the fitz Alans (descendants of Alan fitz Flaald of Oswestry and Mileham) as supporters of the rival Angevin cause and given it to the Chesneys, but was now obliged to make restitution by the peace and treaty of Westminster in 1153. In Domesday the manor of Mileham with its berewicks of Litchen and Great Dunham was valued at 60s. (double its value in the time of king Edward) and said to be three leagues in length and one in breadth. It was then in the king's hand as formerly held by Stigand. The castle is not referred to at all in documents relating to the fitz Alan manor of Mileham in 1218 but was said to be decayed in an inquisition *post mortem* of 1302.

Montgomery

In 1223 in the course of a punitive expedition against Llywelyn the Great the royal army reoccupied Montgomery, i.e. Hen Domen (p. 131), on 30 September, the day before Henry III's sixteenth birthday. The young king's advisers pointed out to him a great rock above the river Severn, one mile to the south as 'a suitable spot for the erection of an impregnable castle', and orders were issued at once for the construction of the new Montgomery. Timber was brought up for the initial enclosure of the site with palisades, and miners were sent for from the Forest of Dean to level and scarp the rock and cut the great ditches. Work continued for at least thirty years, first upon the Inner Ward at the highest, northern end of the rock (c. 1224–c. 1235), then upon the Middle Ward (1251–3?) and the outworks and approach from the new town of Montgomery also founded at this time. It is not certain that the castle was finished when it was granted by the king to his son the lord Edward, i.e. the future Edward I, in 1254. Certainly there was further activity in the 1270s and 1280s after the new Welsh prince Llywelyn ap Gruffyd, grandson of Llywelyn the Great, built his castle of Dolforwyn only four miles away to challenge both Montgomery and the new king. Works then included a new hall, chamber, kitchen, bakehouse and granary in the castle, and the building of the walls about the town hitherto defended by palisades.

The result must have been one of the finest castles in the March until its ruthless demolition by England's only republican government in 1649. Its position is dramatically impregnable; its defences in series up from the town; its ultimate strength the Inner Ward (revealingly referred to as 'the donjon' in contemporary documents) with its huge twin-towered gatehouse (solid at the base), its equally formidable Well Tower on the west side, and another great D-shaped tower projecting at the northern apex; and all this beyond the rock-cut ditches and other defences of the Middle Ward. Yet soon after its maximum development the outright conquest of Wales by Edward I removed some of the importance of Montgomery, and the king's resources certainly became concentrated upon his great castles about Gwynedd in the north. There are signs of neglect in the fourteenth and fifteenth centuries, including little evidence of expenditure upon the fabric. In the 1530s, however, Leland found it recently 're-edified', and as late as 1622 Lord Herbert of Chirbury, whose family then owned the castle as they still do, built a grand new brick house in the Middle Bailey. This was swept away with everything else by the Parliamentary Commissioners of 1649 and only since 1964 have the ruins been excavated and conserved (by the former Ancient Monuments branch of the Department of the Environment) to restore some impression of lost majesty.

FURTHER READING

J. D. K. Lloyd and J. K. Knight, *Montgomery Castle*, Cadw Official Handbook, Cardiff.

Naworth, *Cumberland*

Fourteenth-century Naworth shows the difficulty of using the word 'pele' as a term of art (p. 26 above), for it is sometimes considered to have been originally a pele tower (Dacre Tower, south-west) with a curtained courtyard, and sometimes to have been a late and minor castle built on the traditional keep and bailey plan. Either way the Dacre Tower, though later heightened, is small by any standards (8.8 m × 8.8 m, cf. Sizergh), but the castle occupies a strong position at the point of a triangular rocky promontory, cut off on the third side by two ditches (one filled up) in classic fashion. Founded in *c.* 1335 (the date of the licence to crenellate) by Ranulf de Dacre, it has been much developed, and therefore changed, over the centuries, as its lords, first Dacre and then Howard, ascended the greasy pole of nothern politics and war. In *c.* 1520 Thomas lord Dacre (d. 1525), Lord Warden of the West Marches, heightened the Dacre Tower and added a barbican to the gate it covered, built (if he did not finish) another tower, later the Howard Tower at the opposite, south-east, corner of the court, and built also the magnificent great hall, 24 m long, running north along the east curtain behind it. The end of the Dacre

period is foreshadowed by the shameful, turn-coat, gyrations of Leonard Dacre in the Northern Rebellion of 1569–70, which seemed also to presage the end of the castle. Reported 'partly decayed' in 1580, it was 'nowe in very great decay' in 1589. Then in 1604 lord William Howard came into possession via his wife, a Dacre, and embarked upon great works to restore and modernize the place. Amongst other things he restored the Dacre Tower, rebuilt or finished the top of the Howard Tower, and rebuilt also the long range of lodgings on the south front between the two towers. He is also known to have bought in material from the demolished Kirkoswald, including the ceiling of the third floor of his Howard Tower. Less happily, over two hundred years later, a fire in 1844 severely damaged the building which was subsequently rather more than restored by Anthony Salvin, the best known castle architect of the day. Additions by him evidently include the two northern towers, Stanley and Morpeth.

Norham, *Northumberland*

Norham, like Durham, was an episcopal castle, pertaining also to the bishop of Durham as the head of Norhamshire and Holy Island which were a northern outlying part of the bishopric and palatinate. It was founded in 1121 by bishop

Ranulf Flambard (1099–1128) on the bank of the Tweed, by an ancient ford, and very close indeed to the Scottish border, to protect the district against the incursions of robbers and Scots. It was taken and ordered to be destroyed by David I of Scotland in 1138 and rebuilt by bishop Hugh du Puiset (1153–95) at the king's command (*precepto regis*) soon after Henry II's resumption of Northumberland from the Scots in 1157. In the endless Border wars, raids and forays of the fourteenth, fifteenth and sixteenth centuries, which were the *damnosa hereditas* of Edward I's attempt to conquer Scotland, the castle was repeatedly attacked and damaged, held or surrendered and returned. In the early fourteenth century it was reputed 'the most dangerous and adventurous place in the country' when, in the legend, the young knight, Sir William Marmion, came here to prove himself to his lady. (Hence the West Gate, through which he charged to take on the Scots single-handed, may still romantically be called 'Marmion's Gate'.) As late as 1513–21 the castle was extensively rebuilt, after its breach and capture by James IV and the great Mons Meg in the former year, to be again 'with the help of God and the prayer of St Cuthbert' impregnable: hence much of the remaining walling of both inner and outer baileys is sixteenth-century even if on twelfth-century foundations, and hence also the triangular-headed bastions facing south on both curtains, designed for artillery.

The castle was planted on a site of great natural strength above the river. There is no reason to doubt that Hugh du Puiset's castle followed the line and plan of

Flambard's just as it forms the core and basis of all later rebuilding and strengthening. The overall plan is of a great and part natural mound, with a bailey, the Outer Ward, to south and west, and a very large outer enclosure or barmkin beyond, to the south, after the manner of Barnard Castle. The mound bears an inner enclosure, the Inner Ward which, as at Barnard Castle and Alnwick, is the donjon, the ultimate strength of the castle and packed with the main residential accommodation of hall, chambers, kitchens and chapel. Here at Norham, however, there is also the rectangular tower keep of Hugh du Puiset, ruined like all else but visibly much altered and partly reconstructed in the earlier fifteenth century, when its own accommodation was increased from a basement and two floors to a basement and four. The inner and outer (West) gates, too, are basically Pudsey's work, though now within considerable development and rebuilding respectively of the sixteenth and fifteenth centuries, and a long stretch of his curtain still stands along the east side of the Outer Ward.

In the second half of the sixteenth century, Norham, having been taken over by the Crown in 1559, was characteristically neglected. Elizabeth I in particular refused to spend money upon it, and the castle fell into that long decay which has only been belatedly arrested in our own day.

FURTHER READING

C. H. Hunter Blair and H. L. Honeyman, *Norham Castle*, English Heritage Handbook, London.

Norwich, *Norfolk*

The Norman Conquest was the making of modern Norwich. The castle was planted here (about 100 houses or messuages taken for its site) perhaps as early as 1067 with the first Norman penetration of East Anglia, and a new burgh founded for the 'Frenchmen' west of the Old English burgh. The East Anglian bishop's see was moved here in 1095 from Thetford (formerly at North Elmham) and the foundation stone of the present cathedral priory church laid in 1096. Both castle (centre) and cathedral are clearly visible on the accompanying photograph, surrounded by the modern conurbation; yet when the medieval city was fortified in the thirteenth century the walls had a circuit of two and a quarter miles.

The castle was placed on a ridge by cutting off and ditching round its end, to form a gigantic mound which is thus part natural. Nothing else of the site remains today, the baileys to south and east being mainly given over to car parks. But standing proud upon the mound there is one of the largest rectangular tower keeps anywhere and claimed to be the fifth largest in England. It is unique, moreover, in the degree of its external decoration by Romanesque blind arcading, which is a genuine feature of the original building though now a reproduction as part of an entire refacing in Bath stone (wrong) in the late 1830s. The keep is usually attributed to Henry I and has close affinities with Falaise in Normandy (known

also to be his) and Castle Rising in Norfolk, the latter evidently something of a copy of it and built *c.* 1140 by William of Albini II who had married Alice, second queen and widow of the same Henry I. It is of that type of keep which is more a cube than a tower, of two storeys only, a basement and a residential suite of great hall, great chamber, chapel and kitchen at first-floor level. It had, too, a splendid forebuilding on the east side, after the manner of Castle Rising, with a grand staircase leading up to an entrance vestibule in the form of an open arcaded loggia with the richly decorated main entrance which almost alone survives. Little other detail survives, for the keep and the castle have had an appalling post-medieval history, neglect followed by increasing use as a prison which mutilated what it did not destroy. When that phase ended in 1887 the keep was gutted to make the present Museum in *c.* 1890, so that the true nature of the interior of a once noble building is obliterated by incorrect floor-levels and inappropriate collections.

The castle was besieged, and taken, in 1075 when Ralph de Gael held it against the Conqueror in the mysterious 'Rebellion of the Earls', and remained royal thereafter in spite of the early ambitions of the house of Bigod to obtain it.

Odiham, *Hampshire*

The large manor of Odiham was royal demesne in Domesday and had formerly belonged to earl Harold. In Henry I's time at least there was a royal residence here

on some scale, since the king held his Easter court at Odiham in 1116. The castle, however, was built by king John on a different site, in twenty acres of meadow acquired from Robert the Parker, between 1207 and 1212 at a cost of over £1,000. A contemporary chronicler refers to it as 'a castle . . . set in fair meadows and close to the woods which the king had built for his sport'. There is no doubt that Odiham lay in good hunting country much favoured by Angevin kings, and everything so far seems to emphasize its residential rather than the military role. Nevertheless, in that world the two were indistinguishable, and when the test came in July 1216 the castle, more specifically the keep, was heroically defended for fifteen days by a mere three knights and ten 'sergeants' until they came out honourably, with horses and arms, and 'to the great admiration of the French' (i.e. the forces of prince Louis of France, then leading the opposition to king John). The place was evidently well maintained throughout the thirteenth, fourteenth and even fifteenth centuries, in spite of being usually assigned to the queen in dower, and in surviving accounts we hear not only of the great tower but of palisades and walls, moats and bridges, hall, chapel, chambers and kitchen. There was a park (probably ante-dating the castle) with a royal stud in it, and an enclosed garden for the queen.

By the sixteenth century, however, the castle is thought to have been in irreparable decay and references to it cease. All that remains now is the substantial ruin of the great tower or keep, unusual in being octagonal (cf. Richard's Castle and Tickhill) and formerly three storeys high.

Okehampton, *Devon*

After the siege and surrender of Exeter early in 1068 the Normans imposed their rule upon Devon, and this is the context of the foundation of Okehampton castle, which was certainly there by the time of the Domesday Survey. The founder was Baldwin the Sheriff (i.e. of Exeter), *alias* Baldwin de Meules, son of count Gilbert of Brionne and thus brother of Richard of Clare. The castle which was the centre or *caput* of his wide estates was built upon a narrow ridge high above the river Okement, with the motte upon its highest point but not its end. There thus appear to have been two baileys, one on either side, after the manner of Windsor, the site of which Okehampton rather resembles; though if the surviving earthworks west of the motte (to the right on the photograph and not recently excavated) were an original bailey it was evidently early abandoned. Recent excavations (1973–80) have confirmed that the motte bore from the beginning a small, square stone tower keep which is therefore one of the earliest in the country. In the twelfth century, probably marking the acquisition of castle and lordship by the family of Courtenay in the 1170s, archaeological evidence indicates the development of the western bailey with stone-built lodgings and a towered curtain and gatehouse (east). The early fourteenth century, however, witnessed the greatest development, to produce the castle whose ruins still dramatically survive. On the motte the keep was extended to the west to form the present (ruined) irregular oblong

two-storeyed donjon, while in the (eastern) bailey ranges of accommodation were built and rebuilt along the north and south sides, and a long barbican down the slope from the gatehouse to terminate in an outer gate.

As all this grandiloquent early fourteenth-century display is attributed to Hugh II de Courtenay, who was elevated to the earldom of Devon in 1335, so the history of Okehampton ends with the fall of that family in the sixteenth century,and the execution of Henry, marquis of Exeter, by Henry VIII in January 1539. After that came dismantling and decay until modern times.

Orford, *Suffolk*

Orford on the Suffolk coast (though now cut off from the sea by the ever-extending shingle bank of Orford Ness) is an East Anglian example of a new castle on a new site built well after the first Norman settlement. For that we should seek a reason, and can probably find it in a new combination of circumstances. The castle was royal, built between 1165 and 1173 by Henry II, a new king from a new dynasty, with different affiliations, a great castle-builder succeeding after a prolonged civil war. On his accession in 1154 there were in fact no royal castles in Suffolk, while the region was dominated by Hugh Bigod, earl of Norfolk or East Anglia, with his four castles of Bungay, Framlingham, Walton and Thetford, and evident designs upon Norwich. That relations between king and earl were strained is clear from the confiscation of the latter's castles in 1157 and the

retention of the other two after 1165 when Bungay and Framlingham were restored. One cannot but note that 1165 was also the year when Orford was begun, nor that it was finished just in time to be munitioned and manned against the rebellion of 1173–4 in which earl Hugh played a leading role and Suffolk was a principal theatre. It is possible that important works of this period at both Bungay and Framlingham, including the rectangular tower keep at the former, were carried out by the Bigod earl in and after 1165 – and it is a fact that all his castles were demolished by the king after the defeat of the rebels in 1174. It is also a fact that the town of Orford was being developed at this time (the church is of the same date as the castle) as a port on what was the invasion coast of England.

Because Orford castle was built by the king in the second half of the twelfth century, we know from the annual accounts rendered by the sheriffs and preserved upon the Pipe Rolls both the date and the cost of its building. The latter amounts to some £1,400, which scarcely compares with the *c.* £7,000 which Henry II spent upon the rebuilding of Dover, but compares very well with the *c.* £1,200 which king John spent upon his new castle of Odiham in Hampshire between 1207–14. Certainly Orford when completed was a first-class castle. Though only the keep now stands, it is known from John Norden's seventeenth-century view (1600–2), from the site and from other evidence, that this was surrounded by an extensive bailey whose stone curtain was systematically set with projecting rectangular mural towers to provide flanking cover, after the manner of contemporary Dover and Framlingham. The keep itself is very unusual in design, belonging to that experimental class of the later twelfth century, neither rectangular nor cylindrical but something in between. As such it may be compared with Chilham, Tickhill, Conisborough and Odiham, but is in fact unique. The tower proper is in plan polygonal without (cylindrical within) but strengthened by three rectangular buttress towers and a rather awkwardly set forebuilding adjoining the one to the south. Within, the accommodation provided is of a basement for storage (with a well) and two residential floors, of which the upper was the grander, intended for the king, all connected by a spacious vice mounting to the roof in the southern turret. Each residential floor comprises a circular hall, well lit by three two-light window embrasures, a chamber in the northern turret and a kitchen in the western, together with a garderobe and fireplace and sundry closets in the great thickness of the walls. There are also two mezzanine levels, the first of which, between the first and second floors, contains the chapel (in the forebuilding, above the entrance vestibule) connecting by a passage with the chaplain's chamber and his garderobe, and the second, above the second floor, contains what is evidently a cistern (in the west turret). The three turrets rise above the roof level and the northern contains a large oven.

Edward I was here on 11 April 1277, but the castle has little history after its dramatic beginnings and was alienated from the Crown by Edward III to Robert of Ufford, later earl of Suffolk, in 1336.

FURTHER READING

R. Allen Brown, *Orford Castle*, English Heritage Handbook, London.

Oxburgh Hall, *Norfolk*

'Please God, I will build me such a house as thieves will need to knock at ere they enter': thus Patrick Forbes, building Corse Castle in Aberdeenshire in *c.*1500. These words adequately express the practical needs of domestic security behind many 'fortified manors' of the Middle Ages, though the traditions of a military aristocracy and the status symbolism of towers and battlements are present in them also. Oxburgh Hall is never called a castle, which it is not, and lies at the far end of the range of defensible houses, beyond which is only Wingfield, Derbyshire, without any serious defences at all. Oxburgh may be weak by castle standards but it has its wide moat and great gatehouse; and if the latter is more symbolic than practical, with its great windows to the field and bogus machicolation on its turrets, yet the machicolation between the turrets over the gate is real and the whole was once closed by a drawbridge. It is also to be remembered that what we see now, albeit beautiful, is much altered, the east wing damaged and burnt by seventeenth-century East Anglian Roundheads, the south range (hall, chambers, kitchen and offices) demolished in the eighteenth century, and almost all the fenestration (save the gatehouse) nineteenth-century when,

paradoxically, the south-east tower was built (*c.* 1835). Apart from all that, what we have is a great fifteenth-century courtyard house, built in superb and then fashionable brickwork, under a licence-to-crenellate dated 1482, by Sir Edmund Bedingfield who obtained the manor of Oxburgh through his wife, Margaret Tuddenham. Sir Edmund stood well with the Yorkists and stayed in place with the Tudors, Henry VII visiting the new house in 1497. The great and lofty gatehouse was ever the *chef d'oeuvre* and has remained so, mercifully unaltered. Mercifully also, the Bedingfields who built the house still occupy it. Many of them lie in the Bedingfield Chapel in the parish church. In the troubled centuries ahead they were to stay both Catholics and Royalists, which accounts for the damage and losses of the Civil War and for the nineteenth-century chapel now in front of the house, attributed to A. N. Pugin in 1835.

Oxford

Oxford castle, like Cambridge castle, tends to be ignored, placed well away from what became the academic quarter, university and collegiate buildings, and finally mutilated and engulfed by its own solely surviving function as gaol and centre of local government. Nevertheless it has more notable remains than Cambridge, the impressive motte which dominates the New Road to the station (bottom, left of centre), St George's Tower (below the motte) and the crypt of the church of St George-in-the-Castle which went with it, and all three of the eleventh century. It was founded (on the authority of the annals of nearby Oseney) as early as 1071 by Robert d'Oilly (d. *c.* 1093), a powerful tenant-in-chief in Oxford and Oxfordshire (cf. Wallingford) who is usually said to have held it for the king as constable rather than of the king in fee, though his foundation (on the same authority) of the collegiate church of St George within the castle three years later in 1074 does not seem like the act of a mere custodian. The Romanesque crypt of that otherwise vanished church survives and must be his work, as is the motte and also the obviously early and massive tower of St George (its top hamper later) which originally served both as the belfrey of the church and a powerful mural tower of the *enceinte* of the castle. It is of particular interest also that it was Robert d'Oilly who, with the king's consent, acquired a meadow outside the walls of the town from the monks of Abingdon to pasture the horses of his knights within the castle. Oxford had been an Anglo-Saxon burgh (it is in the Burghal Hidage) and the castle, on the motte-and-bailey plan, was placed at its west end, by the river which fed its ditches. It acquired, at an uncertain but probably early date, both a towered stone curtain and a decagonal shell keep upon the motte, demolished in the seventeenth century and excavated in 1794 (*sic*). The castle was described by a contemporary writer in the mid-twelfth century as impregnable and with a very high tower. King Stephen besieged his rival the empress Maud here in 1142, and she made her famous and dramatic escape, perhaps from St George's Tower, on a cold winter's night in December, crossing the frozen river on foot and so, in a white cloak as camouflage, through the snow and ice, with three intrepid knights

for escort, made her way to Wallingford. The castle, which was certainly royal from Henry II's time onwards, was adequately maintained throughout the twelfth and thirteenth centuries, a new, round, mural tower being built in 1235; but in the fourteenth century we hear of serious dilapidations, and by the end of that century it was said to be ruinous though it continued in use as a prison. It was not called upon to play an active role in the seventeenth-century Civil War when the walled city of Oxford itself was the king's capital, but the ruins were largely demolished afterwards. In the nineteenth century new prison buildings, a new Shire Hall (1841) and the construction of the New Road almost obliterated even its site – except for the motte, the tower and the crypt of St George, and also a thirteenth-century subterranean well-chamber which was once within the vanished shell keep.

Painscastle, *Radnorshire*

The great days of Painscastle, *alias* Maud's Castle, in the parish of Llanbedr Painscastle in Lower Elfael, were in the twelfth and thirteenth centuries when the site, in the valley of the Machawy, controlling one of the gateways between England and central Wales, was much disputed between the Welsh princes and the Anglo-Norman marcher lords, notably Braose. It gets its first and lasting name from Pain fitz John (d. 1137) who founded it, and its second from Maud, wife of William III de Braose, who heroically defended it against the lord Rhys, although to no avail, in 1196. It is just possible that the first castle of Pain was on a different site one mile to the east, marked now by the motte in Newchurch parish (Talybedwyn Tump), but there is no doubt that William de Braose's castle was here, raised (together with Colwyn), and no doubt raised in stone, after he had seized the cantref of Elfael from the Welsh in *c.* 1191. The new castle was attacked by Gwenwynwyn of Powys in July 1198 and its defence thought sufficiently important for Geoffrey fitz Peter the Justiciar to bring a royal army from England to relieve the siege and defeat the Welsh in a battle nearby. After the fall of the house of Braose, this too was rebuilt or refortified, evidently with the adjacent burgh, by Henry III as the principal achievement of his great but otherwise abortive expedition against Llywelyn the Great in 1231—'a most noble castle built at vast expense with stone and lime' (*Annales Cambriae*). In 1233 the king granted his new castle to the marcher house of Tosny who retained it until the beginning of the fourteenth century when it passed by marriage to the Beauchamp earls of Warwick. References cease in the fifteenth century.

Of all this now only the underlying earthworks remain, a huge motte and formidable banks and ditches with only undulations showing the former towering masonry. It stands, therefore, as an example of how inadequate and thus misleading the archaeological term 'motte-and-bailey' can be, for if the proud buildings of Braose and Henry III still stood, one would no more label Painscastle a mere 'motte-and-bailey' than, say, Windsor or Warwick, Warkworth or Berkeley.

Peak, *Derbyshire*

A site as dramatic as that of the castle of the Peak, on its near-impregnable rock with a precipice on either side, is rare in England and more reminiscent of the Normans in southern Italy or perhaps, nearer home, in Wales. The castle was placed here soon after 1066 by William Peverel, who in Domesday appears as one of the Conqueror's greatest vassals, holding this castle and all those lands which were to form the Honour of Peverel (of Nottingham), and to whom the king had entrusted the custody of the new royal castle of Nottingham in 1068. He died in 1114 and was succeeded by his son, William II, who, however, was disinherited in 1153–4, accused of poisoning Ranulf, earl of Chester. From then on the Peak was a royal castle, with only occasional alienations as, for example, by Richard I to his brother John, count of Mortain, or by other kings to the queen in dower, until in

1372 Edward III exchanged it with John of Gaunt for the honor of Richmond, whereupon it became and remained a parcel of the duchy of Lancaster. Apart from its military potential, the castle was set in the heart of the Peak Forest, of which it became the administrative centre, and served also as a prestigiously fortified hunting lodge for kings and princes, but in the fourteenth century seems to have lost its importance on either count. In the 1370s some of its buildings were demolished to obtain materials for use elsewhere, and by 1480 the castle was said to be 'greatly decayed'.

On such a site the castle was, necessarily, fortified in stone from the beginning, as a precipitous enclosure with no motte, the north wall of the bailey, with herring-bone work, being attributed to the eleventh century, and the west wall, also with herring-bone work, to the early twelfth. The rectangular tower keep, comparatively small and with no forebuilding, is known from documentary evidence (Pipe Rolls) to have been added by Henry II in *c.* 1176, near the original hall and chambers to the east of it. The ruined gatehouse north-east towards the town is thought to date from the same period, and there was another gate south-west close by the keep. In the thirteenth century a new hall, and, doubtless, chambers and offices, were built in the north-west quarter by the north curtain, and two drum towers added to the west curtain. The township of Castleton, fortified by bank and ditch 90 m below the castle on the only approachable, north, side, is thought to have been founded in the twelfth century.

Pembroke

Superbly sited on a precipitous rock at the highest point and end of a promontory between tidal creeks (as they then were) with the town behind it, the castle of Pembroke was founded by earl Roger of Montgomery (see also Arundel, Hen Domen) the first Norman lord of Dyfed. Castle and lordship were settled by him upon his younger son, Arnulf, and, after his fall with the house of Montgomery-Bellême in 1102, were successively held by kings Henry I and Stephen, and from 1138 to 1176 by the Clare earls of Pembroke. Of this first castle, however, nothing remains, and almost all the standing masonry (save for extensive modern restoration) dates from the time of William Marshal, who married the Clare heiress Isabel in 1189, was created earl of Pembroke in 1199, and died in 1219.

Since the Marshal's day the castle has comprised a large outer ward (south-east) towards the town and a smaller inner ward (north-west) whose inner gatehouse (foundations only) provides an unusual example of a bent entrance via a central lobby (cf. Denbigh). The outer ward is dominated by the splendid and complex outer gatehouse (of which the adjacent Barbican Tower to the east is an integrated part), and the inner ward by the great keep which, indeed, intentionally dominates the whole castle. This is not only massive but also cylindrical, in the fashion popular especially in France when it was built *c.* 1200. It stands 23 m high and has three residential floors above a basement, with a fourth floor beneath and within its most unusual stone domed roof. The other principal residential accommodation of the lords of Pembroke is also in the inner ward, north-east of the keep, where there are two first-floor halls, the Old Hall dating from the time of William Marshal and his sons, and the Great Hall, a tower-like structure jutting out beyond the eastern curtain, which dates probably from the time of William de Valence who succeeded them in 1247. This later hall is built

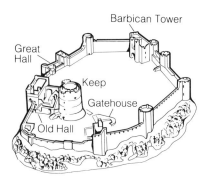

Barbican Tower
Great Hall
Keep
Gatehouse
Old Hall

above the Wogan or cavern beneath it, which served as a water-gate and dock to the castle.

The castle survived to play an active part in the seventeenth-century Civil War when it was held successively both for Parliament and the Crown, which accounts for the internal thickening of the southern curtain and also for the modern restoration of much of the fabric to make good the slighting carried out perhaps by Cromwell himself in 1648.

FURTHER READING

D. J. C. King, 'Pembroke Castle', *Archaeologia Cambrensis* CXXIV.

Pevensey, *Sussex*

We are told by William of Jumièges, in a statement confirmed by William of Poitiers, that upon his landing at Pevensey (on 28 September) the Conqueror 'at once raised a strongly entrenched castle'. This, then, is the, so to speak, first official castle raised in England by the Normans in 1066, though there had been others such as Richard's Castle and probably Ewyas Harold and Clavering founded by individual Norman lords invited into England by Edward the Confessor in the first decade of his reign. The site and pattern chosen was an enclosure of ditch and bank (and palisade) within the larger pre-existing Roman fort, and utilizing its stone walls on two sides in the same way that early Norman castles were planted, for example, within the towns or burghs of London or Portchester.

The castle of 1066 is thus represented by the ditch of the present one on the same site, though a further section of ditch to be seen running north on the line of the present North Tower may also have something to do with it. The accompanying photograph also shows clearly within the enclosure of the castle the

foundations of an early chapel (its north aisle a later addition) which has itself been identified with great probability as the pre-existing church of the Anglo-Saxon township or burgh which in 1066 occupied the Roman fort, expansion of the town beyond the walls to the east being largely a post-Conquest development. The ancient walls of the eleventh-century town were those of the Roman Saxon Shore Fort of Anderida built in the late third century A.D., most unusual in its irregular as opposed to rectangular plan. It was sited upon a peninsula rising above the marshes and in Roman and medieval times the sea reached its walls to afford a port in Pevensey Haven. Taken without resistance, Pevensey was thus an ideal landfall and bridgehead for the Normans in 1066, though having occupied it and planted his castle the Conqueror soon moved his main force on to what for him was the even better base of Hastings. Pevensey Castle was in due course assigned to the king-duke's half-brother, Robert count of Mortain, and became thenceforward the *caput* of the newly established Norman rape or lordship of Pevensey.

The dominating stone curtain walls of the castle on the north, west and south sides, with their projecting D-shaped towers (each of three storeys) and twin-towered gatehouse, are fine and characteristic work of the mid-thirteenth century, presumably commissioned by Peter of Savoy, earl of Richmond and uncle of the queen, Eleanor of Provence, upon whom Henry III bestowed the lordship of the castle and rape of Pevensey in 1246. Vestiges of the grand residential accommodation of his time can be seen on the inner face of the walls and within the towers. The ruined tower keep on the east side of the castle remains, however, something of an enigma. Ugly now in its truncated profile, it was basically rectangular in plan but with at least four unusually large, projecting bastions or buttresses (once called *insule* in a document of 1370) thrust out to west, north and east. It has been

180

attributed to the early twelfth century, but it has also been suggested that the projections are a late twelfth-century addition to a more regular tower, to make of it one of those sophisticated great towers of that period, with projecting warheads supported on great bastions or corbels, as, say, at Niort (Henry II) or Château-Gaillard (Richard I).

With the gradual withdrawal of the sea the importance of Pevensey declined and certainly in the Tudor period if not before decay set into the fabric of both feudal castle and Roman fortress. In consequence not only much of the keep but also almost all the Roman and medieval wall to south and east have long since gone – though the position was in part refortified in 1940 and some of the gun emplacements of that period still remain.

FURTHER READING

A. J. Taylor, 'Evidence for a Pre-Conquest Origin for the chapels in Hastings and Pevensey Castles', *Château-Gaillard*, III.

Pickering, *Yorkshire*

The history of Pickering may be briefly told: it was royal from the beginning soon after the Conquest until 1267, and thereafter pertained to the earls and subsequently dukes of Lancaster as it still does. Penetrate a little deeper and, though the castle is not mentioned until Henry II's time, its foundation is thought to go back to the first Norman settlement of Yorkshire after the 'Harrying' of 1069–70, and was certainly planted on the lands of earl Morcar which came into the Conqueror's hands after the former's final rebellion and capture at Ely in 1071. Such martial beginnings, however, must not obscure the castle's residential role, for it was thereafter popular with kings and princes because of the hunting it could afford in the Forest of Pickering which was administered from it. In 1267 Henry III granted the honour and castle of Pickering to his youngest son, Edmund 'Crouchback', whom he created earl of Lancaster, and from him and the earls and dukes who succeeded him, sovereigns since 1399, the castle descends in unbroken line to the present queen. It was, however, decayed in the sixteenth century and ruined in the seventeeth.

The castle was sited north of the town on a limestone bluff overlooking the Vale of Pickering and is built of the rock on which it stands. It began, however, as a motte-and-bailey with presumed timber defences crowning impressive earth-works, and, indeed, the present Outer Ward or Barbican to the south and east – which strengthens the castle on its weaker side, and may or may not be a later addition – retained its palisades until the fourteenth century. The curtain wall of the Inner Ward and the Coleman Tower at the foot of the motte (west) are attributed to Henry II, mainly on architectural grounds, and the present ruined shell keep upon the motte to the early thirteenth. The curtain wall of the crescent-shaped Outer Ward, with its towers from Rosamund (housing a postern) at the

north end via Diate Hill Tower to Mill Tower at the south, is known to be early fourteenth-century (1324–6), by Edward II when the castle was in his hand. Of the various buildings of which at least the foundations remain in the Inner Ward, the Old Hall, against the west curtain (11 o'clock on the photograph), dates from the earlier twelfth century, the New Hall to the south of it was a timber-framed hall and solar built on earlier foundations for the countess Alice by Thomas, earl of Lancaster, in 1314, and the chapel jutting out to the east (complete but much restored) was built in *c.* 1227. Of particular interest is the separate and once walled off Constable's Lodging north of the motte, which comprised its own range of timber-framed hall, chambers, domestic office and storage buildings.

FURTHER READING

M. W. Thompson, *Pickering Castle*, English Heritage Handbook, London.

Pleshey, *Essex*

J. H. Round once observed that: 'There is no county perhaps that bears more clearly than Essex the imprint of the Norman Conquest.' He was thinking then especially of place-names (Hatfield Peverel, Stansted Mountfichet . . .), and was the first to show that 'Pleshey' too is French, from *le pleissie*, enclosure (as in the early castle of Le Plessis Grimoult in Normandy). Indeed nothing perhaps can better show the imprint of Norman settlement and new Norman lordship upon the English countryside than an aerial photograph of Pleshey, new castle and new fortified township planted in the open country of High Easter as the *caput* or centre of his honour chosen by the new Norman lord, Geoffrey I de Mandeville (Manneville, Seine-Inf., arr. Dieppe). The castle, too, though the prodigious earthworks (but surely not the motte?) may owe something to refortification in the second half of the twelfth century, stands revealed as a classic motte-and-bailey site. The motte, constructed of rammed-down layers, stands some 15 m above its water-filled moat. The present bailey has ramparts up to 12 m above their moat, and is still connected to the motte-top by an ascending bridge, albeit of fifteenth-century brick. The early entrance to the castle here was probably hard by the motte to the north-east where there is an island in the ditch. There are traces of another (earlier?) bailey to the north where Back Lane curves round in the village.

Nothing, save a lingering prestige, remains of the splendours, architectural and other, once recorded here. Few sites would more reward a comprehensive programme of research, though up to the present only part of the (upper) bailey has been seriously and recently excavated by trial trenches.

The Geoffrey I de Mandeville of Domesday died about 1100, to be succeeded by his son William I, d. 1129, and his grandson Geoffrey II de Mandeville. The latter, created earl of Essex in 1140 by king Stephen, who subsequently betrayed him, is that (formerly notorious) Geoffrey de Mandeville who played so prominent a role in Stephen's reign, to die in arms and in rebellion in 1144. His son, Geoffrey III, was granted the earldom and his patrimony by Henry II in 1156 although the Mandeville castles (Pleshey and Saffron Walden) were demolished about a year later. Earl Geoffrey died in 1166 to be succeeded by his brother, William, to whom a licence to refortify Pleshey was granted some time between his succession and 1180, in which year his marriage is known to have taken place in the castle. Pleshey goes proudly on, ever more splendid, to the end of the Middle Ages, via the great house of Bohun, earls of Hereford, and ultimately the duchy of Lancaster. In Richard II's time it was held by Thomas of Woodstock, duke of Gloucester, the king's uncle, murdered in Calais. Hence the reference in Shakespeare —

> With all good speed at Pleshey visit me,
> . . . empty lodgings and unfurnished walls,
> unpeopled offices, untrodden stones.
> (*Richard II*, Act I, Sc. 2)

Portchester, *Hampshire*

Portchester could scarcely be more important to the castellologist, its site, especially in aerial photography, showing at a glance the essential difference between the large communal fortresses of earlier periods (which of course continue throughout the medieval period, and after, as fortified towns and cities) and the usually smaller castle which is basically the fortified residence of a lord (cf. Pevensey, Old Sarum). Here the Norman castle, probably in the first generation after 1066, has been inserted into the north-west angle of the ancient enclosure which was first a Roman Saxon Shore Fort of the late third century and later restored and refortified as an Anglo-Saxon burgh by Edward the Elder soon after 904. Subsequently (cf. Dover) the castle took over the whole rectangular enclosure which thus became its outer bailey, though the latter's original function is still indicated by the large Norman church built by William Pont de l'Arche for his Augustinian priory, founded here *c.* 1130 but soon after moved to Southwick (cf. the Norman cathedral at Old Sarum). The church is still the parish church today.

Portchester has recently been subjected to prolonged, thorough and comprehensive archaeological research covering all periods of its occupation, Roman, Saxon, feudal and post-medieval, and the castle is also amply endowed with documentary evidence. The most notable feature of the Roman fortification for our purposes is the systematic use of projecting mural towers as demonstrating that

the builders of early castles must have been aware of the principle of flanking cover at least from surviving examples. The rectangular tower keep of the castle (which breaks out of the Roman *enceinte*) is of particular interest because, though long known to have been heightened, and still lacking firm dates, it is now thought to have begun in the eleventh century as a single-storey hall-type residence (cf. Castle Acre), subsequently to be thickened and heightened as a great tower in the early twelfth-century, then heightened again probably in the mid-twelfth, its forebuilding also a twelfth-century addition. The gatehouse similarly shows a continuous development of extension outward (south), barbican upon barbican, to culminate in its present appearance by the end of the fourteenth century. Of the standing buildings and residential suites other than the keep itself, the finest and most evocative is the range of hall, chambers, kitchen and other offices built by Richard II between 1396 and his deposition in 1399, along the south and west sides of the castle ('inner bailey') between the gatehouse and the keep. Clearly these elegant buildings were to mark a new phase in Portchester's role as a gateway to France, following the king's unpopular peace with France in March 1396 and his marriage to the French princess Isabella in the same month. It seems equally clear that Richard never saw them; and the history of Portchester thereafter is largely one of decline.

The first Norman lord of Portchester and the founder of the castle – or, perhaps one should say at that stage, *maison forte* – was William Mauduit, the Domesday tenant whose son, Robert went down in the White Ship in 1120. Henry I evidently granted the Mauduit castle, lordship and chamberlainship to William Pont de l'Arche, who married Robert's daughter. A charter of 1153 gives repossession to the family of Mauduit but the castle was taken over by Henry II in 1174 if not before and thereafter remained royal until the seventeenth century.

FURTHER READING

S. E. Rigold, *Portchester Castle*, English Heritage Handbook, London.

Prudhoe, *Northumberland*

Prudhoe is among the most satisfying of border castles, with a fine residential continuity through to the modern period (the early nineteenth-century house, north–south between the two wards, was built between 1808 and 1818 on the site of a former chamber block) and its lordship seemingly held only by two families from start to finish, Umfraville and Percy. In the far north the Norman settlement came later than in the south, and it is thought that the present castle was founded soon after 1100 by Robert II of Umfraville, who had been granted the barony of Prudhoe by Henry I and was already lord of Redesdale by grant of the Conqueror to his father, Robert I (alias *cum barba*, 'with-the-beard'). The Umfravilles (Offranville near Dieppe? or Amfréville-sur-Iton?) became earls of Angus in 1243 and were succeeded by the Percies in 1398. Possible vestiges of earlier fortification on the site, however, may date from the later eleventh century and the time of Robert de Mowbray, earl of Northumberland from 1086 to his fall in 1095. Constantly attacked or threatened by the Scots in the twelfth century (not least in 1173–4 when it figures prominently in Jordon Fantosme's account of William the Lion's invasion), and again in the fourteenth and fifteenth centuries and later, Prudhoe could still be described in 1537 as 'a very stronge fortresse standying opon an hill', though by 1596 it had become 'an old ruinous castle'. By then, and thereafter, it was chiefly leased out by the Percies to tenants until the second Percy duke of Northumberland built the 'modern' house referred to above.

The castle is strongly situated upon a natural promontory above the Tyne, and is sufficiently protected by a steep slope behind it to the river on the north, but to the south had two ditches, the inner and the outer moat. Its principal feature now is the early gatehouse (*c.* 1100?) whose upper storey was converted into a chapel in the thirteenth century and a chamber inserted above that a little later. In front is a long barbican added in the fourteenth century, with access on the left or west to a basecourt or pele between the inner and outer moats. The castle proper, its curtain walls surviving, consists of two wards, east and west, the former recently excavated and having contained the great hall (opposite the gate) with the

kitchens to the east of it. The west court houses the twelfth-century rectangular tower keep, more or less complete in 1786 but now reduced to a mainly south-west fragment. This had a forebuilding (east) but otherwise seems somewhat primitive in design. The west court has or had two round towers open to the gorge of thirteenth-century date, respectively at the north-west and south angles. The curtain between them, and between them and the gatehouse, has two lines of arrow-loops and holes for a timber hoarding.

FURTHER READING

Laurence Keen, 'The Umfravilles, the Castle and the Barony of Prudhoe, Northumberland', *Anglo-Norman Studies* v.

Pulverbatch, *Shropshire*

Pulverbatch in Shropshire is a good example of a motte-and-bailey castle classically placed on a ridge, with its attendant vill or township, here on the slope of the hill at a road junction, laid out beneath it after the manner of neighbouring Kilpeck or Richard's Castle. The Domesday tenant was Roger Venator, i.e. the Huntsman (the district was forest), who held the place of Roger of Montgomery, earl of Shrewsbury. To him the foundation of castle (and vill?) is attributed, in which case it is a mesne castle, held of some other lord than the king. The forfeiture of earl Roger's successor Robert of Bellême in 1102, however, meant that thenceforth it was held in chief. By Henry I's time Roger Venator was succeeded by Roger II, and he early in Henry II's time by Reginald de Pulverbatch, who was probably his son. Reginald left only his daughter Emma as his heir, married to Herbert de Castello who thus held Pulverbatch in her right in addition to his own castle and lordship of Holgate. Emma died without direct heirs in 1193, whereupon the barony of Pulverbatch passed to a collateral, John of Kilpeck, lord of Kilpeck, who in 1195 was pardoned most of the £100 he had promised for it 'on

account of the poverty of the estate and because it is only assessed as one knight's fee' (*pro paupertate tenementi et quia non habet feodum nisi j militis*), i.e. scarcely a barony rating a £100 baronial 'relief'. This does not necessarily mean that the castle was then derelict as is sometimes said, and indeed in February 1205 the king ordered the sheriff to put it in the custody of William de Cantilupe 'with the arms and chattels which you found there', after the death of John de Kilpeck whose heir, Hugh II, was a minor. By 1292, however, it may well have been abandoned, when it was stated that there was no manor house at Pulverbatch.

Raby, *County Durham*

Envy not they neighbour's house, but Raby is among the most enviable of stately homes. The place, the land and the lordship were reputedly first given to St Cuthbert by Cnut, and by the prior and convent of Durham were alienated in 1131 to one Dolphin son of Ughtred, whose grandson, Robert son of Maldred, married Isabel, heiress of Neville of Brancepeth and Sheriff Hutton, their son Geoffrey taking his mother's name. Thus Raby pertained to the rising and great northern house of Neville – also of Middleham – from the thirteenth century to their fall in the lost cause of Mary, queen of Scots, in 1570. By then Raby had been described by Leland as 'the largest castel of logginges in al the north cuntery'. In 1626 it was bought by the family of Vane, later lords Barnard, who themselves rose to the heights of earls of Darlington and dukes of Cleveland in the eighteenth and

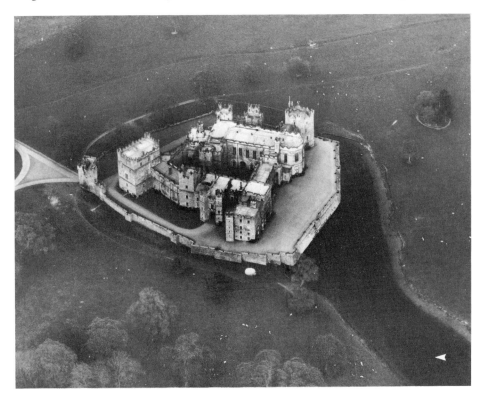

nineteenth centuries. Inevitably in those same centuries the interiors of the castle were mostly altered out of all recognition, not least by the rebuilding of the main residential southern side in the 1840s and, in the late eighteenth century, the driving of a carriageway through the medieval chapel and into the hall to make of its undercroft a sort of grand, private terminus. Yet externally the fourteenth-century fabric has not been added to, nor even greatly altered, save for the lowering of the outer curtain to a mere revetment all round, the rebuilding of the south front, modern fenestration throughout, and the draining of the moat except on the south where it is landscaped into a lake.

The one medieval date we have is 1378, when John lord Neville obtained licence from the bishop of Durham to make of his manor of Raby 'a castle freely according to his will and to crenellate and embattle all the towers, houses and walls'. There is now no trace of any earlier residence from the twelfth or thirteenth century which might account for the irregular plan of the fourteenth-century building, but of that it is thought that some (e.g. the lower hall, the chapel and the inner, tunnel-vaulted part of Neville's Gate) was built well before 1378, and much of it later by John's son, Ralph lord Neville, created earl of Westmorland in 1397, after his father's death in 1388. There were two gatehouses, an outer (north) and an inner (Neville's Gate, west), and nine towers of which one, south of the great hall, has gone to be replaced by the octagonal dining room of the 1840s. The most rewarding medieval interiors now are the splendid kitchens (cf. Durham) north of the mutilated great hall, and the Servant's Hall, south of the imposing Clifford's Tower at the north-west angle.

Raglan, *Monmouthshire*

In any attempt to categorize, Raglan in Monmouthshire would have to be listed as a later castle, yet, as is so often the case, it has an early foundation. Nothing now visible is earlier than the fifteenth century, yet the whole is the ultimate development of a castle in all probability dating back to the eleventh century and the first Norman penetration of Gwent and south Wales by William fitz Osbern (cf. Chepstow) and his vassals. It is further very probable that Raglan in the beginning was raised in the motte-and-bailey form, and that of the present castle the donjon, 'the Yellow Tower of Gwent' (centre, nearest camera), represents the Norman motte and its superstructure (with exactly the same function) and the two courts the Norman bailey. Of that early castle, however, we know almost nothing save that it was held from fitz Osbern's successors by the family of Bloet until in the late fourteenth century it passed by marriage first to the Berkeleys and then (c. 1405) to one William ap Thomas. William (d. 1445) – later Sir William, 'the Blue Knight of Gwent' – and his son William (d. 1469) – who took the name of Herbert and in 1468 was created earl of Pembroke – both did very well, by service in the wars in France, by marriage, and by association with the Yorkist cause which triumphed with the first accession to the throne of Edward IV in 1461. Between them they built the present castle, the greater part being the work of the second

William (Herbert) as befits his ever-rising wealth and status, though on the best authority the keep is attributed to the first phase, and there were further embellishments (e.g. the Elizabethan Long Gallery), in the later sixteenth century. Most notable is the Yellow Tower of Gwent, hexagonal and probably one storey higher before its slighting in 1646, a late medieval example of the tower keep, in no way different in purpose from its eleventh- and twelfth-century predecessors. Scarcely less notable are the palatial ranges of accommodation about the principal Fountain Court, centred upon the magnificent great hall. Notable also are the hexagonal towers of the curtain, and the machicolation (less common in England than in France) which crowns the Great Gatehouse and the adjacent Closet Tower (north-east). Then came the tragedy of the seventeenth-century Civil War, when Edward Somerset, marquis of Worcester, was the king's most generous supporter and Raglan became a principal royalist centre, the first castle, it was said, to be fortified for the king and the last to be surrendered (on 19 August 1646, in the great hall). The slighting and destruction, plundering and looting, which followed were vicious, and the great building has never been reoccupied or restored, the family after the Restoration building the new house of Badminton and becoming dukes of Beaufort (1682).

FURTHER READING

A. J. Taylor, *Raglan Castle*, Cadw Official Handbook, Cardiff.

Restormel, *Cornwall*

Restormel, with Launceston, was one of the two major castles in Cornwall, both of which pertained to the earldom or, after 1337, dukedom. The first known reference to the castle occurs only in 1264 but its origins are much earlier, soon after the Norman Conquest. In the beginning Restormel was part of the manor of Bordardle (in Lanlivery), held in 1086 of Robert, count of Mortain, by Turstin the Sheriff, whose descendants and successors continued to hold it as tenants and vassals of the earl for some two centuries. In *c.* 1270 Isolda de Cardinan, widow of Thomas de Tracy and heiress in her own right, made over to Richard, earl of Cornwall, the castle of Restormel and certain lands which only then became a distinct unit and lordship, held in demesne by the earls and dukes. The first castle, on a spur above the river Fowey, comprised, not a motte but an inner enclosure

(cf. e.g. Castle Acre), of a type labelled unnecessarily by modern archaeologists 'ring-motte', here circular and powerfully ditched and banked on the highest point of the spur, with a roughly quadrangular bailey to the west, now largely vanished. It is attributed to Baldwin, son of Turstin the Sheriff, in c. 1100, and had at least some stone work from the start since the surviving lower courses of the ruined gate-tower into the inner enclosure, i.e. the donjon, are assigned to that date. The ring-wall of this enclosure, built up from the natural ground level inside the bank which is cut back to accommodate it, buts onto the gate-tower and is thus later, possibly late twelfth-century. In the late thirteenth century the projecting barbican was added to the gate-tower, and this also is the date given to the splendid range of lordly accommodation within, consisting of (in anti-clockwise order from and to the gate) kitchen with buttery and pantry, hall, solar, chapel and ante-chapel, and two chamber blocks. The principal rooms are all at first-floor level and the chapel projects boldly beyond the curtain wall (cf. e.g. Kidwelly). All this, the last and grandest phase in the castle's development, is best attributed to Edmund earl of Cornwall (d. 1299; son of earl Richard and nephew of Edward I), who evidently made Restormel his principal residence when in Cornwall. There was also, of course, other accommodation in the now vanished bailey, a survey of 1337 for the young Black Prince, the first duke of Cornwall, referring to a great hall and kitchen, chapel, chambers and bakehouse and stables for twenty horses. It also refers to a lead conduit bringing water into the castle from a spring without, to supplement the well.

In the sixteenth century the castle fell into ruin, Norden lamenting 'to see so stately a pyle so longe a fallinge', and, though it was put into some state of defence in the seventeenth-century Civil War, the Parliamentary Commissioners in 1649 found it not worth demolishing. In guardianship of the Office of Works and its successors since 1925 (though still pertaining to the duchy), the surviving buildings are generally regarded as a classic example of that type of shell keep whose accommodation is ranged round the curtain wall and thus about a central courtyard.

Rhuddlan, *Flintshire*

Edward I's Rhuddlan, like Flint, both with their attendant new towns, was the product of the First Welsh War of 1277, founded to reoccupy and hold the disputed land of Englefield. Militarily it replaced Henry III's castle of Dyserth, destroyed by the Welsh in 1263, as a major fortress at the northern end of Offa's Dyke; but it also replaced the early Norman castle and new town of Rhuddlan, planted here by Robert of Rhuddlan in 1073 and now henceforth abandoned. The motte of that castle still stands some two or three hundred yards south and east of Edward's castle (i.e. above it on the photograph), on the same side of the river. Traditionally it occupied the site of Gruffydd ap Llywelyn's hall, destroyed by Harold in 1063, and it certainly stood in the north-west section of the Norman borough, flourishing in Domesday but now almost vanished save for traces of its

perimeter defences and vestiges of its Dominican priory (founded *c.* 1258) in the farmyard and buildings of Plasnewydd.

Having launched the works at Flint, Edward I arrived at Rhuddlan to establish his headquarters in the third week of August and work began at once upon the new castle and the new town to the north-west of it. Castle and town are still laid out as the king willed, and the virgin site was carefully chosen so that sea-going shipping might reach it. For this, however, the meandering course of the river Clwyd had to be altered and a new deep-water canal cut between two and three miles long; hence the prominence on the accounts in the early years of prodigious sums paid to diggers and dykers. In these years also the works at Rhuddlan took priority over those at Flint and by the autumn of 1280 the castle is thought to have been substantially finished. Two years later, by 1282, when the weight of effort had been transferred back to Flint, a total of some £9,500 had been spent on Rhuddlan, castle, town defences, bridge and canal. Some £365 more was needed over the next four years to finish off the defences and make good the damage inflicted by the Welsh in their rising of 1282.

Though no other of king Edward's works can quite compare with Conway and Caernarvon, Harlech and Beaumaris, Rhuddlan and Flint are most impressive and, like the others, were built or at least planned as one operation with little regard to expense, and employed at once all the latest techniques of fortification available to the warrior king and his master masons in the last quarter of the thirteenth century. At Rhuddlan the result is a concentric castle, the outer ward wrapped exactly round three sides of the inner, and a broad, dry moat round that, though both outer ward and moat descend the slope to the new-cut river, whose waters thus washed the castle on the west and entered the extended eastern arm of the moat to form the dock. The outer curtain, now much ruined, was comparatively low because commanded by the Inner Ward behind it, but was strengthened by a series of rectangular turrets and buttresses (the former having steps down to form a series of sally ports into the moat) and a regular series of arrow slits at alternate levels. There were four gates in the Outer Ward, the Town Gate, the Friary Gate (later blocked), the River Gate and the Dock Gate, the last having the rectangular Gillot's Tower beside it to defend the dock. The Inner Ward in plan is best described as a square set diagonally to the points of the compass, with a great cylindrical tower at the north and south angles and two great twin-towered gatehouses set dramatically opposite each other east and west. The curtains are 3 m thick, wider adjacent to the towers, and again are pierced by arrow slits. All the towers are four storeys high, the southern having a basement in addition, and contain residential chambers. The principal accommodation for the king and queen was in the Inner Ward against the walls which bear faint traces of it.

After and because of the conquest of Snowdonia and all Wales and the founding of even greater castles and attendant boroughs in the Second Welsh War of 1282–3, Rhuddlan never entirely achieved the pre-eminence originally intended for it. The town defences were never built in stone but remained mere ditch and bank and palisade like Flint; the king's proposal to bring the cathedral of St Asaph here was abandoned; and the status of country town passed to Flint. At the end of the seventeenth-century Civil War, when it was held for the king, the castle was ordered to be dismantled, and thereafter remained a quarried ruin until granted by its owner into guardianship under the Ancient Monuments Act in 1944. A passing glimpse of the captains and the kings departed is still given by a payment in 1283 to Adam the Tailor for four pieces of red silk for pennons and royal standards to be flown from the castle.

FURTHER READING

A. J. Taylor, *Rhuddlan Castle*, Cadw Official Handbook, Cardiff.

Richard's Castle, *Herefordshire*

Richard's Castle in Herefordshire, three miles south-west of Ludlow, as one of the rare instances of a pre-Conquest castle, is one of the earliest castle sites in England. It stands thus for the introduction of the castle into this country by the Normans. It

was founded by Richard son of Scrob, one of those Norman lords settled by Edward the Confessor on the Welsh border under his nephew Ralph of Mantes, made earl of Hereford. The context is therefore of early Norman settlement and aristocratic colonization in the late Anglo-Saxon kingdom before the drama of Hastings, and the date has to be before 1051, when Godwin, earl of Wessex, and his sons rose against increasing Norman influence in the realm, and the prospect of an eventual Norman succession to the throne, both of which threatened their dominance. It is to be noted that the new Norman settlement evidently incorporated not only the castle but also a vill or township, itself no doubt fortified, after the manner of Pleshey in Essex, while the siting of the whole position upon a hill top may remind one of such Norman fortified towns with castles as Domfront (or Ste-Suzanne in neighbouring Maine which came under Norman lordship before 1066). The photograph shows Richard's Castle from the south-east, with the triangular vill clearly visible, the castle beyond the church, hidden by trees, on the highest ground, its motte at the extreme north-west limit of the hill. The castle is of the motte-and-bailey type: recent excavations (1962–4) did not disprove that it was so from the beginning, and showed that the true height of the motte was some 9 m with a diameter at the top of some 20–21 m. In the twelfth and thirteenth centuries at least the castle received stone fortification of curtain walls, gatehouse and towers, and a polygonal (in this case octagonal) tower keep after the manner of Tickhill was raised upon the motte probably in the last quarter of the twelfth. The present banks and ditches of the vill are early thirteenth-century, but nothing visibly medieval remains inside except the church, the modern village having moved down the hill to the Leominster–Ludlow road. The church is basically twelfth-century with additions on either side of 1300. An interesting feature is the bell-tower, free-standing and placed at the east end instead of the more usual west where it would have overlooked the castle. Within the area of the otherwise deserted old town there are one or two good post-medieval timber-framed houses including the seventeenth-century Court House.

The Richard fitz Scrob of Richard's Castle was not driven out with others of the Confessor's French and Norman friends by the triumphant Godwin in 1052 and was succeeded after 1066 by his son, grandson and subsequent descendants. In short, the castle founded as the centre or *caput* of a new Norman lordship so remained until its final abandonment, probably in the fifteenth century.

FURTHER READING

P. E. Curnow and M. W. Thompson, 'Excavations at Richard's Castle, Herefordshire, 1962–1964', *Journal of the Archaeological Association* (3) XXXII.

Richmond, *Yorkshire*

The context of the foundation of Richmond, like that of so many castles in England and Wales, is exclusively that of the Norman Conquest and settlement, here of the

north of England, necessarily a few years later than that of the south. The castle was founded by Alan Rufus, 'the Red', as the headquarters of his huge fief in Yorkshire and elsewhere, and the traditional date of 1071 is most likely as following the 'Harrying of the North' in the winter of 1069–70, the retribution for the last great northern rising against Norman hegemony from the south. Count Alan himself, a Breton count and cadet of the ruling house, whose descendants were to become dukes of Brittany in the twelfth century, was the most distinguished member of the substantial Breton contingent in the Norman invasion of 1066, and their leader at Hastings. He was rewarded with all the lands of Edwin, the Anglo-Saxon earl of Mercia, either in 1068 or 1071, the dates respectively of the latter's first revolt and subsequent death. He placed his castle not at Gilling or in any of the earl's former manors but on a strong, virgin site on the cliff above the river Swale, the symbol and substance of new lordship, a new town growing up at its foot. And so matters have remained. The castle played little part in the later wars with Scotland, or in the Wars of the Roses or the seventeenth-century Civil War. A fifteenth-century register of the Honour of Richmond (B L Cotton Faustina B. vii; cf. Dugdale, *Monasticon*, v. 574) says that Alan the Red placed his castle in that strong place near his manor of Gilling for the safety of his men and household against the attacks of the native English and Danes then everywhere disinherited. He named it 'Richmond' in his Gallic idiom, and for centuries it stood as the *caput* of the great honour and earldom of Richmond, called

198

a 'castelry' in Domesday Book, lavishly supplied with the castle-guard services of knights, which itself is a sign of early foundation and the immediate urgency of the circumstances which called it into being.

The castle forms a large triangular enclosure of $2\frac{1}{2}$ acres overall, with a later twelfth-century rectangular tower keep and barbican thrust forward at the northern apex where the principal entrance was and is (now renewed), and the main residential complex on the south front high above the river which naturally defends it. There is also an outer ward called the Cockpit thrust out from the south front to the east beyond Scolland's Hall (right on the photograph), with its own gateway covered by a tower (the Fallen Tower) on the main curtain, and clearly serving as a barbican to protect the private or seigneurial entrance straight into the great hall and its subsidiary chambers. The principal archaeological interest of the castle is that it was a stone walled enclosure from the beginning, without any motte or other early keep, its massive curtains dating from the eleventh century, as do the mural towers (rectangular) which strengthen them, three along the east curtain and one at the south-west angle. Scolland's Hall, in the south-east corner of the Great Court, with its integrated solar or chamber block, garderobe tower (the Gold Hole Tower) and entrance from the Cockpit, also dates from the eleventh century and is thus one of the earliest first-floor halls in the kingdom. It was ever the centre and pivot of the main domestic complex of the castle: further buildings including domestic offices were added to the west in the twelfth century, and a great chamber and chapel (again at first-floor level) to the north in the earlier fourteenth century. There were evidently two early or original chapels, St Nicholas (a Norman dedication) in the Robin Hood Tower (the most northern of the three towers on the east curtain) and a larger free-standing chapel on the west side of the Great Court, now gone but marked by a wide, round-headed arch towards the south end of the west curtain, and given by Alan Rufus to the monks of his foundation of St Mary's at York. The present keep at the north end of the castle is built up from the original eleventh-century gatehouse (cf. Ludlow), a new gate being cut in beside it and a barbican (mostly gone) thrust out in front. This is twelfth-century work attributed to Conan, fifth lord of the honour, earl of Richmond and duke of Brittany, but finished by Henry II, into whose hand the castle came on Conan's death in 1171. The present ruined walls of the Cockpit are of the same date, and it was in this period that William the Lion, King of the Scots, was imprisoned in the castle (traditionally in the Robin Hood Tower) after his capture at Alnwick in 1174. The third important building phase in the history of Richmond occurred in the earlier fourteenth century in the time of John II, duke of Brittany, when at least the chapel and chamber block north of Scolland's Hall were built and the upper levels of curtain walls and towers rebuilt or heightened. A fifteenth-century illustration of the castle still very much in its glory survives in the Richmond Register referred to above, but less than a century later, in a survey of 1538, it was in grave decay and Leland in *c.* 1540 referred to it as a 'mere ruine'.

FURTHER READING

Sir Charles Peers, *Richmond Castle*, English Heritage Handbook, London.

Rochester, *Kent*

The first castle at Rochester was founded soon after 1066 and is mentioned in Domesday Book (1086). One would expect the Normans to plant a castle here early, in an important city and to guard the crossing of the Medway by the great road from London to Canterbury and Dover, the former Roman Watling Street. It was placed directly beside the river (the present Esplanade is modern), more or less within the line of the ruined Roman city wall at the south-west angle, and at the head of the medieval bridge which (demolished in 1857) ran south of the present road and railway bridges. In form it was simply an enclosure within the city, making what use could be made of ancient defences on two sides, but for the most part of bank, ditch and palisade. Between 1087 and 1089 this castle was rebuilt in stone on the same site, i.e. a curtain-wall was raised about it, by Gundulf, bishop of Rochester, at William Rufus' request. Gundulf, a former monk of Bec and a protégé of Lanfranc, had supervised (perhaps still did) the Conqueror's work of the White Tower at London and was 'very competent and skilful at building in stone', as was necessary on this rather awkward site. Next, in and after 1127, the great rectangular tower keep was raised by archbishop William de Corbeil, to whom and his successors at Canterbury Henry I in that year granted perpetual custody of the royal castle and permission to build a tower therein (cf. plans p. 14). With that the development of Rochester was almost complete. The only other major phase, under Edward III between 1367 and 1383, was mostly devoted to restoration and reparation, though it included the construction (northern) and reconstruction (southern) of the two mural towers on the east curtain and the strengthening of the main gate to the city (north-east, now vanished). Richard II added the northern bastion, by the bridge and river, restored and converted into an entrance in *c.* 1872.

The close juxtaposition of castle and cathedral at Rochester (the latter now basically Norman and Gundulf again) is not so surprising as might appear, for they represent the twin authorities of church and state, *regnum et sacerdotium*, the Two Swords of secular and ecclesiastical jurisdiction, and seen together (from the other side of the river – or from an aerial photograph) they symbolize, as they were meant to do, a panoply of power, in a view second only to Durham. Here, too, as at Durham, the relationship of *regnum* and *sacerdotium* was, for a time, especially close. It was to the See of Canterbury that Henry I granted the perpetual custody of Rochester in 1127, and that arrangement lasted until 1215 when archbishop Stephen Langton, in John's words that 'notorious and barefaced traitor', let in the king's enemies and so failed to 'render up our castle of Rochester to us in our so great need'.

The military history of Rochester castle has been unusually strenuous, with three sieges: one in 1088 by Rufus, when the defenders surrendered and rode out with the honours of war; one in 1215, when king John took the castle by storm; and the third in 1264, when the assailants, earl Simon de Montfort and earl Gilbert de Clare, were obliged to withdraw from the fortress, this time held for the king (Henry III). Of these occasions the second is the most important and still leaves its mark upon the fabric, visible in the accompanying photograph. In an investment lasting almost two months in October and November 1215, John entered first the

bailey and then the keep itself, bringing down the south-east quarter of the great tower by undermining, the mine sprung by fire fed with the fat of forty pigs, brought in for the occasion and slaughtered on the spot. To this day a monument to those forty pigs stands at Rochester in the south-east angle of the keep, rebuilt cylindrical in the next reign (in Poitevin fashion?), and in the contemporary curtain wall and drum tower in front of it.

No further work of any note is known at the castle after Richard II's bastion, and by the sixteenth century it was certainly in decay. James I alienated it from the Crown to one Sir Anthony Weldon and it remained in private hands until the City Corporation acquired it in the 1870s. Since then it has passed to the Department of the Environment and English Heritage.

FURTHER READING

R. Allen Brown, *Rochester Castle*, English Heritage Handbook, London.

Rockingham, *Northamptonshire*

That Rockingham was founded by the Conqueror himself, evidently upon a virgin site, is explicitly stated by Domesday Book – 'The king holds Rockingham . . . It was waste when the king commanded a castle to be raised there.' It remained a royal castle throughout the medieval period, moderately developed and adequately maintained, until the usual neglect of the Tudor period, when Henry VIII first allowed building materials to be taken from the ruins and then, in 1544, leased it to the Watson family, who subsequently bought it outright and made it into the country seat it has ever since remained. Nevertheless, it played an active role in the seventeenth-century Civil War, being seized and held by the Parliamentarians and repeatedly attacked by the Royalists, and was thereafter slighted. Hence the cutting-down of the motte now planted out as a garden (like a dartboard on the accompanying photograph), hence the mainly Tudor and Stuart residential buildings (with some nineteenth-century work by Salvin), hence landscaping and parterres as well as medieval remains. The result, it must be confessed, is very agreeable. Beneath all this one can still see the lay-out of the Conqueror's castle, classically sited, cut off by ditches at the end of a promontory above the river Welland. It had a large central motte with a bailey on either side (north and south) after the manner of Windsor and Arundel. Only the northern bailey, however, seems thereafter to have been much developed, and contained the main lodgings, as it still does, much of the fabric of a thirteenth-century hall and chamber block surviving in the present house. The motte once bore a polygonal shell keep, comprising many chambers and apartments about a central courtyard but heavily fortified in the Civil War and now vanished. This, with the motte, was clearly the 'great tower' of the documents, and both Leland's 'dungeon' and 'keep exceeding fair and strong'. Nevertheless, there was another strong tower north of this, on that side of the motte ditch. Of the curtain once surrounding the bailey or baileys a length survives, albeit restored, on the east front between the former motte and the gatehouse (also restored). That gatehouse, comprising two projecting drum towers added in Edward I's time to an earlier gate tower of *c.* 1200, is now the principal remains of the medieval castle.

Sandal, *Yorkshire*

Excavations in 1964–73 (following others of 1893) dramatically confirmed what a surviving survey and contemporary drawing of 1565 had shown, that the derelict site at Sandal (Magna) was once one of the grandest castles in the realm, as befitted its lords, the Warenne earls of Surrey (to 1347), Edmund of Langley and his successors, dukes of York, and king Richard III. The great manor of Wakefield was royal demesne in Domesday and was only granted to William de Warenne, the second earl, by Henry I, before 1121 and probably in *c.* 1107. Hence the comparatively late foundation of the castle, evidently as a motte-and-bailey with timber buildings and defences, by one who was already lord of Castle Acre, Conisborough, Lewes and Reigate. The rebuilding of the castle in stone and its development into a towering edifice with the romantic majesty of an illustration in the *Très Riches Heures* (or of the drawing of 1565) was the work of the thirteenth century, from *c.* 1200 to *c.* 1280. It is thus a splendid example of that development on the same site of an early, 'primitive', and in this case motte-and-bailey, castle, which is so often the pattern of the architectural history of English castles, and more especially of the development of the early motte and its timber superstructure into a most formidable complex and desirable donjon. One may think, as another example, of the Seven Towers of the Percies at Alnwick, but here at Sandal the outcome was an elaborate shell keep with projecting cylindrical towers four

storeys high, a projecting gatehouse block, also four storeys high, with a barbican descending the motte, and, at its foot and thrust into the bailey, a great Barbican Tower with its own revetted moat and drawbridge. All this was not only impressively formidable but also residential, while the bailey, with towered curtain and gatehouse, contained other residential suites and a great hall.

Comparatively minor modifications and modernizations with some rebuilding were carried out for Richard III between 1483 and 1485, but in the sixteenth century the castle was allowed to decay before being granted out by Elizabeth I to one Edward Carey in 1566. In the seventeenth-century Civil War Sandal was put into a state of defence and held for the king until its surrender on 1 October 1645, after a punishingly damaging cannonade. Demolition, robbing and total ruination followed.

Old Sarum, *Wiltshire*

Old Sarum, i.e. Old Salisbury, exhibits the fortifications of three epochs and differing societies, and, in an aerial photograph especially, emphasizes the difference between the castle and the generally much larger communal fortresses which were or became fortified towns and cities. Here, as at Dover, the large

enclosure (29½ acres) evidently began as an Iron Age hill-fort, and in the late Anglo-Saxon period was serving as a burgh in fact if not in name. Alfred is said to have ordered the (re)fortification of Salisbury which, though it is not listed in the Burghal Hidage, nor directly referred to as a burgh in Domesday, yet in the pre-Conquest period had a mint, more than one church, and paid the third-penny to the king. Though suburbs were to develop east and west, there is no good reason to doubt that this late Anglo-Saxon town was principally within the hill-top defences – which explains the presence of the new Norman cathedral, placed in a precinct carved out of the north-east section by bishop Herman following the conciliar decree of 1075 that sees were to be moved from rural sites to urban centres. The Normans characteristically and drastically remodelled the city, vastly strengthening the now outer bank and ditch to its present scale and building a wall upon the former (three-quarters of a mile in circumference: the upstanding section of curtain by the cathedral is early twelfth-century upon the earlier work), levelling up the whole interior, and planting within not only a cathedral but also a castle which is the smaller enclosure (1¾ acres) on the artificially levelled summit of the hill. Further, one must suggest if not insist that this whole formidable development of fortified city, cathedral and castle pertained in the early Norman period to the bishop (*Idem episcopus tenet Sarisberie*, thus Domesday), on the analogy of Durham (a site scarcely more dramatic), and that bishops Herman and St Osmund held the castle of the king as their successor Roger, bishop of Salisbury, certainly did. On Roger's fall in 1139 the castle was seized by Stephen and only thereafter remained royal, the resultant cumulative friction being one contributory cause of the transfer of the church to the present (New) Salisbury in the early thirteenth century, the citizens and thus the city thereafter following piecemeal.

The castle of Old Salisbury is or was thus, in overall plan, simply an enclosure, here placed centrally within the town (cf. Dover), which is sometimes confusingly referred to as the 'outer bailey', which it doubtless became when the canons and the townsmen moved out (cf. Dover, and also Portchester, where the castles similarly took over the whole once congested site). Its stone buildings are mostly twelfth-century and reduced to little more than foundations revealed by the excavations of 1909–15. There is a curtain wall about the formidable bank with a gatehouse (east), a strong tower, *viz.* the Postern Tower (west) and a thirteenth-century hall (south). The most interesting building is what is erroneously called the 'Great Tower' but is in fact a courtyard complex attributed to the great builder Roger, bishop of Salisbury (1103–39), and very like his similar work at Sherborne. The castle evidently lost its importance after the fourteenth century and by 1446–7 was said to be 'now fallen into decay'. In the sixteenth century Henry VIII allowed the ruins to be demolished for their materials.

Scarborough, *Yorkshire*

Scarborough castle has a long history, in this instance continuity being more upon the military than the residential side. Some seven sieges are recorded, including

two (1644–5 and 1648) in the seventeenth century, and it was even shelled by the German fleet in 1914. No slighting followed the seventeenth-century triumph of the Parliamentary cause, though by then the castle was both severely damaged and decayed. It was founded by William 'le Gros', count of Aumale (cf. Castle Bytham), whom Stephen created also earl of Yorkshire in 1138, but was resumed with the town, together with many of his lands north of the Humber, as former royal demesne by Henry II soon after 1154. The king at once embarked upon an important series of works which cost over £650 between 1157 and 1169, and his son John spent over £2,000 upon the castle in the course of his reign. Nothing comparable is recorded later, and the twelfth and early thirteenth centuries are thus the period of principal development, though the barbican which still gives the only access was evidently not complete until c. 1343. From Henry II's time the castle remained royal until it was alienated by James I.

The most impressive features of Scarborough are the site itself – a rocky headland bounded on three sides by the sea, with entry only via a narrow strip of land fortified by the barbican and gates – the great ditch on the south-west rendering that side as inaccessible as the others, the long, turreted and towered south-west curtain above the ditch, and the fine but ruined (by seventeenth-century bombardment) rectangular tower keep hard by the entrance. The curtain is of composite date. The keep is always attributed to Henry II who undoubtedly spent money upon it, but it should perhaps be stressed that its affinities are with the keeps of Rochester and Castle Hedingham, both dating from the second quarter of the twelfth century, i.e. the time of William le Gros. The unusually large area of the castle was determined by the site, which occasions a kind of all-or-nothing military situation (cf. Dover), though the castle is principally concentrated on the west, with the barbican, gates, inner bailey and keep. On the rest of the plateau the only medieval buildings known are two hall and chamber blocks of twelfth- and fourteenth-century date respectively, and the twelfth-century chapel of Our Lady (with later domestic buildings once adjacent) on the site of the former Roman signal station and on the edge of the cliff.

Sizergh, *Westmorland*

In 1769, evidently before the alterations of *c.* 1770, Sizergh was succinctly described as 'an ancient hall house with a very large tower, embattled; the rest of

the buildings added to it are later'. The tower itself is nowadays attributed to c. 1340 and to Sir Walter Strickland, who had inherited the manor from his Deincourt mother and whose family have retained it until modern times. It is one of the largest 'pele towers of the North' (cf. Belsay), measuring some 18 m by 12 m on a (more or less) east–west axis, and rising to a height of 17.5 m, with the addition of a large, projecting turret on the south-west front (*viz.* the Deincourt Tower) originally for garderobes and staircase and rising 3 m higher. It has a tunnel-vaulted basement and three floors above, but was much altered internally in the Elizabethan period, which accounts for the plaster ceiling and splendid (and dated) fireplaces and panelling, all of which emphasize the continuing residential role of what was always a strong house. Some of its larger windows are c. 1770. Sir Nikolaus Pevsner thought the hall range adjoining to the north might itself go back to the fourteenth century in some of its masonry, but now, like the tower, it is overwhelmingly Elizabethan internally, with windows and external façades owing most to the 1770s. The projecting wings or ranges of service buildings forming two sides of a courtyard on the present front of the house are basically sixteenth-century. There are traces of a moat.

Stokesay, *Shropshire*

Stokesay, like Acton Burnell in the same county or Little Wenham in Suffolk, falls into the indeterminate category of fortified manor or strong house rather than castle proper, crenellated to give prestige and strong enough to afford security to a man of wealth, in this case an *arriviste*. It was built (for the most part) in the late thirteenth century by Lawrence of Ludlow, a very successful wool-merchant, *mercator notissimus*, and a financier making loans to the Crown, who obtained a licence to crenellate his manor house from Edward I in 1291 as a sign of his arrival. He evidently built upon the site of an older and also defensible house formerly belonging to the family of Say (hence Stoke-Say), for the lower two storeys of the present North Tower are dated back to 1240 and even earlier foundations of c. 1200 have been noted beneath the existing solar block. Degraded to farm use in the eighteenth century but restored and conserved since the mid-nineteenth, Lawrence's new residence has survived remarkably unaltered. Basically it consists of a ground-floor hall and attached solar block (south) with a tower at either end, the South Tower being deliberately the stronger and more impressive. The hall still retains its central hearth, original window openings part glazed and part shuttered, and an open staircase at the north end leading to the upper chambers of the North Tower; while the first-floor solar at the south end can only be reached by an external stairway from the courtyard. If the South Tower (of two residential floors above a basement) is the more impressive, the North Tower is perhaps the more interesting, for it is now known that the timber-framed top stage is mostly the work of Lawrence of Ludlow's time, and, being jettied, comes close to being also a rare example of surviving timber hoarding. All this, however, did not stand alone, but was, and to an extent still is, the west range of a moated enclosure which

certainly contained other, if subsidiary, buildings. The curtain wall on three sides of this enclosure, moreover, was reduced to its present ineffective height after the seventeenth-century Civil War, and once rose higher with an embattled parapet, while the present merely picturesque timber-framed gatehouse is also a seventeenth-century construction replacing something less frivolous in stone.

FURTHER READING

J. F. A. Mason, *Stokesay Castle*, Official Guide, English Life Publications.

Tamworth, *Staffordshire*

The castle of Tamworth is an early Norman foundation in the south-west corner of Ethelfleda's burgh which was itself the fortification of the ancient centre of the Mercian kings. It stands thus as a motte-and-bailey site just above the confluence of the rivers Tame and Anker, with the old town to the north behind it. Of its early history we are ill informed. It was held until the end of the thirteenth century by the family of Marmion (Fontenay-le-Marmion, Calvados) but evidently not from the beginning, for a charter of the Empress Mathilda granting the castle and honour of Tamworth to William de Beauchamp (who did not long retain it) specifically refers to both castle and honour as having been formerly held by Robert the Despenser, brother of Urse d'Abetot, i.e. in the time of the Conqueror and/or Rufus. Marmion scarcely appears in England before the time of Henry I, and Robert must be the founder of the castle.

The bailey to the east has all but vanished (even in Leland's time the 'base courte and great warde' was 'clene decayed') and what remains is principally the motte with its complex superstructure, remarkable especially for the continuity of its residential occupation. This consists basically of a shell keep in the shape of an irregular polygon and strengthened on the east or bailey side by a strong rectangular tower which is contemporary (cf. e.g. Lewes). Shell and tower are dated to the (early?) twelfth century, but a stretch of wing-wall, i.e. curtain wall, descending the motte on the east side is earlier and built in herring-bone fashion – though excavations in 1977 found evidence of a timber palisade elsewhere in the area of the bailey (north-east). The residential buildings whch now occupy almost all the interior of the shell keep are mostly Jacobean (the Ferrers family) but doubtless stand upon medieval foundations and in arrangement comprise a central hall with chamber blocks on either side (north and south).

Tattershall, *Lincolnshire*

It is impossible not to treat Tattershall as an example of a later, fifteenth-century, castle, even though it was built upon the site of, and incorporated, an earlier castle founded *c.* 1231 by one Robert of Tattershall. The old castle occupied what is now

the Inner Ward: Ralph lord Cromwell, Treasurer of England, between *c.* 1432 and 1448 (some accounts survive to provide some precision) added an outer moat, thus providing two further wards, the Outer (west and north) and the Middle (north and east), with a 'Pleasaunce' or garden to the south, no doubt rebuilt or refurbished much of the existing castle, almost all of which has vanished, and certainly built 'the great tower called le Dongeon' which still proclaims his status over the flat countryside for miles. Nor was this all, for a grand college of secular priests was founded in 1440, east of the castle but pertaining to it, to serve in the parish church which was rebuilt on its present splendid scale to accommodate them. There were also almshouses, north of the church, which survive in a seventeenth-century rebuilding. So here, with the adjacent township then more important than it is now, was an impressive centre of lordship in fifteenth-century fashion, and it is sad to relate that Ralph, lord Cromwell, died in 1456 without any direct heirs.

There was never any outer curtain but an elaborate entrance from the north by three gatehouses and three bridges, traversing both outer wards, to reach the Inner. The inner curtain retained seven or eight thirteenth-century drum towers (the stumps of three survive) and the Buck view of 1726 shows what are evidently the ruins of hall, kitchens and chapel, now entirely gone. But the *pièce maîtresse* of Ralph lord Cromwell's work is the great brick-built tower, not very strong by castle standards (e.g. those large traceried windows) but magnificently ostentatious. It comprises a vaulted basement and four residential floors each of one great apartment with ancillary chambers (and garderobes) in the turrets and the thickness of the walls. The top three floors, with no direct communication with those below, were evidently the state apartments of the lord, interpreted as hall, audience chamber and privy chamber in ascending order. All the fireplaces above the basement are superb. The great tower juts out into the moat in Rhinelandish fashion, and south of it new kitchens to serve it do likewise. In the Buck view the turrets have conical caps or spires. The castle, abandoned since *c.* 1700, was in process of demolition when rescued by Lord Curzon in 1910, restored and subsequently presented to the nation.

Thetford, *Norfolk*

An enormous motte still very much marks the site of a motte-and-bailey castle inserted into a decayed Iron Age fort in the later eleventh century (on archaeological evidence), i.e. soon after the Conquest. The bailey lies to the east of the motte and there are traces of an outer bailey to the north. Clearly here is a major castle much in need of investigation. As it is, almost the only known fact of its history is that it was demolished by Henry II evidently in June 1173, i.e. at the very beginning of the rebellion of his son, the Young King, and not afterwards as a punishment (*Pipe Roll 19 Henry II*, Pipe Roll Society, p. 117). The foundation and lordship of the castle are almost invariably attributed to Warenne on the authority of Martin's *History of Thetford* (1779, citing no evidence), but Bigod foundation

and lordship make more sense and must be accepted. In Domesday Roger Bigod shared the borough of Thetford with the king, whereas there is no mention of Warenne, and it was Roger Bigod who founded the Cluniac priory at Thetford in 1103–4. In 1173 earl Hamelin de Warenne (he had married the Warenne heiress) was loyal and, indeed, the king's half-brother, whereas Hugh Bigod, earl of Norfolk, was a leading rebel. Thetford had been taken into the king's hand in 1157 with earl Hugh's other castles of Bungay, Framlingham and Walton, but, like Walton, was not restored in 1165. Now, in 1173, Thetford was slighted as an opening move in the struggle for power in East Anglia, and has never been refortified.

Tickhill, *Yorkshire*

Tickhill stands as a splendid example of an early motte-and-bailey castle subsequently developed but little altered, whose context and explanation is entirely the Norman Conquest and settlement of Yorkshire. It was planted in the pre-Conquest manor of Dadsley (which thereafter lost its name to it), and on a site not naturally defensible, by Roger de Busli (from Bully, near Neufchâtel-en-Bray, in Normandy) as the *caput* of the extensive lands he received at the Conquest, thereafter the honour of Tickhill. Both castle and honour were in the early years often referred to as 'of Blyth' (Notts.) from the nearest place of consequence, where Roger de Busli also founded his priory of St Mary in *c.* 1088 as a dependency of Holy Trinity, Rouen. Roger de Busli seems to have died *c.* 1098–1100 and appears only to have had one direct male heir and successor to his honour, Roger II, who was dead by, or perhaps in, 1130. The castle played an active role in Norman and Angevin England, being taken by Henry I in 1102 from Robert of Bellême, who for some reason held it (perhaps in wardship or custody) at the time of his rebellion, and by both Stephen and his rival Henry of Anjou in the civil wars of the former's time. The latter as Henry II held it throughout his reign and built the stone tower keep on the motte. It was also actively disputed between John as count of Mortain and the royal government of Richard I's absence between 1190 and 1194. But the honour of Tickhill, like the honour of Eye, having lost its direct and, as it were, residential lords at an early date, was never for long an active lordship again but,

rather, a prize of patronage and diplomacy, held by kings and queens (Isabella and Philippa) and princes as part of some larger whole, until it came in the end, in 1372 via John of Gaunt, into the vast conglomeration of the duchy of Lancaster, and so back to the Crown. As a royal castle it was finally besieged by Cromwell.

Though the barbican in front of the gate is attributed to the fifteenth century on the analogy of Tutbury, and the bailey is occupied by a modern house (itself on the site of medieval buildings which it partly incorporates), the physical remains of the castle otherwise reflect almost exclusively the first century of its history. The motte, part natural and part artificial, is formidable, some 23 m high with a summit some 24 m in diameter, whereon are the foundations of Henry II's polygonal tower keep (references on the Pipe Rolls between 1178 and 1180 to 'the work of the tower of Tickhill'), in its unusual plan to be compared to the contemporary keeps of Orford, Chilham, Odiham and Richard's Castle. The oval-shaped bailey covers about two acres. While the ditch between this and the motte has largely vanished, the outer ditches mostly survive, some 9 m wide with a strong counterscarp and still partly filled with water. The gatehouse on the west is of the early two-storeyed rectangular type with a degree of decoration (diapered triangular panels with 'rude figures'). Together with the curtain wall it is attributed to Henry I on no very strong evidence and may be earlier. In 1130 the barons of the honour recognized an obligation to maintain 'the wall of the castle of Blyth', which sounds like an early arrangement. A sixteenth-century view of the castle survives in the Public Record Office (MPC 96), though a survey of 1538 shows the keep and much else in decay.

Totnes, *Devon*

The castle of Totnes was thrust into the oval-shaped Anglo-Saxon burgh by Judhael son of Alfred (Alured), henceforth Judhael of Totnes, a Breton follower of the Conqueror who granted him the town and over a hundred manors in Devon for his services. With the foundation of his castle and his new Benedictine priory hard by (an 'alien' priory and cell of St Serge at Angers) Judhael made the former royal burgh, which profited from his coming, the *caput* of his honour, but lost all in 1088 by supporting the losing side, i.e. Robert Curthose as opposed to Rufus, in the struggle for the Anglo-Norman succession. (Restored to favour under Henry I, he went on to become lord of the honour and castle of Barnstaple but never regained Totnes.) Thereafter the history of the lordship of Totnes was somewhat chequered, but always distinguished – Nonant, Braose, Cantilupe, de la Zouche, down to the modern dukes of Somerset – though the castle was decayed by the sixteenth century, if not before, and not used in the seventeenth-century Civil War. The town was given stone walls and gateways in the thirteenth century.

The castle is a fine and large example of an early Norman motte-and-bailey, set, like the ancient burgh into which it intrudes, on a ridge above the river Dart. The motte is one of the largest in the realm, artificial above a natural rock base. Of particular interest is the evidence that it originally bore a small timber tower upon

its summit, after the manner of the mottes upon the Bayeux Tapestry. That evidence is the stone foundations for it, certainly carried well down into the motte and presumably built up with it from the rock beneath. The shell keep now upon the summit, and no doubt the curtain of the bailey (which ascends the motte in classic fashion to meet the keep), were first raised, it is thought, in the early thirteenth century (by Reginald de Braose), though both were rebuilt and/or strengthened, and the whole castle restored, in the early fourteenth century (by William de la Zouche). It appears that the shell keep never had a complete range of lodgings about its inner circumference like Restormel, and the whole castle is now denuded of internal buildings though great hall, chambers and chapel once stood in the bailey.

FURTHER READING

S. E. Rigold, *Totnes Castle*, English Heritage Handbook, Edinburgh.

Tretower, *Breconshire*

The two principal interests of Tretower are the great cylindrical donjon inside a shell keep (cf. Launceston), and the continuity of occupation with a difference from the eleventh century to the eighteenth. The house called Tretower Court

(centre left on the photograph), is said to have replaced the castle as a residence as early as the early fourteenth century, thereafter remaining a country seat down to the 1780s.

The castle was first planted here by the Norman Picard, a vassal of Bernard of Neufmarché who overran Welsh Brecknock at the end of the eleventh century. It took the form of a motte-and-bailey (the motte revetted in stone), as it indeed still does though the bailey to the east is now occupied by a farmyard and only the motte with its later stone buildings are accessible and have been surveyed and conserved. About the middle of the twelfth century Roger the son of Picard, or Roger's son John, replaced the supposed palisade and timber buildings on the motte with a stone shell keep, with a gatehouse and an L-shaped hall and chamber block within. In the earlier thirteenth century and probably before 1230 the same family of Picard rebuilt the castle again, the works comprising principally the cylindrical great tower upon the motte within the shell, and the enclosure of the bailey by a stone curtain with a cylindrical angle tower and twin-towered gatehouse. The great tower is one of the finest of its type in the realm, complete save for floors and roof and the embattled parapet which crowned it. Its walls are 3 m thick above the battered base. There were three residential floors above a basement, the entrance was at first-floor level by an external staircase, and a covered bridge led from the second floor to the wall walk of the shell keep, which stands very close about the tower. The building of the great tower involved the demolition of the twelfth-century hall and chamber block save for the outer walls which were part of the shell (their window openings then blocked up) and the heightening of the shell keep itself.

Though said to have been abandoned as a residence from c. 1300, the castle was put into a state of defence against Owen Glendower a century later, while an early sixteenth-century sketch seems to show it intact. Tretower Court began as a fourteenth-century house (the present north range) and was greatly extended and altered in the fifteenth century by Sir Roger Vaughan, with further substantial alterations in the seventeenth. The Vaughan family continued to reside here until they sold the property as a farm in the 1780s.

FURTHER READING

C. A. Ralegh Radford, 'Tretower: the Castle and the Court', *Brycheiniog*, VI.

Wallingford, *Berkshire*

Wallingford is first and foremost a good example of a surviving Anglo-Saxon burgh with a Norman castle placed within it (in the north-east sector – top right) soon after 1066, on the analogy of Portchester, Winchester, London itself and several other places. The burgh is, of course, the large, communal fortification, here a rectangular enclosure of ditch and bank (and vanished wall) placed beside the Thames to guard its crossing. It is listed in the Burghal Hidage and called a

The Anglo-Saxon burgh at Wallingford, the line of its rectangular defences running down to the Thames particularly clear on the left of the photograph. The castle earthworks lie amongst the trees beyond the church spire.

burgh in Domesday. In 1066 William the Conqueror was here, and received the submission of Stigand, archbishop of Canterbury, soon after Hastings and before his entry into London and subsequent coronation. The castle must have been among the first to be raised in England: the Abingdon Chronicle refers to it as early as 1071, and the Domesday Survey notes that eight burghal tenements or messuages were taken for its construction. Presumably it was thus royal in the beginning; but the castle soon became mediatized as the *caput* of the extensive lands which became the honour of Wallingford – held by Miles Crispin (d. 1107) in the Conqueror's day and after; evidently by Robert d'Oilly before him (Robert is the reputed founder of the college of St Nicholas in the castle: an inquest of 1212 states that Miles married his daughter, Maud, and obtained the honour of Wallingford through her); and certainly by Brian fitz Count (the second husband of the same Maud according to the same inquest) who was famously lord of the honour and castle in Stephen's reign. Three times, though to no avail, in 1139, 1146 and 1152, Stephen besieged the castle and its burgh, held by Brian for the empress Mathilda. Henry fitz Empress, after the entry of Brian and his wife into religion without heirs, obtained both castle and honour, which remained royal or quasi-royal after his accession as Henry II in 1154. Later alienations were in effect royal appanages, for Richard earl of Cornwall in 1231, Gaveston in 1307, and Edward the Black Prince in 1337. Little remains now save the earthworks of the Conqueror's motte and bailey(s), though Leland could still note 'goodly building(s) with the tourres and dungeon' as well as decay, and records of the thirteenth and fourteenth centuries refer to the great tower, the great hall and chambers, kitchens, buttery and other offices, and the college of St Nicholas in the outer ward.

Wark-upon-Tweed, *Northumberland*

Almost nothing remains save the site, itself encroached upon, of this, one of the most important border castles, with a dramatic history of repeated action against the Scots, though as late as the sixteenth century Henry VIII modernized it, developing the keep to take guns ('so that grete bumbardes may be shot out') and it was being put into a state of defence in 1592.

The foundation of the castle of Wark – i.e. the (new) work – is attributed to Walter l'Espec, the founder of Rievaulx Abbey, to whom Henry I granted the new barony (after 1118?) as he also granted him the lordship of Helmsley in Yorkshire. It was set at the east end of a high ridge on the south bank of the Tweed, guarding a ford and not far from the Scottish border. The motte was at the west end, where the castle ditch cut it off from the ridge, the bailey ran to the east and north, finishing against the river, and a township was developed east and south of the bailey. This castle was finally taken by the Scots in 1138 and demolished. After the death of Walter l'Espec without direct heirs in 1155, in the odour of sanctity as a monk at Rievaulx which he had founded, Henry II chose to keep the castle in his hand, and rebuilt or completely restored it, over £380 being spent upon it between

1158 and 1161. The new works probably included a polygonal shell keep upon the motte, stone curtains and a gatehouse where later the 'great gate' is known to have been. The king's castle, under the command of Roger de Stuteville, successfully held out in 1174 against a hard-pressed siege by William the Lion, king of Scots, described by Jordan Fantosme. Henry later granted Wark to the Ros family who had also succeeded Walter l'Espec at Helmsley, and they continued to hold it until William III de Ros exchanged it with Edward II for other property in 1317. Edward III granted it to Sir William Montagu who was created earl of Salisbury in 1337, and thereafter border warfare was interrupted by romance when, we are told, the warrior king wooed the beautiful countess of Salisbury here, to no avail and therefore *Honi soit qui mal y pense*. At the end of the fourteenth century the castle passed from Montagu to Gray, and so remained until this present century. In the time of the first Elizabeth the castle comprised three wards, the inner 'called the Ring' consisting of the donjon and the ancient motte, the middle ward, where stood the constable's house, and the nether or outer ward with the 'great gate' towards the town on the south-east side and the river on the north.

Warkworth, *Northumberland*

Though no less involved in Border wars for centuries, Warkworth is the very opposite of Wark, castle and attendant town still standing in much of their medieval glory. The castle guards the narrow neck of a bold loop in the river Coquet and thus bars entry to the town stretching down the hill behind it to the north (cf. Bungay). The place is one of ancient settlement, going back to the eighth

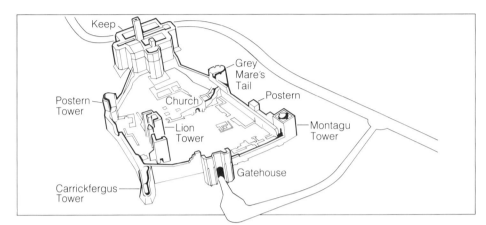

century at least, but now owes almost everything to the lords of the castle and their town planners.

The precise date and occasion of the castle's foundation is unknown but is probably to be attributed to the Norman settlement and the Norman earl of Northumberland, Robert de Mowbray, disinherited for political reasons in 1095. After him Henry of Scotland, son of king David I, held the earldom until deprived of it by Henry II in 1157. The first reference to Warkworth castle occurs in 1158, when the same king granted it and the manor to one Roger son of Richard, clearly an up and coming man, whose mother was a Bigod and wife a de Vere, though his father is now unknown. With his descendants it remained until 1332 when it passed to the Percies of Alnwick, first earls, then dukes of Northumberland and Wardens of the March, who made of it their principal castle and in name are lords of it still.

In the beginning a castle of the motte-and-bailey type, it has retained that form ever since – though losing a stretch of its bailey when the eastern curtain was built, as the aerial photograph clearly reveals. Since then it has been built and developed in masonry of every date from the twelfth century to the sixteenth, but its crowning glory is its early fifteenth-century keep of unique design upon the ancient motte. Basically a square with the angles mortared off, this has four rectangular bays (the angles similarly cut off), one to each face, and a central lantern bringing both light and water to the interior. The ground floor has entrance vestibule and service rooms; the first floor, chapel, great hall and chamber, kitchen, buttery and pantry; the second floor, two further great chambers, one with access to the oriel of the chapel below. In the bailey the principal chapel lay west of the splendid gatehouse which is the centre of the south front, and up the west side, south to north from the Carrickfergus Tower to the Postern Tower, lay a grand residential range of solar, great hall, buttery, pantry and kitchens. The entrance to the hall is the Lion Tower, with the Percy emblem of a lion carved in deep relief – and another Percy lion looks down on the town from the north face of the keep. On the other, eastern side of the bailey, from north to south, are the tower called the Grey Mare's Tail, the stables, another postern, and the Amble or Montague Tower at the south-east angle. Right across the bailey, towards the north end beneath the keep, a cruciform church was intended (never finished and now down to the foundations) to be served by a college of secular canons, after the manner of Windsor.

By the seventeenth century, at least, all these splendours were in decay. James I looked at the castle with dismay and his courtiers were 'much moved to see it soe spoyled and soe badly kept', sheep and goats in the chambers and the gates open day and night. In the nineteenth century Salvin carried out some restoration (1853–8) and now the duke can still lodge in the keep and the whole building is in the care of English Heritage.

FURTHER READING

C. H. Hunter Blair and H. L. Honeymoon, *Warkworth Castle*, English Heritage Handbook, London.

Warwick

Superbly sited on its sandstone cliff above the Avon, Warwick, like Arundel and Alnwick, or indeed like Windsor, stands above all for continuity of noble residence. And if now in these evil times the noble lords have here departed, that was only yesterday, while this castle has been far less afflicted by rebuilding and transformation in the modern period than is the case with the other two, or three, examples. What one sees now, in spite of seventeenth-, eighteenth- and nineteenth-century alterations especially of the domestic complex, is overwhelmingly fourteenth-century, and, moreover, stands upon the foundations of a motte-and-bailey planted here by the Conqueror in 1068, partly within the burgh or fortified town of Ethelfleda, daughter of King Alfred (914). The Conqueror entrusted his castle to Henry de Beaumont, from whom descended the line of

Newburgh earls of Warwick who were succeeded by the Beauchamps in the late thirteenth century. It is likely that the castle was fortified in stone at least in the course of the twelfth century, to which period the surviving but much revamped polygonal shell keep on the motte may be attributed; but it owes most now to the two Thomas Beauchamps, earls of Warwick, of the fourteenth century, and especially to the second of them (1370–1401). Thus the palatial residential range, originally comprising the great hall, two chamber blocks and chapel, securely set above the river where the main domestic complex had always been, is still basically fourteenth-century though with additions, and the Watergate Tower in the filled-in ditch between motte and bailey is contemporary. The medieval pride of Warwick is, however, the splendid fourteenth-century north-east front of central, lofty gatehouse and barbican, and two great flanking towers, Guy's Tower and Caesar's Tower, one polygonal, the other tri-lobed, respectively north and south (left and right on the photograph). It is to be noted that here each unit, including the barbican, is residential, and each (let alone the whole) elaborately defended to near-impregnability.

In the fifteenth century Warwick passed to both Richard Neville, i.e. Warwick the King-Maker (slain 1471) and Richard duke of Gloucester, i.e. the future Richard III (slain 1485). Of works in their time, which was the apogee of the castle's eminence, we know nothing, save on Leland's testimony, of how the latter 'began and halfe finishid a mighty tower, or strengthe, for to shoute out gunns'. This is the keep-like structure in the centre of the north or north-west curtain (with a later entrance driven through it), of which only the outer half is visible and only stands to first-floor level (topped with later battlements), but is equipped with gun-loops. Its two extant corner turrets are now named the Bear and Clarence Towers. In 1604 James I granted the castle to Sir Fulke Greville, whose family (created earls of Warwick in 1759) held it until its recent sale.

Little Wenham, *Suffolk*

Little Wenham in Suffolk, south-west of Ipswich, is a less well-known example of the thirteenth-century fortified manor or *maison forte* (cf. Acton Burnell and Stokesay). It is attributed to the period *c.* 1270–*c.* 1280 and to John de Vaux (d. 1287), representative of a family of second rank but considerable substance in East Anglia, very considerable tenants of the Bigod earls of Norfolk, founders of Pentney priory and benefactors of the houses of Sibton, Castle Acre, Thetford (St Mary's), Blythburgh and Leiston. The standing building (centre) is best described as a small tower house, strong in construction, crenellated for lordship and resistance to armed marauders (arrow-slits also at roof level, though this has sixteenth-century restoration), but not otherwise very defensible, as its two-light windows emphasize (three lights for the east window of the chapel). It is built of (local) brick, with stone only for the dressings (flint septaria for the footings), and is one of the earliest buildings in England to be so. It is L-shaped in plan, the main block on a north–south axis comprising the hall upon a vaulted undercroft, and

the subsidiary block of one bay only containing the chapel facing east. The chapel, reached handsomely from the upper (north) end of the hall, also stands upon a vaulted undercroft and is vaulted itself, with the great chamber or solar above – an irregular arrangement in that no apartment should stand on a chapel, but not unprecedented. A turret in the re-entrant angle of the L contains the vice and rises above both the two storeys of the hall block and the three storeys of the chapel wing. Entrance to the whole was at first-floor level into the south end of the west front, i.e. into the lower end of the hall. A pleasing detail, if it can be accepted, is that the boss of the vault in the chapel shows a carved figure usually identified as St Petronilla to whom the chapel was dedicated; and Petronilla was the name of John de Vaux's elder daughter and co-heiress who died in 1326 and was buried at Pentney. Wenham, however, went with the younger daughter to William de Roos of Helmsley.

The tower house at Wenham may have been built freestanding (Pevsner) but it cannot have stood alone as now (on the lawn of the modern house of *c.* 1700), and is presumably to be envisaged with an attendant courtyard of service rooms and offices, like the not dissimilar Markenfield in Yorkshire or the 'pele-tower' of Sizergh in Westmorland. There are extensive moats on the site, and the now deserted contemporary church (*c.* 1300) and a fine sixteenth-century barn stand nearby.

Windsor, *Berkshire*

The Normans came early to 'New' Windsor, then the manor of Clewer, to fortify with a new castle the escarpment above the river which is about the only naturally strong site in the Thames valley between London and Wallingford. The scale of the castle was great from the beginning, and in plan it is to be compared with Arundel,

with two baileys one on either side of a central motte. Its foundation, history, development, and any aerial photograph of it, are full of significance. From the beginning soon after 1066 until the present day it has been one of the major royal castles of England and its structure records almost every passing period. Within at most a generation of the Norman Conquest it had become a principal royal residence, replacing the unfortified Old Windsor, where Edward the Confessor had lain and held his court. It was at 'New' Windsor that Henry I is known to have worn his crown in 1110, i.e. held a crown-wearing, the largest and most formal of courtly assemblies. Henry II built new royal lodgings here and Henry III spent prodigiously upon others. Edward III, Edward of Windsor, between c. 1350 and his death in 1377, made of it a veritable fortified palace, the Versailles of the age, the ultimate centre of his court and chivalry, and of his new Order of the Garter still based upon his College of St George within the castle and now served by the magnificent St George's Chapel begun by Edward IV in 1477. Charles II celebrated the Restoration by refurbishing Edward III's state apartments in the Upper Ward as a Baroque palace by Hugh May. George III and George IV had them largely rebuilt again by Wyatt and Wyatville between 1800 and 1840, when the new Romanticism brought castles back into fashion as stately homes. State banquets are still held in royal Windsor, prepared in Edward III's kitchens which Wyatville brought up to date. Until very recently ladies in waiting might ascend the long twelfth-century pentice and stairway to the keep upon the Conqueror's motte to reach their bed-chambers. And in that shell keep Edward III placed the earliest mechanical, weight-driven clock in England in 1354. Windsor not only stands for continuity and regality but also, though its strength was never neglected in the Middle Ages, emphasizes above all the lordly residential role of castles which was always more than half their *raison d'être*, and is now the only function that a fortunate few among them may retain (cf. Arundel again). The park within which the great castle stands still covers some 4,800 acres, fourteen miles in circumference, though this is a sad diminution of its appurtenances in Edward of Windsor's time, when its parks, chases and forests, studded with hunting lodges, made of the Thames Valley a royal pleasaunce, almost from Oxford and almost to London – the sound of the horn borne on the morning air, royal barges gliding on the water.

For such continuity one pays a heavy price. The authoritative *History of the King's Works* (vi, p. 392) observes that 'Windsor Castle today is to all intents and purposes a nineteenth-century creation, and it stands as the image of what the early nineteenth century thought a castle should be'. But this is harsh. Superficially in appearance the Upper Ward owes more to Wyatville between 1824 and 1840 than to anybody else, and his hand and that of Salvin in the 1860s are very apparent in the restoration of the Lower. Yet beneath all this, the motte and two baileys of the Conqueror predetermined all that came after. Henry I (rather than Henry II) is probably responsible for the shell keep upon the motte – maddeningly doubled in height by Wyatville in 1830–1 as the present so-called Round Tower – as he may be also for the earliest known great hall of which traces remain in the Lower Ward on the site of the former Denton's Commons. No one has altered the characteristic rectangular profile of Henry II's mural towers about the Upper Ward, while Henry III's great drum, or D-shaped, towers still dominate the town on the west front of the castle (Curfew, Garter and Salisbury from north to south) as they stand also south of the motte on either side, west and east (respectively Henry III's Tower and Edward III's Tower). His spirit also lingers in the Dean's Cloister in spite of Edward III's remodelling of it, in wall-paintings there and elsewhere in the Lower Ward, and in the magnificent ironwork on the doors of the narthex of his chapel, rebuilt by Queen Victoria as the Albert Memorial Chapel. But above all, in spite of Charles II, George II and George IV, Wyatt and Wyatville, Salvin and Queen Victoria, Windsor is Edward III's: in its overall magnificence as a castle become a fortified royal palace; in the fundamental construction of the State Apartments in the Upper Ward; in the presence of the Order of the Garter and in the Dean's Cloister, Canons' Cloister and Treasury or Aerary of the College of St George; in the splendid timber-framing of the apartments within the keep or Round Tower; in endless sumptuous details still unobscured, not least the vaults beneath the State Apartments, or in the so-called Norman Gate between the Middle and Upper Wards, or in the little tower now called King John's Tower but once (from its vault) the tower, and chamber, 'called la Rose'. And then, as the crown of this regalian site, there is St George's Chapel, begun by Edward IV as his memorial especially, completed by Henry VII, and deliberately rivalling Henry VI's chapel at Eton College, clearly visible from the castle.

Wingfield, *Derbyshire*

Wingfield is included here, like Camber, as a non-castle. Camber was purely military with no domestic residential purpose: Wingfield was purely residential. The two functions, military and residential, are uniquely combined in the castle, which does not exist when they are separate. Wingfield, though often included amongst the 'fortified manors' of the later Middle Ages, in fact has no serious defences and is no *maison forte*, but was and is a very splendid example of a mid-fifteenth-century unfortified but noble house. Such great residences, of course, were not then new (e.g. Woodstock, or Clarendon, or Westminster itself), nor do they signify the castle's end.

Wingfield Manor was built upon an old site cleared for the purpose, between 1439 and *c.* 1450, by Ralph lord Cromwell, Treasurer of England (1433–43), a man of modest origins who had reached the top by royal service both in peace and war (he had been amongst the happy few at Agincourt), and who also built Tattershall to express his new-found rank and fortune. The great building is mostly of the highest quality, and, though grievously ruined and in some parts in the past abused, has never been substantially altered. It is set about two courts, the outer (south and now with modern farm-buildings south and south-west) given over to offices and staff accommodation and separated from the inner by a cross range (east–west) pierced centrally by the inner gate lavish with heraldic display. The inner court contained the great hall, kitchen and offices and the accommodation and lodgings for lord Cromwell and his noble guests. There are now no state apartments at the upper (east) end of the hall, nor any buildings down the east side

of the court, though these were presumably once provided or intended, and the house has no recognizable chapel as it now stands. The grandest lodgings for the grandest guests were in the south-west High Tower. The great hall (north-east) was the largest known of its period until Edward IV built Eltham a generation later. Though not only ruined but mutilated when converted into a house in the late seventeenth century, it still retains its deliberately impressive bay window at the high-table end as well as the porches of the screens passage north and south. Beyond the north range of hall and private apartments lay the gardens, bounded by a large ditch which doubtless dates back to an earlier and fortified manor upon the site.

Lord Cromwell died at Wingfield in January 1456 and the great house was sold to the Talbot earl of Shrewsbury, whose family occupied it until the seventeenth-century Civil War. Twice then attacked, in 1643 and 1644, it was thereafter slighted and has remained a noble ruin ever since.

FURTHER READING

A. Emery, 'Ralph Lord Cromwell's Manor at Wingfield', *Archaeological Journal*, CXLII.

Wingfield, *Suffolk*

Wingfield, the foundation of which is associated with a licence to crenellate dated 1384, is a later castle, described by the *Victoria County History* (1911; i, p. 622) as 'an ideal example of that type of residence transitional from the feudal castle to the moated manor house'. The description will do very well so long as it is remembered that in all periods there were castles less strongly fortified than others. What is typical of its date is its neat and tidy quadrangular design, set on a moated platform with a tower at each angle. What remains apart from the moated site is the south front, with a deliberately impressive gatehouse of three storeys in the centre and an angle tower, polygonal in plan like the gatehouse, east and west, all in local flint with the minimum of dressed stone and brick. There are possible traces of subsidiary enclosures to the east and one may suppose an outer court to the south. The attractive but inappropriate timber-framed Tudor house now occupying the west side of the castle is an insertion of the 1540s built after the castle's demolition in the earlier sixteenth century.

Much unhappiness lingers at Wingfield. It was built by Michael de la Pole, 'favourite' of Richard II, married to Katherine, daughter and heiress of Sir John Wingfield (d. 1361; monument in the church), to mark the elevation of his house in 1385 to the earldom of Suffolk, from humbler beginnings as wool merchants and financiers of Hull. But seldom glad confident morning again. Michael de la Pole himself was deprived of his earldom by his political enemies in 1388, and died in exile in 1389. His son and successor, Michael II, splendidly commemorated by his tomb with effigies in the church, died on Henry V's Barfleur campaign in

September 1415, and his son and heir, aged twenty, was slain at Agincourt one month later. William de la Pole, brother and heir and duke of Suffolk from 1448, was murdered at sea off Dover on his way to political banishment in 1450. He spent six weeks at Wingfield before his last departure, and left a well-known letter to his son which ends

> Wretan of myn hand
> The day of my departure fro' this land,
> Your trewe and lovyng fader, Suffolk.

Another political murder ends the story (unless we add all surviving relations including the Cardinal Pole), when Henry VIII executed Edmund de la Pole, the 'White Rose' and last earl, in 1513, for having blood better than his own.

Wolvesey, *Hampshire*

Wolvesey is no true castle but the defensible medieval bishop's palace (cf. e.g. Wells), in the south-east corner of the walled city of Winchester beyond the east end of the cathedral. Winchester Castle is on the other side of the city, running north from the south-west corner, founded by the Conqueror and royal ever after. There was an episcopal residence on the Wolvesey site, north of the present ruins, from the tenth century and attributed to bishop Ethelwold's reorganization of the Winchester churches, i.e. the Old Minster (replaced by the present Norman cathedral), the New Minster very close to the former on the north side (and moved to Hyde Abbey outside the north gate of the city in 1110) and the 'Nunnaminster' for the ladies, i.e. St Mary's Abbey, to the north-east. This Old English house was replaced early in the twelfth century, by bishop William Giffard (1100–29), by an exceptionally grand stone-built residence comprising an immense first-floor hall, chambers and chapel. The hall was 53 m long and the largest at that time in England save only royal Westminster. These buildings, which are on the left or west of what is now a courtyard as one enters from the south, served as the more private apartments of the bishop until the seventeenth century. The equally ruined and very grand hall and chamber block on the right or east, and the curtain walls to the north and south joining the two complexes and making a courtyard of the whole, were built by bishop Henry of Blois between *c.* 1138 and *c.* 1170. Henry of Blois, bishop of Winchester, papal legate and brother to the king, was the most powerful man in Stephen's England. We are told that he built at Winchester 'a house like unto a palace' – *domus quasi palatium* – and this at a time when 'palace' was a rare and regal word. We are also told that he fortified his palatial official residence *ad instar castelli* in *c.* 1141, and two strong towers remain, both on the east side towards the open country, i.e. an almost keep-like structure north of Wymondestour, and the latter which is at the south-east angle. Wolvesey thus, though not a castle, is an early and splendid example of a 'fortified manor' or *maison forte*. The modern bishop's palace, shown on the photograph due south of the medieval ruins, seems almost humble by comparison.

Yelden, *Bedfordshire*

An aerial photograph of Yelden shows not only the surviving earthworks of a castle of motte-and-bailey (in fact two baileys) form, but also the regular grid-pattern, east but also west of the village street, of the crofts or messuages of the original settlement, into which, surely, the castle has been inserted. If this interpretation is correct, then it seems most likely that the castle was founded soon after 1066 and as part of the Norman settlement, when such things were most likely to be done. In Domesday, Yelden (rated at ten hides) was held of Geoffrey, bishop of Coutances, by Geoffrey de Trailly (Trelly, Manche, near Coutances), a man of moderate estate who may be the founder. His successor, Geoffrey II, married Aubrey, a co-heiress of Walter Espec (d. 1155) of Old Wardon in Bedfordshire (and also Helmsley, Yorkshire), fining for her lands in 1158. Yelden passed to the honour of Gloucester after bishop Geoffrey's time and continued to be held of that honour by the Trailly family until the late fourteenth century. Almost the only known reference specifically to the castle occurs in 1174 when first five, and then three knights were paid for their service there by the king during the summer and autumn. In 1360 the site of the manor, which is presumably the castle, was said to be in ruins.

We are dealing, therefore, with a mesne castle, held of some other lord than the king, which may help to explain the paucity of reference to it. Archaeologically it

has not been investigated since 1882, when slight traces of masonry were found on the disturbed top of the motte (12 m high from the base of its ditch), and about the inner bailey (south-west) which evidently had a towered curtain. The small mound due south of the inner bailey contained the foundation of a cylindrical tower 9 m in diameter. The ditches of the castle were fed by the water of the Til stream which now runs in a straight and artificial course through the unusually wide west moat.

York: Clifford's Tower and the Old Baile

The two castles founded by the Conqueror here in 1068 and 1069 mark not only the importance of York in general but more particularly the immediate danger of the Anglo-Scandinavian city to the Norman take-over of England in the years following 1066. Harold Hardrada of Norway, after all, had invaded England as well as duke William in 1066, and two great battles, Gate Fulford and Stamford Bridge – the latter Harold of England's last triumph – had been fought near York only a few weeks before Hastings. In 1068 the Norman king came north for the first time, at the threat of revolt. The city surrendered to him and he raised his first castle there. He also raised castles at Warwick and Nottingham on his way up and at Lincoln, Huntingdon and Cambridge on his way back. In 1069 he was obliged to return to York twice, on the first occasion in the late winter or spring when the new castle was attacked. The Conqueror relieved it and planted another. In the autumn the threat was greater, when a large Danish fleet raided England and approached the Humber, and all over England the king's enemies, Danish and English rose up, but especially in York where both Norman castles were overwhelmed. This time the answer was the notorious 'Devastation of the North', during which the king held his Christmas feast in York, where both castles were refortified.

While it is not possible to be certain, it is generally supposed that the first York castle of 1068 was that which is now known as Clifford's Tower (below centre, right), on a triangular strip of land between the two rivers Fosse and Ouse, on the south-east edge of the city, while the second castle was that long known as the Old Baile, and now almost forgotten, placed directly opposite on the other (west) bank of the Ouse (by the south end of the modern Skeldergate Bridge) and in the southern angle of the city's defences.

Unlike so many castles, the Old Baile did not survive very long after the dramatic circumstances which brought it into being. It passed into the keeping of the archbishop, probably in the late twelfth century, and was going out of use by the fourteenth. The motte, which excavation in the 1960s showed to have been constructed in a series of rammed-down layers, now alone survives, as a tree-covered grassy mound, while the bailey to the west, having been sold off in 1880, is now mostly covered by a nineteenth-century housing estate.

The Conqueror's first castle also, which in practice became York Castle, is in effect now reduced to its motte, standing as a monumental roundabout with

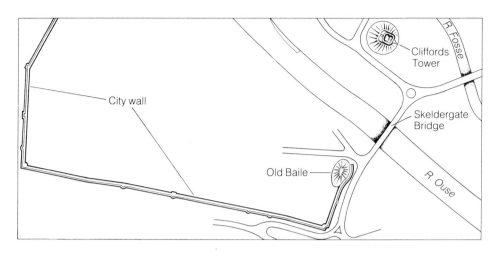

Clifford's Tower upon it, the bailey to the south having been almost obliterated by the public buildings placed in and about it mostly in the eighteenth and nineteenth centuries. When it was raised, or at its refortification in 1069, the Fosse river was dammed just below it to bring water into its ditches and to form an artificial lake on the east side further to defend it. The same dam created the great Fishpond of the Fosse farther to the north and east beyond Walmgate, already there as 'the king's pool' in Domesday. These water works, the 'missing links in the defences of the city' which has retained its walls and gates, are now vanished even on an aerial photograph. The castle, however, still retains Clifford's Tower, the tower keep upon the Conqueror's motte, though burnt out and gutted by a great fire on 23 April 1684. Unique in England in its quatrefoil plan, it was built on the orders of Henry III between 1245 and 1272 to replace a timber keep which had evidently stood here as late as 1228 when blown down by the wind. It was probably never finished as the king had intended, for the additional height of a third storey would make it look much better and more like its French prototypes (Etampes, Ambleny).

A note on further reading

The following may be recommended amongst the comparatively few books dealing sensibly and authoritatively with the subject of castles, mainly (but necessarily not exclusively) in England and Wales:

Ella S. Armitage, *The Early Norman Castles of the British Isles*, London, 1912.
R. Allen Brown, *English Castles*, 3rd edition revised, London, 1976.
M. W. Thompson, *The Decline of the Castle*, Cambridge University Press, 1987.

To compile anything like a full bibliography for individual castles would be quite beyond the scope of this book, and in many lesser known cases not even very rewarding. What has been done here is to cite, where such exists, any one particularly useful monograph at the end of the text dealing with the castle in question. This is often but not always the official guidebook issued by what was the Ministry of Works, then the Department of the Environment, and is now 'English Heritage'.

Finally, reference should be made to certain specialist journals and other publications of a more general kind which will be found to contain valuable accounts of individual castles, although usually, like most of the available literature, confined to an architectural or archaeological point of view. These include most notably the volumes where available of the *Victoria County Histories* and of the Royal Commission on Historical Monuments; the first two volumes especially of *The History of the King's Works* ed. H. M. Colvin, *viz.* vols. 1 and 2, *The Middle Ages*, by R. Allen Brown, H. M. Colvin and A. J. Taylor, HMSO, London, 1963; and the bi-annual volumes of *Château-Gaillard: Etudes de castellologie médiévale*, Université de Caen, Centre de Recherches Archéologiques Médiévales.

Photographic details

All photographs are from the University of Cambridge collection unless otherwise stated

Acton Burnell *EY 19 (4.6.1950)*
Alnwick *BHD 65 (2.8.1971)*
Anstey *TZ 8 (23.3.1957)*
Arundel *AR 10 (19.6.1948)*
Bamburgh *BHD 52 (2.8.1971)*
Barnard Castle *CVH 88 (21.9.1978)*
Old Basing *DY 11 (19.7.1949)*
Beaumaris *EI 73 (24.7.1949)*
Belsay *CQM 11 (30.7.1984)*
Berkeley *BW 23 (26.7.1948)*
Berkhamsted *PO 91 (20.3.1955)*
Bodiam *DZ 4 (19.7.1949)*
Bolton-in-Wensleydale
  BS 92 (23.7.1948)
Bramber *DZ 29 (19.7.1949)*
New Buckenham *PP 46 (14.4.1955)*
Old Buckenham *AIL 76 (6.4.1964)*
Builth *EO 17 (26.7.1949)*
Bungay *BYI 85 (29.6.1976)*
Caernarvon *ASR 82 (9.7.1967)*
Caerphilly *BW 55 (26.7.1948)*
  CGB 41 (19.6.1978)
Cainhoe *BFI 93 (19.5.1971)*
Camber *ARR 90 (13.6.1967)*
Cambridge *BEN 4 (21.10.1970)*
Castle Acre *RC 8–EV 136 (15.10.1982)*
  BYP 27 (2.7.1976)
Castle Bytham *CNL 75 (4.10.1980)*
Castle Hedingham *LZ 55 (29.6.1953)*
  AXL 101 (13.5.1969)
Castle Rising *BLO 32 (31.1.1973)*
Cause *AUE 74 (24.4.1968)*
Chepstow *AN 57 (16.6.1948)*
Chilham *BFY 63 (7.7.1971)*
Christchurch *CM 47 (20.6.1949)*
Clare *BEQ 31 (19.1.1971)*
Clavering *CQV 20 (9.7.1986)*
Clun *AUB 34 (12.4.1968)*
Colchester *EP 127 (27.7.1949)*
Conisborough *ARC 27 (2.5.1967)*
Conway *BO 51 (19.7.1948)*
  CKS 51 (8.8.1979)
Corfe *ML 43 (6.7.1953)*
  AQB 16 (16.9.1966)
Denbigh *TJ 7 (14.6.1956)*

Dover *AU 25 (26.6.1948)*
  7 OH–X 1 (16.7.1974)
Durham *BLK 66 (16.1.1973)*
Edlingham *CMZ 72 (2.8.1980)*
Ewyas Harold *EP 66 (26.7.1949)*
Exeter *ANO 45 (29.4.1966)*
Eye *BWB 11 (8.9.1975)*
Farnham *DY 18 (19.7.1949)*
Flint *TJ 18 (14.6.1956)*
Framlingham *BU 21 (24.7.1948)*
  PP 96 (14.4.1955)
Goodrich *BFS 92 (5.7.1971)*
Guildford *CV 64 (29.6.1949)*
Harlech *TQ 71 (27.7.1956)*
Hastings *BU 78 (24.7.1948)*
Haughley *CQW 22 (15.7.1986)*
Helmsley *BHH 13 (10.9.1971)*
Hen Domen *BVQ 27 (4.8.1975)*
Kenilworth *BQ 89 (22.7.1948)*
Kidwelly *TE 60 (13.6.1956)*
Kilpeck *AKS 95 (13.4.1965)*
Kirby Muxloe *RI 25 (21.7.1955)*
Launceston *ANM 71 (28.4.1966)*
Leeds *CPN 23 (7.6.1982)*
Lewes *AR 16 (19.6.1948)*
Lidgate *BPK 17 (6.2.1974)*
Lincoln *RC 8–CN 129 (5.4.1978)*
The Tower of London *7OK–GQ 38*
  (29.10.1986)
Ludlow *CKR 52 (2.8.1979)*
Mettingham *HO 29 (19.6.1952)*
Middleham *BLM 62 (22.1.1973)*
  BA 8 (5.7.1948)
Mileham *AMU 41 (3.1.1966)*
Montgomery *COK 20 (29.6.1981)*
  COK 25 (29.6.1981)
Naworth *DI 62 (6.7.1949)*
Norham *BHC 54 (1.8.1971)*
  CKK 46 (31.7.1979)
Norwich *AEZ 27 (5.6.1962)*
Odiham *BUP 46 (18.7.1975)*
Okehampton *CMC 53 (24.6.1980)*
Orford *HC 55 (2.8.1951)*
Oxburgh Hall *ARO 88 (10.6.1967)*
Oxford *AOK 2 (18.6.1966)*

Painscastle *AFR 24 (23.6.1962)*
Peak *EE 52 (23.7.1949)*
Pembroke *CY 52 (30.6.1949)*
Pevensey *RC 8–B 92 (8.8.1967)*
  BU 81 (24.7.1948)
Pickering *BBF 4 (24.4.1970)*
Pleshey *BVA 42 (24.7.1975)*
Portchester *CGI 17 (6.7.1978)*
Prudhoe *BUQ 44 (19.7.1975)*
Pulverbatch *TN 30 (25.7.1956)*
Raby *CLR 37 (10.5.1980)*
Raglan *BFT 28 (5.7.1971)*
Restormel *BON 65 (26.7.1973)*
Rhuddlan *AKX 81 (20.5.1965)*
Richard's Castle *BHP 2*
  (14.2.1971)
Richmond *BB 12 (6.7.1948)*
Rochester *AQZ 77 (26.4.1967)*
Rockingham *AW 13 (27.6.1948)*
Sandal *GV 29 (16.7.1951)*
Old Sarum *CFD 62 (25.1.1978)*
Scarborough *COG 56 (10.6.1981)*
Sizergh *MY 88 (10.8.1953)*
Stokesay *BM 36 (18.7.1948)*
Tamworth *SB 88 (6.4.1956)*
Tattershall *BT 62 (23.7.1948)*
Thetford *AIL 70 (6.4.1964)*
Tickhill *BRU 94 (29.11.1974)*
Totnes *AFG 84 (8.6.1962)*
Tretower *BVP 28 (1.8.1975)*
Wallingford *AMP 103 (6.12.1965)*
  GA 38 (19.6.1951)
Wark-upon-Tweed *GT 48*
  (16.7.1951)
Warkworth *ADU 9 (17.7.1961)*
Warwick *BAZ 54 (16.3.1970)*
Little Wenham *HC 34 (2.8.1951)*
Windsor *PZ 91 (25.6.1955)*
Wingfield (Derbyshire) *XN 52*
  (23.7.1958)
Wingfield (Suffolk) *AFM 68*
  (15.6.1962)
Wolvesey *BSK 98 (19.5.1975)*
Yelden *BIF 18 (3.5.1972)*
York *RC 8–V 199 (17.4.1971)*

Index